Danger

'Much the best book by Michael Apter th

'Fascinating glimpses into the complex world of human motivations.'

Mihaly Csikszentmihalyi, Ph.D., Author of *Flow* and
Professor of Psychology, University of Chicago

'This book is a dazzling success. Michael Apter has triumphantly succeeded in producing a book of real substance on topics of interest to all of us. Sex, war, antisocial behavior, the pursuit of danger, and much else besides are analyzed insightfully by an internationally respected psychologist.'

Michael W. Eysenck, Ph.D., Professor of Psychology,
Royal Holloway, University of London

'I found this an insightful and useful analysis, capturing the remarkably oppositional nature of human motivation. The book is well written and makes for fascinating reading. Dr. Apter clears up the paradoxical aspects of human behavior and draws useful implications for many of today's personal and social problems.'

Joseph F. Rychlak, Ph.D., Professor of Psychology,
Loyola University, Chicago

'Freud supposed that what human beings most wanted was a state of tranquility following the discharge of all tensions. Freud was wrong. Professor Apter rightly stresses man's need for arousal and excitement; a need so pressing that it must find an outlet even if it leads to danger and destruction. Apter argues that juvenile crime could be diminished if society provided enough exciting alternatives. This is an important, challenging book.'

Anthony Storr, Author of *Solitude*

ABOUT THE AUTHOR

Renowned psychologist Michael J. Apter has taught and researched in a number of universities, including Yale, Georgetown, and Chicago in the United States, and Toulouse, Bergen, Cardiff, and Louvain in Europe. His revolutionary work on reversal theory led to the foundation of the Reversal Theory Society, and the organization of a biennial international conference. In 1998 he co-founded Apter International, a management consultancy firm offering products and services to businesses and organizations, which has resulted in the development of a worldwide network of management consultants and trainers.

In the course of his career he has written or edited sixteen books and over 100 articles and book chapters, including *Reversal Theory* (Oneworld Publications, 2006), and his books have been translated into eight languages. He currently resides in Manassas, Virginia.

DANGER
Our Quest for Excitement

Michael J. Apter

ONEWORLD
OXFORD

DANGER

Published by Oneworld Publications 2007

ISBN-13: 978–1–85168–481–6
ISBN-10: 1–85168–481–6

Typeset by Jayvee, Trivandrum, India
Cover design by Mungo Designs
Printed and bound by Bell & Bain Ltd., Glasgow

Oneworld Publications
185 Banbury Road
Oxford OX2 7AR
England
www.oneworld-publications.com

To Mitzi
And to Clifton Suspension Bridge
NEW YEAR'S EVE 1989

Contents

Preface   ix

 1 Playing with Fire   1
 2 The Protective Frame   13
 3 Danger's Delight   36
 4 Into the Safety Zone   53
 5 On the Sidelines   64
 6 How People Differ   80
 7 Getting Turned On   93
 8 Fueling the Flames   111
 9 The Fallacious Frame   125
10 Crime and its Pleasures   145
11 The Glamor of War   164
12 Risk, Rebellion, and Change   186

Notes   211
Index   231

Preface

One of the most obvious, but at the same time most puzzling, features of human behavior would appear to be the pointlessness of so much of it.

Even as I sit in my study, considering these opening words, I can easily turn my head and gaze through a window overlooking the bay of this seaside resort. A light drizzle is falling, the smooth sea as gray as gunmetal. Yet there are people out on the water, going on with their various activities. Far in the distance, I can see three men in a speedboat pulling a fourth behind them on water skis. Nearer the shore, a man in a wetsuit is teetering precariously on a sailboard. Now he falls in. Presently two teams of rowers emerge from a misty area, racing each other across the inlet.

Why, I ask myself, in a momentary mood of detachment and self-induced perplexity, are people freely engaging in such strange activities —activities that are uncomfortable, unnecessary, and even unsafe? Why would people exert energy when they do not have to; or set up goals for themselves that lead nowhere beyond themselves; or take unnecessary risks? One answer that immediately presents itself, of course, is that such activities are pleasantly stimulating, even exciting. But this answer only raises a host of new questions.

The aim of this book is to explore this quest for excitement, and to try to answer at least some of the questions it spawns. For example: Just what is excitement? Why do most of us experience the need for it at various times? What are the different ways in which we go about trying to achieve it? What biological or other functions does it serve? What happens when it goes wrong?

The search for answers to these and many other relevant questions will lead us into some strange byways of human experience, as well as allow us to see "normal" and "everyday" aspects of human behavior in a new—and sometimes surprising—light. Indeed, one of the underlying themes of this book is the way that even the most bizarre, horrendous, and seemingly inexplicable types of human activity can often be understood as variants on things which all of us want or do from time to time. As the Roman writer Terence put it: "I am a man. I consider nothing human to be alien from me." This sentiment is the basis for all that follows here. More specifically, one argument will be that we can go some way towards understanding such deviants as the reckless adventurer, the social misfit, and the hardened criminal—not by looking at them as if they were members of a different species, but by looking inwards at ourselves and discovering them at the very heart of our own normality.

It might seem that my preoccupation in this book with danger and violence (not to overlook sex) means that my book is merely an exercise in sensationalism. In fact my intention is much more subtle and interesting: it is to investigate what it is about human nature that *makes sensationalism possible.*

I make no apologies for the fact that this book is primarily for the general reader rather than the professional psychologist. This means neither that it is not a serious work, nor that the ideas and evidence on which it is based are not part of the "legitimate" psychological literature. What it *does* mean is that my primary aim here is to make the ideas involved as accessible as possible to the reader who possesses no special psychological knowledge. I have attempted to do this in the main by using concrete illustration drawing on personal reminiscences, newspaper reports, autobiographical writings, and the like. In this way, I believe that I have brought the ideas to life in a manner which would not otherwise have been possible. But I am well aware that in using these materials for this purpose I may be misunderstood by my professional colleagues. So let me emphasize again that although this book is not an academic one (it does not refer in detail to laboratory research, or make continual reference to the scholarly literature, beyond brief notes of some of the more important studies), the theory on which it is based—"reversal theory"—is one that has been developed in a rigorous way and led to a growing field of empirical research. Such development and research having been described at length elsewhere, this is not the place to go over it all again. (Reference to some books on reversal theory will, however, be found in a footnote to the final chapter.)

Most of the material to be presented here, therefore, is in the nature of illustration rather than proof, of exposition rather than demonstration. But I should also add that the variety of types of illustrative material that it has been possible to use does, in my view, demonstrate in a particularly compelling way something of the explanatory power and elegance of the underlying theory. And the ease with which it can be shown to be applicable to matters which are part of everybody's everyday experience does provide a kind of strength lacking in some other psychological theories of emotion. Nor is the theory just a trivial redescription of what people already know; it also leads to some rather unexpected conclusions concerning the psychology of risk-taking, aggression, sexual perversion, and other important psychological topics.

The introduction of some new technical terms drawn from reversal theory has been unavoidable. True, terms of this kind can often make a passage of writing seem awkward and stilted. Indeed, in the worst excesses of writing in the human sciences, especially in sociology, one sometimes sees banal ideas wrapped up in a ludicrous cloak of obscure terminology. My reason for using the terms I have is partly as a kind of shorthand, to avoid having to spell certain ideas out over and over again. And partly it is a way of bringing out the strength of the theory, by showing how the same concepts are useful in a variety of different situations and settings, and how they relate to a diverse range of psychological questions.

While I was writing this book, usable material thrust itself at me from all directions. I could not open a magazine or a newspaper, turn on television, read a book, or listen to the radio without being presented with new illustrations of my theme. Nor could I observe the everyday behavior of myself, and of others with whom I came in contact, without being frequently struck by its relevance. The problem of writing then became more one of selection, of choosing the most appropriate from a wealth of examples, than of searching out and carefully polishing precious pieces of hard-won information. There was no need to do any special reading. Passages from my normal everyday reading seemed to jump out of the page at me. Nor, with the exception of a visit to Pamplona, did I have to do any special fieldwork: wherever I went, the field went with me.

As it happens, since I have been traveling a great deal, the examples tend to have an international flavor. Quite fortuitously, this emphasizes the universality of the psychological processes involved. Much of the book was, however, written while I was a Fellow at the Netherlands Institute of Advanced Studies, and I would like to express my gratitude to that splendid organization for presenting me with an ideal opportunity for uninterrupted writing. I would also like to thank my many friends and colleagues in the reversal theory community for their advice and also for their help in drawing my attention to relevant materials. I am particularly grateful to my colleagues at Apter International: Steve Carter, Marie Shelton, and Gareth Lewis, and also to Ludmilla Rickwood, Randall Braman, John Kerr, Sven Svebak, Jay Lee, Kathleen O'Connell, Kathryn Lafreniere, Mark McDermott, Jennifer Tucker, Mary Gerkovich and to many others who are no less valued for not being mentioned here.

Juliet Mabey, Kate Smith and Kate Kirkpatrick at Oneworld Publications and Justine Gore-Smith were all a delight to work with, and I would like to thank them here for their dedication and support.

My wife Mitzi Desselles was brave enough to act as a friendly critic. I can report that this has not damaged our marriage, but rather has greatly enhanced this book—which I am delighted to have the opportunity to dedicate to her.

Michael J. Apter

1

Playing with Fire

THE PARADOXES OF EXCITEMENT

Some years ago I was lying on an empty beach, sunbathing. It was the end of the summer vacation season, but the autumnal air was still deliciously warm. I was peacefully listening to the murmur of the waves when I heard a distant droning sound get nearer and louder. Sitting up, I could just make out a light aircraft that seemed to be swooping down towards the beach. As it got closer, I realized with sudden panic that it was heading straight towards me, and might even be intending to land on the part of the beach where I was lying. I stood up and started running. But before I had time to cover much distance the plane roared overhead, perhaps 30 feet above the beach: as it swept past, I quite clearly caught a glimpse of the pilot waving. Then, as it climbed steeply away, glinting in the sun, the pilot tipped the wings several times. And as he did, I realized with amazement that my feelings had switched from panic to exhilaration—and I jumped up and down, waving like an idiot. Later, thinking about it all, it came to me that my panic *and* the exhilaration that followed it so quickly were intimately related in some way. But how could such opposite emotions be so closely tied together?

Panic and exhilaration are deliberately linked in fairgrounds and leisure parks, where the rides are designed to take the control of one's body out of one's own hands, and to throw one's body around in various ways. Here people can experience what it is like to fall out of the sky, to be held upside-down, and to loop-the-loop—often in quick succession. "There's a marvelous mood of frenzy as everybody screams together," says the marketing director of a leisure park, referring to a ride known as the Corkscrew:

> It's the exhilaration of whizzing through G-forces, snaking through a double helix upside down with no idea of what awaits you one second ahead, subjecting your body to pressures and physical sensations that are available nowhere else. You don't feel lethargic when you come off that ride. It's the nearest you can get to flying. And when you've experienced the Corkscrew once, you want to experience it again. One man rode it 50 times in one day.[1]

But why do people (at least *some* people), enjoy putting their bodies under these kinds of stresses? Why do they enjoy the sensations that go with the impression of being physically at risk? And how is it that screams can represent joy?

Some people also scream when they watch horror films: The popularity of film series such as *Halloween, Scream*, and *A Nightmare on Elm Street* gives evidence that there is a fascination among many people for the macabre, and a delight to be had from shock and terror. Now, it might be argued that this is a minority taste; not everyone goes to horror films, reads books about vampires, or buys lurid comic-strip magazines. But who will deny that they have read—and read with a certain thrill—the newspaper account of some grisly murder, or paused over photographs of some terrible natural catastrophe? And who among us will not admit to having slowed down while passing a car accident, to have a good look? We may not be proud of such reactions. But they would appear to exist as part of normal human psychology. And they require explanation, especially since they do not seem to fit very well with the idea most of us have about ourselves that we are kind and caring people.

What is even stranger is that some people go beyond being observers and take *real* risks, and expose themselves to *real* harm of one kind or another, and that they do so completely voluntarily. Why do people, of their own free will, participate in such activities as sky diving, mountaineering, bungee-jumping, white-water rafting, big wave surfing, pot-holing, base jumping, cave diving, and hang-gliding?

In this respect, it is interesting that new forms of voluntary risk are continually emerging or being invented in different parts of the world, and this seems to have been particularly true in the last decade or so. Here are just a handful of examples. In "coasteering," which started in Wales, people scramble around coastline cliffs in a mixture of rock climbing, swimming, and cliff jumping. In "canyoneering," as practised in the Swiss Alps, they slip, slide, and jump down canyons, and through rapids and waterfalls. In "downhill sliding," largely practised in California, riders career down steep city streets on skateboards, using slider gloves to help control their descent. In "heli-skiing," skiers in the American Rockies jump from helicopters onto virgin snow and ski down far from crowds (or the possibility of help). In a variation, skiers parachute from planes onto the slopes. In yet another use of ski slopes, this time in the summer when the snow has gone, "downhill mountain-biking" involves bikers taking the ski lifts with their bicycles up to the top of the slopes and then riding them down as fast as they can. The variations on climbing, falling, scrambling, and other risks seem endless as different permutations and combinations are created and experimented with, come in and out of popularity, remain marginal or are institutionalized and commercialized. We seem to be in a golden age of risk-activity invention.

The best known of recent forms of voluntary risk must be the collection of sports known as "extreme sports." Although these have been around individually in various forms for some years, they came to more general public attention when the television network ESPN set up and broadcast what they called the "X games," which have been held annually since 1995. At the heart of the X games are a set of activities which all involve the thrill of getting airborn by riding skates, skateboards, snowboards, bikes, BMX bikes (i.e. bicycle motocross bikes), and other devices, all of which can be used to shoot you into the air from ramps or in other ways. The aim of most of these activities is to perform various tricks and gyrations in the air before landing. The majority of the competitors are amateur, and injuries occur on a regular basis.[2]

In these and similar cases, it would appear that people do things not just *despite* the risk but, at least in part, *because* of it. They enjoy being, at least in certain circumstances, at what I shall call the dangerous edge of things. Nor is this phenomenon limited to the young and healthy. Once something is labeled as dangerous, it seems to exert a magnetic attraction to young and old alike. For example, from the moment the council of the seaside town in Wales where I was living at the time pronounced that the promenade along the seafront was in a dangerous condition, the crowds flocked, not just to see it, but to walk along it. The chance of the whole structure collapsing into the sea made it more popular than ever. Certainly the rope cordon intended to keep everyone out made not the slightest bit of difference. The young ducked under it, the old stepped over it, and those in wheelchairs—and even mothers pushing babies in prams—had it lifted for them.

· To take another (and rather larger-scale) example: business consultant Iben Browning announced that, according to his calculations, there was a 50–50 chance of an earthquake occurring in the area of New Madrid, Missouri on 3 December 1990, give or take a day. Interest in the quake built up until on the day itself traffic was snarled up by visitors from all over the country who had come to sightsee and to relish the atmosphere of danger. Many of them finished up at Hop's Tavern, where a Shake, Rattle, and Roll party went on all day.[3] The question that this happening raises is: why is danger so glamorous, and for some people so irresistible?

In some parts of the world such risk-taking is not only condoned by authorities, but even encouraged and institutionalized. Consider, for instance, the "fire festivals" that take place in towns in Catalonia in northeast Spain. These are usually associated with the annual town festival, the organizers including in the festival procession numerous *diablos del fuego*—fire devils. Men, dressed as ferocious satanic figures complete with tails and horns, carry with them arsenals of fireworks which they are expected to use in an aggressive way against the spectators lining the route. What they do is attach each firework to a pole, light it, and then run amok in the crowds. The fireworks all have within them a reed device which makes them whine and whistle like artillery shells, and they all similarly finish by detonating loudly. After a while everything is covered by a thick pall of smoke, while wave after wave of devils continue their attacks, even running into open shops with their poles or attacking with "flame-thrower" fireworks those watching from balconies. And, where the sidewalks open out sufficiently to allow terrace cafes, they dart among the tables, leaving a floating confetti of still-sparkling cinders —causing the customers (who shortly come out from behind the chairs they have been holding up for self-protection) to furiously brush off their hair and clothes.

The danger at these festivals of literally playing with fire, even if generally believed small, is real. Every year a number of people are treated in hospitals for burns, and all the spectators on the route of the procession are likely to suffer from small pinprick burns, burnholes in their clothes, and a ringing in the ears that lasts for hours afterwards. Again, the question is: why do people [including the present writer] willingly expose themselves to these dangers and discomforts? Such behavior, like other behavior cited above, is paradoxical in that it increases rather than decreases the chance of coming to harm. It seems in fact to work against our own natural interests.

It is also possible, it seems, for the fun and thrill to come in a more sinister way: through violence towards others. A much publicized example has been the practice of "wilding," a term used most notably by, and about, bored and disaffected youths to describe the way in which they band together into "wolf packs" and rove around looking for trouble and generally raising hell. Such trouble can include shoplifting, pickpocketing, mugging, rape, and gratuitous aggression towards those unfortunate enough to cross their paths. Starting in New York, both the term and the phenomenon have spread around the world.[4] What originally brought wilding to public light back in the 1980s was the much discussed case of the

Central Park jogger, a 28-year-old female investment banker who was accosted while jogging in New York City's most prominent park. She was beaten, gang-raped, and left unconscious and near death by a gang of youngsters aged 14 to 17.

The mayhem of such groups seems neither to have any special racial basis (victims can be of any color), nor to be motivated primarily by a need for money (not all victims are robbed), nor to be a result of drug-taking (typically, those involved are not on drugs at the time). Indeed, there seems to be little sense or reason to the pattern of the rampages, except the desire for violence itself and the "high" that goes with it. What the term "wilding" seems to mean is "being wild for its own sake," which is another way of saying being violent to keep boredom at bay, and for the sake of the thrills that such violence brings. But how is it that hurting others can produce thrills?

When we look at all these kinds of behavior, many questions arise which are clearly interrelated: they all have to do with the quest for excitement, and the way in which excitement is somehow tangled up not only with anxiety but also with other unpleasant emotions, such as horror, panic, and disgust. The aim of this book is to disentangle this knot. It is to show that there is in fact a clear underlying structure which, once discerned, can help us to make sense of all the strange kinds of behavior that have just been exemplified. And strange they are, because they involve people enjoying things they are not supposed to enjoy, and willingly doing things that are widely considered unpleasant, risky, or both.

Certainly we shall be able to look at many of the intriguing phenomena that have to do with excitement-seeking and explore and map the particular ways in which it expresses itself in different times and places, and in different people. This essentially descriptive task is in itself both interesting and worth doing. But if the book were to do *only* this it would represent little more than a systematic extension of the sort of magazine article that appears fairly regularly under such headings as "The Thrill-seekers" or "The Dare Devils." What this book really endeavors to contribute is something much more—namely, a general and coherent account of the phenomena that enter into excitement-seeking, in all their amazingly varied forms; and an explanation of the paradoxical behavior so often associated with it.

The aim of this study, in brief, is to answer questions of the kind raised in the opening paragraphs of this chapter. This is worth doing for three reasons. First, psychology should be concerned with *all* aspects of human behavior and experience. But excitement and other kinds of pleasant "high arousal" emotions have on the whole been strangely neglected by psychologists—especially in comparison with anxiety, which has tended to take all the limelight. Second, excitement-seeking, and phenomena related to it, raise some problems about human nature which are, as we have just seen, especially puzzling. They fairly cry out for explanation. Third, some of these problems are more than merely intellectual. They are societal. For example, it may be asked: How do we prevent vandalism? How do we reduce the incidence of rape? How can we stop people from indulging in risky sexual behaviors? How, in what might be called "The Age of Boredom," do we help disaffected youngsters to come to terms with themselves and their society, and to enter into more fulfilling activities and relationships with others? And these questions reflect only a few of the practical problems we will touch on in the pages ahead. I cannot pretend that they will be fully solved. But if by examining them we can gain a better understanding of their psychological roots, we shall be in a much better position to start to deal with them more effectively.

Although all this might seem to imply that excitement-seeking is always problematic, such is of course far from the case. Everyday life is full of perfectly normal and healthy activities which provide, among other things, the possibility of excitement. Indeed, a substantial part of our waking life seems to be spent in their pursuit: playing and watching sports; attending stage shows and movies; listening to music; betting on horses; dancing at discos; going to parties, bars, and nightclubs; driving fast; playing cards; trying new kinds of food; visiting foreign countries. One may even, if one is lucky, experience some form of excitement while watching television.

Clearly, then, excitement-seeking is basic to human nature. This does not mean that everyone seeks excitement all the time, or the same level of it all the time, or even that it is involved in every kind of pleasure. Nor does this mean that it is necessarily predominant in many of those activities in which it plays one or another sort of part. What it does mean is that *every normal person seems to need excitement some of the time—some people more often than others—and that we must recognize this if we are to gain a full and accurate picture of human nature.*

We should also not forget that sexual excitement plays a major role in most normal adults' lives, and that this excitement (and especially the excitement that comes with orgasm) is probably the most pleasurably intense form that most of us will ever experience. Indeed, as we shall see in later chapters, excitement from a variety of different sources is frequently described in sexual terms because sexual excitement can be taken as prototypic. The mild stimulation of flirtation, the developing excitement of foreplay, and the climactic ecstasy of orgasm all provide an accessible metaphoric language for describing excitement of other kinds.

The central importance of sexuality in human life was, of course, first emphasized by Sigmund Freud in the early years of the last century. We would expect therefore that Freud would have a great deal to say about the pleasures of excitement. Ironically, the whole tenor of Freudian theory is to see any kind of arousal, including sexual arousal, as something which people try to avoid. He was therefore unable to recognize the obvious fact that sexual behavior in its normal healthy form is all about the enjoyment of erotic stimulation. In the Freudian account sex becomes furtive, sinister, and problematic rather than joyful and ecstatic. Clearly, Freud's theory can therefore contribute little to the arguments of this book.

One other thing needs to be made clear at the beginning. Risk-taking and excitement are closely related, and risk and danger will be central to much of what follows. But this book is not about risk-taking as such, except to the extent that it is used to create excitement. After all, people may need to take risks for all kinds of reasons, and excitement is only one of them.[5] For example, someone may be forced to take a financial risk and do so with no feeling or expectation of excitement, but rather with trepidation. In this case the hoped for benefit will be of another kind. At the same time, we shall see that excitement can be brought about for a whole range of reasons that have little or nothing to do with risk. So, to repeat, the focus of this book is on excitement, and risk will be dealt with in relation to this theme rather than the other way around.

A PREVIEW OF THIS BOOK

The main purpose of this book is to provide an analysis of excitement, especially of the way in which it enters into the whole gamut of human emotional experience and expression. And the aim is to do so in a way that allows us to make sense of such puzzles as those we have just looked at. In fact, in the coming chapters it will be argued that there are universal principles involved. So in order to build up a unifying theory, these principles will be introduced in a step-by-step fashion.

Let us take a fast first look at the overall structure of this book—of what it will cover, and the order in which the different topics will be dealt with. This may not make a lot of sense at this point, but at least it will immediately impart something of the flavor of the fare, and should in any case also provide an orientation to bear in mind as you progress through the chapters ahead.

The first question to be addressed is: what is excitement, and how does it relate to such unpleasant emotions as fear and anxiety? In chapter 2 the relationship between excitement and anxiety will be traced, and from this it will emerge that they can only be understood in relation to each other—that they are in fact opposite sides of the same coin. It is interesting in this respect that much of the psychology of the emotions has, over the years, dealt with anxiety, but very little has dealt with excitement.[6] The starting point of this book then, is not only that excitement is as basic and important in human affairs as anxiety, but also that the two are inextricably bound together, and make sense only when taken that way. Chapter 2 will also show just how excitement and anxiety differ, and what it is that decides which side of the coin will be uppermost at any given time.

In chapter 2 the key explanatory concept of the book will also be introduced, that of the "protective frame." This "frame" is a way of seeing the world at a given time which implies that one is ultimately safe from whatever dangers arise at that time, even in the *danger zone*; that one is in some way disengaged from the brute realities of real life, at least for the time being. By its presence or absence it determines, among other things, whether anxiety or excitement will constitute the emotional response to arousing situations. We shall also see, since the protective frame is something that comes and goes, how our experience shifts around between these different (and opposing) ways of experiencing life. Indeed, it will become appreciated that in some very real sense we are all different kinds of people at different times, with different needs, feelings, emotions, and ways of seeing things.

In the following chapter (chapter 3) we shall also take up the metaphor of the dangerous edge and see how, when the protective frame is firmly in place, we *welcome* risk, challenge, and danger—how, in fact, we *like* to "go to the edge." There is, however, more than one kind of protective frame, and this theme is pursued in the two subsequent chapters (chapters 4 and 5). In the course of the argument it will be shown how not only danger can be enjoyed within the enclave of a protective frame, but also all those situations and events that would otherwise be productive of a variety of unpleasant emotions. In turn this insight allows us to explain some of the most puzzling and paradoxical features of human behavior.

The theme of individual differences—of the different ways in which, and the degrees to which, individuals need, experience, and respond to situations which induce excitement and other emotions—will run throughout the book. But it is taken up and dealt with explicitly in chapter 6, which also asks why people differ in these respects. The range of experiences that can cause strong sensations and emotions is reviewed in chapter 7.

The next three chapters (chapters 8, 9, and 10) are primarily concerned with exploring how things can go wrong in relation to behavior within the protective frame. These chapters map out a kind of pathology of excitement-seeking which complements the more traditional pathology of anxiety. In the first of them we shall look at what happens when different sources of arousal and stimulation are added to each other in the hope of increasing feelings of excitement. Such a process of combining sources of arousal is not in itself problematic. For example, at a professional baseball game the organ music adds its own increment of arousal to the innate excitement of the game. But when, for instance, risk is added to the excitement of a sexual encounter, real problems can ensue. In the second chapter of this set of three we shall focus on what happens when the protective frame is so misleading that people think they are safe when they are not, and therefore carry out foolhardy actions. In the third of these chapters, the topic will be the kinds of antisocial behavior that may arise when the individual treats life like a kind of game, feeling protected from the consequences of his or her actions even when these are immoral or illegal (such as shoplifting, vandalism, or rape).

In a chapter on the psychology of war (chapter 11), it will be suggested that seemingly traumatic experiences, such as those associated with fighting in battle, may in fact be experienced, at least on occasion, as euphoric—provided that methods are found for maintaining the protective frame under these extreme conditions. Also, it will be argued that any sufficiently arousing event (like a war) inevitably becomes just another spectator sport for those not participating in it directly. This view may seem cynical, but it nevertheless is, I believe, an unavoidable conclusion.

Underlying these themes is the most basic and tantalizing puzzle of all, which is examined in chapter 12, wherein a solution is suggested. Given that excitement-seeking can lead to risky behavior, that often such risk is quite gratuitous, and that on occasion it will lead to actual harm, why has the propensity for excitement-seeking remained part of not only human nature but also human *culture?* In other words, why has it not been weeded out by natural selection during the course of human evolution and the span of the development of culture? This question leads to another important issue to be considered: If the need for excitement has, in the difficult evolutionary past, presented certain biological advantages to the human species, will it continue to do so in the supposedly easier technological future? The part that excitement-seeking plays in *individual* development is also examined in this final chapter.

In moving through these issues and arguments, I shall from time to time direct things back to you, the reader. How often do *you* seek excitement in your life? In what ways do you seek it? What are you willing to sacrifice for it? Do you take unnecessary risks? My intention here is that you should finish this book with a clearer understanding of what is, after all, something which, it is reasonable to assume, is of the greatest interest to you: your own personality. It should be clear that this book is about more than dangerous sport—interesting as this is. Rather, it is about a paradoxical yet fundamental aspect of human nature.

2

The Protective Frame

In this chapter I am going to lay down some of the broad foundations of the theory on which the rest of this book is based. The argument, especially early in the chapter, may seem a little dry, but it is essential for everything which follows in this book. Without an understanding of the way in which anxiety and excitement differ from each other, and the meaning of the protective frame in relation to this difference, none of the discussions in later chapters about such phenomena as dangerous sports, thriller movies, sexual risk-taking, psychopathic murder, and the experience of military combat, will make sense.

GOOD AND BAD AROUSAL

Just what *is* excitement? Its most obvious feature, at the outset, is that it has to do with being worked up about something—that is, about being emotionally involved, or having an intense experience of some kind. In physiological terms, it is about what psychophysiologists refer to as being "aroused."

A great deal is known about the physiology of arousal, which has been an enormous area of study especially since Walter Cannon, an American physiologist, carried out his pioneering research in the

1920s.[1] He studied particularly what he called "fight or flight" reactions. These are reactions of the body which prepare it for action, and especially the kind of strenuous action that might be involved in hunting, fleeing from danger, and a variety of serious emergencies. (He could also have included here the preparation of the body for sexual activity.) Generally speaking, when an individual feels emotionally aroused, this is the mental concomitant of such bodily arousal. So when one is worked up, one will also typically experience a number of bodily symptoms which represent the way in which the body is becoming activated. Thus one may detect a pounding of the heart, and deepened breathing (even gasping); one's mouth may become dry; there may be a sinking feeling in the pit of the stomach; one may start to perspire; and so on.

These are all signs that the part of the nervous system called the *autonomic nervous system* is functioning in a particular way. This system, which is spread throughout the body in a diffuse manner, controls the body's "housekeeping" functions. These are functions of which we are normally unaware except when we become aroused, and which are generally not under our conscious control (e.g. the rate at which the heart beats, and the amount of saliva being released into the mouth).

The autonomic system is made up of two branches which work in opposite directions: the *sympathetic* branch (which tends to increase the body's level of arousal) and the *parasympathetic* branch (which tends to decrease it). When we are experiencing being aroused, then, the sympathetic system is dominating the parasympathetic, setting up a pattern of activation designed to marshal the body's resources for action. Faster and deeper breathing brings more oxygen into the body and expels carbon dioxide more rapidly. The pounding of the heart represents the fact that the organ is beating faster so that the blood can carry greater quantities of oxygen and sugar to the muscles where they are going to be needed. Perspiration helps the body to keep cool during exertion. And the dryness of the mouth and discomfort of the stomach mean that digestive processes, which have low priority during an emergency, are temporarily receiving less of the body's resources. One other important effect of the action of the sympathetic nervous system is the stimulating of the adrenal glands into secreting adrenaline. This hormone, as it courses through the body, helps to maintain over a longer period all the changes just described.

We should not forget that while all this is happening to the body, the brain itself is also likely to become aroused, in the sense of becoming more alert and active. This result is actually brought about by a different part of the nervous system, that known as the *reticular activating system*, which exists in the brain stem—a small structure at the base of the brain, roughly where the spine enters it.

Since being excited involves being activated in the ways just described, it might appear that we can equate excitement with such overall activation of the body (and brain). Unfortunately this will not work, since not only is excitement associated with this kind of activation, but anxiety is, too. In both anxiety and excitement we see the body becoming prepared for action in exactly the same manner. And in both cases the degree to which one is worked up appears to relate in a fairly obvious way to the global level of bodily activation that has been induced by the sympathetic nervous system. In other words, there appear to be no obvious patterns of physiological change which differ depending on whether excitement or anxiety is being experienced. Physiological arousal, then, is a kind of gross bodily activation which in itself does not reflect such emotional distinctions.

In a classic and oft-cited experiment carried out by the psychologists Schachter and Singer in the early 1960s, human subjects were given injections of adrenaline in order to increase arousal. Some subjects were told the truth about the injections, while others were misinformed, being told that their injection was a vitamin. Those who were misinformed about the source of their arousal were then put in different situations. Believing that their arousal was due to these situations, the specific emotions they reported depended on the nature of the situations. In other words, the same arousal was experienced differently depending on how subjects, as it were, explained it to themselves. So an emotion involves both arousal, which is physiological, and some kind of subjective interpretation, which is psychological.[2]

So that we may make sense of the difference between the two emotions of anxiety and excitement, we must turn from the physiological to the psychological level, then, seeing those emotions as different ways of experiencing essentially the same bodily arousal. Here we should note straight away the basic qualitative difference between them. Excitement is pleasant and anxiety unpleasant. Excitement merges into, or is part of, such good emotions as thrill, euphoria, and (even) ecstasy. Anxiety is related to, or is part of, such bad emotions as apprehension, fear, terror, and (even) panic. To put it at its simplest, excitement is a kind of good arousal, and anxiety a kind of bad arousal. Excitement is therefore what we experience when watching a tense game of football, during a thriller film, or while making love. Anxiety is felt while waiting to see the dentist, looking for one's name on an examination pass list, or being interviewed for a job.

One common way in psychology of trying to distinguish between the two kinds of emotion has been to claim that they are different in level (i.e. intensity) of arousal. The argument is that anxiety involves much more intense arousal than does excitement.[3] But clearly this simplistic view will not hold. If we think back to the examples of chapter 1, and especially if we think of sexual intercourse, it is obvious that excitement can be very high in intensity— every bit as high as anxiety. For that matter, anxiety can also be relatively mild without turning into excitement: being slightly worried about whether one will be late for work is not the same as feeling excited about the prospect. It should be evident, therefore, that we cannot explain away the difference between the two in terms of intensity. There has to be a qualitative difference which cuts across different levels of arousal.

Yet level of intensity *does* come into things, in the sense that the more intense the excitement, the more pleasant it feels, and the more intense the anxiety, the more *un*pleasant it feels. This suggests that it might be helpful to think of things in terms of a graph, and to plot out what the relationship between intensity and pleasure might look like for different levels of arousal and different levels of pleasure. This has been done in figure 2.1, in which it can be seen

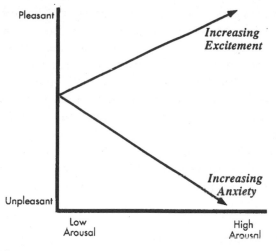

Figure 2.1

that there are two lines, one representing different levels of excitement and the other different levels of anxiety. It will be noted that the two diverge from each other in terms of how pleasant or unpleasant they are as the intensity of the arousal increases.

The excitement line (the upper one in the graph) represents such experiences as the feeling of expectancy and magic building up that many of us experienced as children on Christmas Eve, that people experience on their way to watch championship sports events, and that teenagers feel as they prepare to go to a party. Of course, what goes up must come down. Eventually, in all such cases, the pleasure subsides as one slides back down the excitement line to no more than moderate arousal.

The anxiety line (the lower one on the graph) represents a very different class of situations—those in which, as arousal increases, it is experienced as increasing anxiety, or some similar emotion like worry, fear, dread, or panic. We are now talking about the feelings that build up, say, in a school child waiting to see the headmaster about breaking school rules; in an employee unexpectedly called in to see the boss; or a woman about to meet a devoted boyfriend whom she has decided to leave. The point is not just that these are unpleasant situations, but that the more worked up one gets in them, the worse one feels. As was the case for excitement, as arousal eventually returns to lower levels, so the anxiety subsides with it.

To illustrate the difference between the two lines in more concrete terms, let us look at how a given situation—preparing to perform on stage—can be experienced in these two opposite ways, one involving increasing excitement as arousal builds up, the other increasing anxiety.

Consider first the following extracts from Sir Laurence Olivier's book *On Acting* in which he describes his feelings as he prepares a role (in this case Richard III) and then approaches the first night:

> The excitement was beginning. An actor, when he begins to sense that he is on to something, is a bit like a stoat coming out of its hole and smelling the morning air: the nose twitches and the body starts to tingle. The flash of lightning away in the distance, the thunder still muted, but coming, slowly coming! Everything begins to change: the taste buds improve, the sense of smell is more acute, the mind is constantly wrapping itself round the image which is to be created, then presented to an unsuspecting public.
>
> As an actor approaches a first night the sense of excitement is extraordinary. Like a bullfighter, everything is geared towards that moment, the moment of truth with his audience. [4]

In contrast, there follows an example of someone becoming increasingly anxious before going on stage, and therefore moving along the anxiety line rather than the excitement line. It comes from a description by the British comedian Les Dawson of his feelings while waiting to perform at a Royal Variety Show before the Queen:

> Artiste after artiste went up to the side of the stage like gladiators for the arena. I paced the floor of the dressing room, vainly trying to remember my lines ... how could I, a red nosed club and pub comic ever hope to entertain the Queen? ... Oh Christ the waiting ... my lips are dry and my heart is pounding like a sledge hammer ... Rudolf Nureyev is on stage, and the roar from the audience is a respectful

tribute to his talent. You fool Dawson, you're next on, get up and into the wings for your cue ... I can't go on, I cannot even hope to follow this. Madness all of it; out of my depth ... Meg is out there, my Meg, what will happen if I forget one line? Millions will see my downfall on their screens ... Sorry, Mother, sorry, Dad, I'm going to fail you ... I gape as the great dancer takes call after call from a wildly delighted audience. He stands erect and proud as he accepts the ovation ... I'm on.[5]

In fact, Dawson's performance turned out to be a triumph—but we saw, during the waiting beforehand, someone fearing the worst, and moving towards panic.

In these two accounts are starkly contrasted the two different ways in which increasing bodily arousal can be interpreted, one of them being consistent with the upper (excitement) line in our graph, and the other with the lower (anxiety) line. It would be difficult to find a better illustration of the fact that there are two *opposite* ways of experiencing increasing arousal.

OVER THE WHOLE AROUSAL RANGE

So far we have only looked at half the picture, in the sense that we have been looking at only the *top* half of the arousal range, from moderate to high arousal. What happens at the *lower* end of the range? As with high arousal, there is a common assumption in psychology that it all depends on the level of arousal, with extremely low arousal being unpleasant—boredom—and low arousal which is less extreme being pleasant, i.e. relaxation, tranquillity or calmness. But, just as was the case for high arousal, this view will not stand much examination, and for the same kind of reason. This is that very low arousal *can* be very pleasant; i.e. relaxation can be every bit as low in arousal as can boredom. What could be more pleasant and unaroused than taking a nice soaking bath at the end of a long day's work? Similarly, it is possible to be only a little bit bored without this being experienced as relaxation. We must

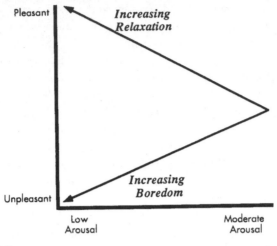

Figure 2.2

therefore infer that the situation is the same as it was for high arousal, with two different lines being required to represent the relationship between intensity of arousal and degree of pleasure or displeasure. These are shown in figure 2.2.

A rather interesting pattern now emerges from this analysis. The lower end of the arousal dimension is a *mirror image* of the upper end, as we see if we combine figures 2.1 and 2.2 in the way shown in figure 2.3. But, more than this, it becomes clear that the lines connect in such a way as to make *two* lines over the *whole* arousal dimension which cross over each other, rather than four separate lines. So, one line (the broken line in figure 2.3) extends from boredom all the way through to excitement, and the other (the solid line) from relaxation through to anxiety. This makes good psychological sense, since boredom is obviously opposite to excitement, and relaxation to anxiety. After all, boredom is what we feel if we want excitement and cannot get it, and excitement is what we feel when we overcome boredom. Similarly, anxiety is what we feel when we want relaxation and cannot get it, and relaxation is what we feel when we get rid of anxiety. Consider the following two concrete examples.

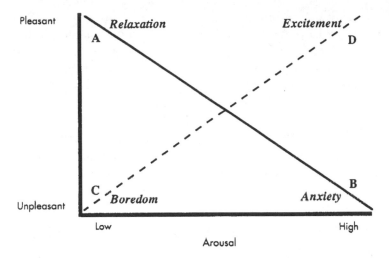

Figure 2.3

Example 1: A child is bored (position C in figure 2.3). He is just hanging around in his backyard, not knowing what to do with himself, desperately hoping for some distraction. Suddenly he sees that someone's infringing cat is in close pursuit of a resident mouse, and decides to try to rescue the rodent. During the ensuing chase, with the cat turning several times and spitting at him, the child gets worked up and excited (position D), especially when the mouse eludes the cat's lips and darts away, across the lawn, apparently to safety. At this point the child starts screaming, trying to frighten off the offending feline but to no avail. Eventually, the cat, complete with mouse in mouth, escapes the field of battle. Then, as the child calms down, he starts to feel bored again (back to position C). Here we see movement all the way up and down the complete boredom-excitement curve.

Example 2: The father of the child in example 1 has come back wearied from work and is slumped comfortably in a deck chair in the garden, sipping a gin and tonic. He is pleasantly relaxed (position A in the figure). Suddenly he hears his son screaming, and imagines that the child has been seriously hurt. His arousal level rises quickly and he feels anxiety (position B). He jumps up, spilling his drink all over himself in the process, and runs over to his son. When he discovers the meaning of the screaming, and the fact that there is nothing to be concerned about, he sighs with relief and trudges to the house to pour another drink. By the time he gets back to the deck chair and settles down again his arousal has subsided (to position A) and he is once more feeling relaxation (not to mention wet spots—but they don't seem to matter).

This is a deliberately everyday pair of examples emphasizing how processes we have discussed enter into everyday life. More dramatic and unusual examples will be given in later chapters.

EXCITEMENT-SEEKING AND ANXIETY-AVOIDANCE

There are, then, two different lines in our graph, each representing a contrasting way of experiencing arousal over the whole arousal range. In one of them, increasing arousal is increasingly pleasant, all the way from boredom to excitement. In the other, the opposite is the case, arousal becoming increasingly unpleasant, all the way from relaxation to anxiety.

It now becomes apparent that what we are talking about is two completely different *states of mind* (or ways of being) which we can call *excitement-seeking* and *anxiety-avoidance* respectively, each of them being represented by one of the lines in figure 2.3. These are opposite to each other over the whole arousal dimension, in that they are associated with contrary ways of experiencing bodily arousal and therefore prompt the individual to seek out *opposite* levels of arousal.

In the one case, arousal is felt as good, and is therefore welcomed—and even sought out. In the other case, it is experienced as bad—and is therefore avoided as far as possible. So not only does each state of mind have an opposition *within* it (excitement versus boredom in one case, anxiety versus relaxation in the other), but each state is in opposition *to* the other.

These contrasting states of mind, then, divide up our everyday experience between them. As we pass through our daily lives and encounter the various people, events, and situations that make them up, so we switch backwards and forwards between one state and the other, sometimes looking to get more worked up and involved, and sometimes to become more relaxed and calm. In this sense we truly are different kinds of people at different times. Indeed, since the two states are opposite, it could even be said that this kind of movement back and forth represents a kind of inherent inconsistency—even a self-contradiction—in human nature. Sometimes we want one thing, but at other times its opposite. A graphic illustration of this kind of inconsistency was related to me by a clinical psychologist who, while passing a fairground, saw a client of his (whom he was treating for chronic anxiety) riding on a roller coaster and apparently enjoying every moment of it. Here was an anxious patient, who supposedly spent his life avoiding arousal, deliberately seeking it out.

When we switch, or reverse, from one state to the other, we jump from one line in the graph to the other (see figure 2.3), with the consequence that arousal is immediately experienced in an opposite way. Thus, if you are experiencing excitement (somewhere around point D in the figure) and you switch to the other state, this means that you will drop perpendicularly onto the other line (somewhere around point B) and experience the arousal as anxiety instead of as excitement. For instance, say you are standing in line to get into a football game and are feeling excited—but someone tells you that your ticket may be forged. Your excitement turns instantaneously to anxiety.

In general, it can be seen that the greater the excitement before a reversal, the greater the anxiety afterwards, and vice-versa. The more extreme your position on the arousal dimension, the more dramatic a reversal will be (the greater will be the contrast between the pleasantness or unpleasantness of the emotions felt before and after the reversal). This of course applies at both ends of the arousal dimension, so that it would also be true to say that the more relaxed you are before a reversal, the more bored you will be afterwards, and vice-versa.

In a questionnaire study that a colleague and I carried out, we asked sports parachutists about how they experienced their dangerous activity. The most common sequence was something like this: they felt anxiety in the aircraft as they waited to jump, and this anxiety increased until the moment of leaping from the plane. It reached its peak while they were falling and before the parachute opened, this being what they estimated to be the moment of maximum danger. The moment that the parachute opened, however, they suddenly found themselves experiencing intense excitement instead of anxiety, and this excitement lasted all the way to the ground and stayed with them for a long period thereafter. In other words, in jumping from the plane they also jumped from point B in the graph to point D. Since their arousal was particularly high, so that they were somewhere towards the extreme right hand edge of the graph, both the anxiety and the excitement were intense, and the eventual excitement lasted a long time while the arousal slowly subsided.[6] Something similar was found in a study of people riding a downhill cable at high speed, with a movement from anxiety to excitement during the ride.[7] A similar switch, but in a very different activity, was observed in a study of dance performers: they experienced their strongest anxiety just before the curtain went up, and felt their most intense excitement immediately thereafter.[8]

This now puts the basic emotions of excitement, anxiety, boredom, and relaxation into a systematic framework which brings out the way in which they are related to, but different from, each other. This also brings out something of the dynamics involved in moving from one of these emotions to another. As you can see, there are two kinds of movement around this "emotional space." In one case, one moves up and down a curve, for example from anxiety to relaxation. In the other case, one switches from one curve to the other, for example from anxiety to excitement. As one person put it to me after I explained all this to him: "To change emotions, one can either jump or slide."

However, we still need to consider more the subjective nature of the two underlying states of mind. So let us come at things from a slightly different angle.

Consider first those circumstances in which you feel anxiety. In one way or another, anxiety always involves a response to some threat which has imposed itself on you, and which you fear you may not be able to overcome, or even cope with. It may be some danger to be avoided, unpleasantness to face up to, or nagging problem to be solved. But in any case it looks as if it will not go away. You fear the worst. And it involves something truly important to you: your health, your self-esteem, your financial state, your marriage. These problems appear to be real, serious, and not quite under your control—if at all. Of course, an outside observer may see your situation differently, but the point is that this is the way that *you* see it at the time.

Your arousal is part of your body's response to the threat that you perceive, but you are not sure of how to use the arousal to overcome the threat. If the threat *does* go away, or you manage to cope with it, then as the anxiety subsides you feel glorious relief. When the pain stops, when the doctor tells you that you do not have a serious disease, when a check turns up out of the blue to meet the demands of your creditors, the result can be joyous relaxation. Consider having had largely a bad day at the office because of a number of problems which, in the end, you solved. You come home through the rain or snow, have a bath, and settle down in comfort to eat your evening meal in your robe and slippers. The experience of no longer being worked up, of being tranquil and undisturbed, can be one of the greatest experiences of life.

Now think of excitement. In some sense this always involves a response to some challenge which has not been imposed on you but which you have freely chosen and which you feel more than adequate to deal with. There may be dangers and threats and problems, but they are all faced within a context of security. Either they do not really matter, when it comes right down to it, or you feel confident in your ability (or the ability of others who are protecting you) to cope. Or it may be that you are so absorbed in what you are doing that the question of whether it matters or not, whether you can cope or not, does not really arise for you at the moment in question. The threat, such as it is, is not to something basic and essential to your existence. You are not on the defensive but on the offensive.

Again, things may not seem that way to an outside observer, who may be aware of serious implications for you which you do not recognize at the time. The point is that *you* feel so optimistic and confident that you are interested in doing what you are doing for itself, rather than to achieve some important solution to a genuinely real and threatening life-problem. Hence you enjoy being worked up in playing tennis, because it does not really matter, in any "ultimate" sense, whether you win or lose. You become absorbed in your hobby and the problems it poses (you are building a boat in the back yard, or painting a still-life, or engraving the Book of Genesis on the back of your watch) and realize that it is the *activity* that is important, rather than the success of the end product. It is the journey rather than the destination that counts. Thus any uncertainty or unexpected snag adds piquancy to the situation, not desperation. But if it all becomes too easy, loses its challenge, descends into a run-of-the-mill ritual, so it becomes less and less stimulating, and your experience degenerates into one of monotony and boredom—the inverse of the relief experience after anxiety.

DANGER AND THE DANGEROUS EDGE

In order to spell out the difference between these two states of mind a little more fully, we need to look more closely at the idea of danger. The word "danger" in the English language is fundamentally ambiguous. On the one hand, it means being at risk in relation to some harm, injury, or loss; on the other, it means the actual harm, injury, or loss itself. If we walk on an unstabilized cliff edge there is a danger of our falling off. But falling off is itself the danger that we must be aware of. *Danger* means both that which constitutes the harm (the fall), and the risk that the harm will occur. Let us then reserve the term "danger" for the first of these (to denote the risk) and introduce the technical term "trauma" to mean the consequence of the risk when things do not work out (i.e., hurt, harm, damage, loss, injury, or pain).

Now, we can imagine every activity in life as having three zones: safety, danger, and trauma. In terms of the literal example of an edge just given, when you are *away from* the cliff edge you are in the *safety* zone, when you are *on* the cliff edge you are in the *danger* zone, and if you *slip or fall* (or are pushed) *over* the cliff edge you are, to put it in an odd-seeming way, in the zone of *trauma*. To help to conceptualize this, let us refer to the simple diagram shown in figure 2.4. (This metaphor of a cliff's edge will, as you no doubt already have guessed, run through the whole of this book.) Here is another example illustrating the three zones. Suppose that you are a bomb disposal expert. When you are at home (*sans* bomb) you are in the safety zone; when you are approaching and starting to dismantle a bomb you are in the danger zone; and of course if a bomb blows up while you are dismantling it you are in (if not all over) the trauma zone.

It may be objected that not every activity has a trauma zone, and therefore involves danger. But this is not strictly true in the very general sense of trauma intended here, even though admittedly in many activities the trauma may be extremely mild and extremely infrequent, and one may spend most of one's time in the safety zone. For example, chatting with one's spouse may not seem like a dangerous activity, but there is always the danger that one or the other spouse will say something that could lead to a bitter and hurtful row.

The boundary line between the danger and trauma zones we shall call the *dangerous edge* (see figure 2.4). The danger zone we may imagine as something like a slippery slope which changes its contours in such a way that at an unlucky, unexpected, or unguarded moment one may suddenly find oneself sliding over the dangerous edge and into trauma. The danger zone is therefore a kind of gray area between the white of safety and the black of trauma, and it may be experienced as relatively wide or narrow (or, to change the metaphor, steep-sloped, or shallow) at any given point and time. The distance one actually feels oneself to be from the dangerous edge (whether one is in the safety or the danger zone) is one's experienced *safety margin*. In the safety zone, then, there is

Figure 2.4

subjectively no immediate likelihood of trauma, whereas in the danger zone there is a possibility which increases subjectively the nearer we get to the dangerous edge.

Let me emphasize that the whole picture being drawn here, as represented in figure 2.4, is about the way the individual person sees the world, and not the way in which it is seen from the outside by someone else. So, by "trauma" is meant what would be traumatic to the involved person; how great the safety margin is at any given time is the distance away that the individual perceives possible trauma to be; and which zone the individual is in at any given time is entirely a matter of the way in which the individual experiences the situation. Thus, to say that the individual is in the *safety* zone means that he or she either is *not* aware of any danger of trauma, or believes it to be sufficiently distant not to be worth worrying about. To say that the individual is in the *danger* zone means that he or she *is* aware of the possibility of trauma.

Because these three types of zones are to be understood entirely *subjectively*, they may be more or less accurate in *objective* terms. For example: while driving, we normally feel that there is a solid margin of safety between us and the edge of the road. In fact, it is very small—in most cases a fractional turn of the steering wheel could mean instant mutilation, or death. Similarly, cars speeding towards us on the other side of the road miss us by only a matter of feet. But we do not normally feel threatened by this. These zones therefore are personal, and often changing, ways both of demarcating different aspects of one's "life-space" and of evaluating the events occurring within it. The perception of these zones may be more or less realistic in different situations.

THE MEANING OF THE PROTECTIVE FRAME

In light of this discussion of danger, we can now look again at the excitement-seeking and anxiety-avoidance states of mind. And here we come to one of the key arguments of this book.

In the excitement-seeking state, I suggest, there is a kind of psychological *protective frame* which one can imagine all along the inside of the dangerous edge. (See figure 2.4, where it is shown as a broken line to indicate that it is not a permanent feature of the situation, and may or may not be present at any given time.) This means that subjectively one feels that, when it comes to it, one will not actually go over the edge. This protective frame may come from one's own confidence, the availability of others to help one, the presence of physical aids, and the like. In the parachuting example that we looked at earlier, the open parachute constitutes the protective frame: it is what prevents one from falling to a certain death, and once it has opened one feels safe even though one is in mid-air and surrounded, as it were, by danger. To take another example, in "shark-cage diving," centered in South Africa, tourists descend below water in a protective cage from which they view and photograph sharks that have been lured to the area by blood that has been thrown into the water. The thrill comes from being very close to the sharks while feeling that one is protected by the cage. The effect of a protective frame is that a person can get very close to trauma without actually being traumatized.

In the anxiety-avoidance state, in contrast, a person feels that there is *no* such protective frame, that there is nothing to stop him or her from going over the abyss. He or she may even feel forces pushing them towards the slippery slope of the danger zone, so that the safety zone itself becomes a kind of *sub-danger* zone with its *own* risks. One then stands seemingly naked and without protection. In the parachuting example, until the parachute opens there is no

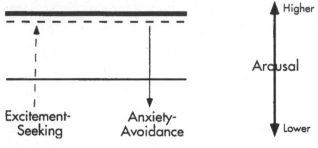

Figure 2.5

protective frame, at least for most people. That is, until it actually does open, one cannot be sure that it will actually open and protect one from a grisly demise.

In the excitement-seeking case, one's "life-world" is essentially benevolent, in the anxiety-avoiding case it is malicious. *So, whichever of the two curves that one is on, as depicted in figure 2.3, depends on whether such a protective frame is being experienced or not.*

In the excitement-seeking state, one can get to the dangerous edge with impunity. And one does indeed often try to get as close to the edge as possible in this state, because that is where arousal is likely to be at its highest. (Figure 2.5 represents diagrammatically the natural tendency of this state, equating arousal level with closeness to danger.) Thus someone might enjoy standing at the edge of a platform at a station and experiencing the overwhelming sensation and noise of an express train racing through—but only if he or she can assume that it will not come off the rails, or that he or she will not fall, or be pushed from behind, onto the tracks. Similarly, one can enjoy the roller coaster at the fairground because of feeling close to calamity even while having confidence that it will not actually occur. As a TV interviewee at an amusement park emphatically expressed himself about a ride: "Why am I getting on it? It's the thrill of being scared, *being on the edge.*"[9]

Think of looking at a tiger in a cage. Both the tiger *and* the cage are needed in order for one to experience excitement: the tiger without the cage would be frightening; the cage without the tiger would be boring. Both are necessary. In order to experience excitement, then, we need both the possibility of danger and something we believe will protect us from it. There is a kind of paradox here, of course, because the danger is needed to produce the arousal, whereas the perceived lack of *real* danger is what produces the feeling of protection that allows the arousal to be felt as excitement. But it is not a question of logic so much as of the "psycho-logic" of the emotions, which works in its own way. In terms of this psycho-logic it is perfectly possible to experience the paradox of danger which is not dangerous.

We should also note that a whole range of situations which cause excitement are also exactly those situations which cause anxiety and fear: being driven in a fast car, standing on the balcony of a tall building, trying to swim in high waves. Nor are the dangers that can cause excitement or anxiety necessarily physical ones. They may for instance be financial, or involve threats to self-esteem. Speaking in public, bidding at an auction, being interviewed on television, negotiating a business deal—all may be either exciting or frightening to different people, or to the same person at different moments. Everything depends on whether or not the arousing objects or events are experienced through a protective frame.

In the anxiety-avoidance state (in contrast to the excitement-seeking state) one attempts to make the safety margin as large as possible, and will feel great anxiety in the danger zone. (Figure 2.5 depicts the tendency of this state to move away from danger and towards safety, and hence from high to low arousal.)

All this may give the impression that the excitement-seeking state is inevitably a good-time state and that anxiety-avoidance is a state of misery. But in fact (in principle, anyway), pleasure and displeasure are equally possible in each state—they simply take different forms. After all, in the anxiety-avoidance state it is possible to feel an absence of threats and obligations, and therefore to be in the safety zone and to feel relaxed and at peace with oneself and the world.

And in the excitement-seeking state it *is* possible to feel oneself to be far away from where the action is, and as a result to be bored and restless (look back at figure 2.3). It should be quite clear, then, that the excitement-seeking state is *not* to be equated with the state of excitement. It is about what one *wants to* experience, not necessarily what one actually *does* experience. Similarly, the anxiety-avoidance state is *not* to be equated with anxiety. After all, one might be successful in avoiding anxiety, and in the safety zone experience the delight of relaxation instead.

The use of the word "frame" to depict that which psychologically limits (and in this sense acts as a containment of) the danger implies two kinds of metaphor. Both of them are helpful in understanding the point being made. The first metaphor implies something like a fortress framed by a wall with battlements. Or one could think of a stockade, or a dyke. Less dramatically, one could think of the railing along a cliff path, the balustrade on a balcony, or the containment barrier at a motorway. In all these cases there is something at the boundary which helps to keep back the danger—be it the danger of an enemy army, Native Americans (at least in old Westerns), inundation, falling, or crashing. The danger in each case is real, and the protective boundary cannot guarantee success. But it does provide a buffer—and perhaps, under normal circumstances, at least, safety.

Contrariwise, the *psychological* protective frame does not necessarily depend on a concrete physical presence of any kind, and that is why the second metaphor, to which we shall now turn, is in some ways more helpful and appropriate. This metaphor is that of a picture frame, the frame of a pair of glasses, or any of various other frames through which, or within which, viewing takes place. What is seen is then a result not only of what is there but also of how it is presented, focused, structured, or organized. A frame of mind is, in this respect, variously like a pair of sunglasses, distorting lenses, binoculars, or even rose-colored glasses, since it helps the viewer to see the world in a particular way at a given time. In these terms, the anxiety-avoidance and excitement-seeking states are different means of seeing what is there, the one focusing on the possibility of real danger, the other involving a frame which brings into view some defence which will provide adequate protection against any danger there might be.

This second metaphor is better than the first in emphasizing the impermanent and changeable nature of the protective frame which can, as it were, slip in and out of place from moment to moment—so that a person fluctuates in the way in which he or she sees the world over time, now feeling the arousal as pleasant, now as unpleasant. As the "lenses" drop in and out of place, so we feel different degrees of boredom and relaxation, anxiety or excitement.

REVERSALS OVER TIME

So that I may illustrate fluctuations of this kind, let me draw on two personal examples. (You will doubtless be able to find similar examples from your own experiences.) The first, a kind of situation I have experienced many times, involves making a commitment to do something in the future. On each occasion what happens proceeds more or less according to the following pattern: I agree to give a paper at a conference. At the time I agree, the conference itself is fairly far off, and so there is a large safety margin between me and the major threat that the conference might pose. This threat is of course to my professional reputation and self-esteem: I might let myself down in some small way, or even make a complete fool of myself. But at this distance in time the prospect is not very threatening. If I accept in the excitement-seeking state, then I may have difficulty raising much interest—although there might be momentary excitement over, for example, the prospect of the travel involved. If accepting in the arousal-avoidance state, however, I may at this stage feel relaxed about the whole thing. Whichever the case, as the conference nears, the threat suddenly looms over the horizon in a way which induces the arousal-avoidance state and simultaneously raises arousal, and I feel anxiety.

As the moment arrives for presenting the paper at the conference itself I feel increasing anxiety, which generally peaks at about the time I start to speak (subjectively the moment of greatest threat).

But at some point after this I find that I become fully absorbed in the whole task. And eventually a moment arrives at which I switch over to the excitement-seeking state and feel pleasure from the arousal I am experiencing. This may well continue until someone asks a difficult question, thus bringing about a switch to the anxiety-avoidance state and actual anxiety. But if I manage to answer the question in a way I feel is satisfactory, then the excitement-seeking state may kick back into operation. Finally, when the presentation is over and I return to the audience, although all threat is suddenly removed, arousal takes some time to return to normal. This is usually the best moment, because (since there is no longer any threat) now I will probably be in the excitement-seeking state. And the high arousal will continue, producing excitement for at least a while. Eventually, to be sure, the arousal subsides, and there may even follow a period of bored depression—although, if I have reverted to the anxiety-avoidance state, there may instead be relief and pleasant relaxation.

One kind of situation in which fluctuations can occur particularly rapidly is that in which there is ambiguity, leading one to see the situation first this way and then that, producing an alternation between the excitement-seeking and anxiety-avoidance states. Here is my second personal example, this time a very specific and concrete one which concerns a visit made to Romania to give lectures at different universities. This was during the period of the brutal and all-encompassing Ceausescu dictatorship.

I arrived at dusk at my hotel in a small town near the Russian border. A telephone message to my room asked me to come down to the hotel foyer, where I was met by a young lady who asked me (without explanation) to go with her to a car waiting outside. Inside the car, in the darkness, was the driver, and a man introduced to me as "the head of the laboratory." There was something they wanted me to see, the young lady explained. So we drove off into the night, in silence. Street followed street, all of them in darkness because of the Romanian energy crisis. The atmosphere seemed increasingly sinister, and I began to feel anxious. What could the purpose of the trip possibly be? We were clearly not going to the laboratory, and indeed we were soon on the very edge of town in an area where the apartment blocks were empty and lying in ruins. In the moonlight I could see the broken windows and doors hanging crookedly off their hinges. There was not a person in sight.

My imagination went to work, and I thought of the end of the novel by Franz Kafka called *The Trial*, in which the hero is taken out into the countryside at night and ceremoniously killed. I also thought of the ruined and desolate streets of Vienna in the film *The Third Man*, and of various spy thrillers set in Eastern Europe. These dramatic images suddenly gave me a thrill of excitement: I was taking part in a piece of fiction!

We drove on, still in silence, my feelings of excitement now alternated with growing feelings of anxiety as I experienced this ambiguous situation alternatively as either menacing or enjoyably melodramatic. Eventually the road turned to a track, and the car came to a halt. We all got out, except the young lady, and I was beckoned to follow as we staggered through the thick mud to what turned out to be the steep bank of a river. There, in the moonlight, I could just make out the shape of a tunnel from which a black river emerged. They appeared interested in that tunnel. I just stood looking at it until directed back to the car.

In the car, the purpose of the visit was at last explained to me by the head of the laboratory, using the young lady as his translator. His research team, including psychologists, was working together with engineers to find creative solutions to problems posed by this tunnel, in relation to a building project they were going to be engaged in. They would explain the whole thing to me tomorrow, but he had wanted me to see the site for myself so that later discussions would be more meaningful. My feelings of anxiety changed to self-deprecating humor, and I smiled to myself in the darkness at my previous suspicions and fears. Then, as we drove back to town, relief began to alternate with mild disappointment. The excitement was over.

3

Danger's Delight

THE USES OF DANGER

As is implied by the everyday examples we have just looked at, once the protective frame is in place, the search for stimulation may get started. We see this particularly clearly in children. Within the protective framework of the playpen, and then the nursery, and later the house and yard, the normal child shows a strong inclination to explore, experiment, and have "adventures." We all no doubt have our own childhood memories of discoveries made, and games played, and we can see them re-enacted by our own children. But once placed in a strange environment, or deprived of the presence of parents, there is typically an anxious withdrawal by the child, a drawing-in of the horns: the world has become a frightening place. With mother there to provide security it becomes thrilling to pet a big dog, visit a new home, or meet a strange adult. Without mother these same things become filled with the terror of the unknown.

Likewise the adult, if he or she feels confident, at home in his or her environment, and generally capable of coping, is also liable to look for interest and stimulation. And indeed, in some people this may take an extreme form, involving going as close to the brink, the dangerous edge, as reasonably possible—and doing so where trauma is serious (injury, or even death). It is this kind of extreme excitement-seeking that will be the focus of this chapter.

To make sense of the examples we are going to look at, it must be remembered that the "trick" of excitement involves exposing one-self to enough danger to obtain high arousal, while experiencing this danger as being in a form which one feels can be handled (that is, within a protective frame). Without the high arousal one will not feel excited, and without the protective frame one will feel anxiety rather than excitement. This is in effect the "tiger in the cage" phenomenon, discussed earlier, for which both things are needed—the danger of the tiger, and the safety of the cage. One must feel that special combination of being simultaneously worked up and secure, in the danger zone but protected.

In the face of different kinds of danger some people are better than others at maintaining this subjective feeling of security, and are therefore able to achieve higher levels of excitement for longer periods of time than others. It is these kinds of people we shall be looking at in the next section of this chapter. But we should remember that we can all experience the same basic phenomenon, albeit in a milder way, in the course of our everyday lives—at least if we are psychologically healthy. The difference between most of us and these others is that they have a greater confidence in whatever it is that they find reassuring, and thus their protective frame is more robust. That is, they may have more confidence in themselves, in others, or be more adventurous, while still feeling adequately safe. This may be a general feature of their lives, or relate to specific areas in which they take risks such as skydiving or white-water canoeing.[1] Either way, they can face up to greater dangers than the rest of us, and in this way achieve greater excitement.

Thus developing ability at some skill, like rock-climbing, means that one will have greater self-confidence when on the mountain-side; and this should translate not only into the pleasures that come from performing well and mastering increasingly difficult climb-ing, but also into the propensity to handle higher levels of arousal while climbing without these becoming translated into anxiety. Of course, a given individual may be misled into taking absurd risks by the safety promised by his or her frame (we shall explore this in a later chapter). The individuals we shall look at next, however, are ones who are reasonably realistic in both their self-expectations and their assessments of their situations. Things can still go wrong, but dangers are faced up to, and taken into account.

It should also be emphasized that in the excitement-seeking state, however robust the frame, there is always the possibility that one will actually fall over the dangerous edge and experience trauma, or alternatively that the protective frame will disinte-grate under threat, so that anxiety will be felt. As we shall see, when you are at or near the edge you are doing a balancing act, and some-times even skilled acrobats fall. In a book on the Vendée Globe round-the-world solo yacht race, Derek Lundy uses the protective frame idea to account for the different feelings that the competitors have at different moments during the race:

> The Vendée Globe sailor's protective frame, so to speak, is the boat – the integrity of its hull and rig, the reliability of its communication and emergency gear. If all this feels intact, then surfing in the South-ern Ocean is exhilarating. When the frame is compromised – the hull is pierced by ice, the rig goes over the side, the whole cocoon of the boat turns turtle and stays that way – or if its integrity is seriously threatened by ferocious weather, the skipper's brain isn't likely to interpret his body's aroused state as pleasure.[2]

UP TO THE BRINK

Perhaps the most literal of all versions of the excitement-at-the-dangerous-edge phenomenon is mountaineering, with its genu-inely dangerous edges, ledges, and brinks. Here the danger of going over the edge is both real and obvious. But so are the means to safety, so that, with appropriate training and equipment, and in the company of competent fellow climbers, a protective frame is set up which converts the fear into excitement. As Sir Chris Bonington, the famous British mountaineer, has said: "I wouldn't say mountaineering is so much a game as a calculated risk. It's not the roulette kind of gamble. The excitement of climbing is going into a danger situation and then using your skill to obviate danger."[3]

The result can be exhilaration. According to the legendary American climber, Smoke Blanchard: "The real reason I [take part in high-altitude trekking] is because of the charge ... Because I get turned on. For several excellent reasons I have never sampled psychedelics, but I know what it means to be turned on. Some things turn me on as if I'd swallowed a neon sign."[4] And the greater the risk and hardship, the greater the joy. As Bonington has written:

> And through it all is the undercurrent of danger; for this is what
> climbing is all about—staking one's life on one's judgment, playing
> the calculated risk ... certainly my most memorable, and in a way
> most enjoyable days' climbing have been in violent storms in the
> Alps, when the wind and snow have torn my anorak-covered body;
> when my wits and judgment have been extended to the full and yet,
> in spite of all I have remained on top of the situation.[5]

In a similar vein, the French mountaineer Maurice Herzog, celebrated conqueror of Annapurna, reports: "A fierce and savage wind tore at us. We were on top of Annapurna; 8,075 meters, 26,493 feet. Our hearts overflowed with unspeakable happiness."[6] This literal "peak experience" was clearly enhanced by the continuing menace of the conditions.

The ultimate climbing risk arises in "free soloing," in which the climber is on his or her own without support, uses no technological equipment like that necessary for driving in pitons or drilling bolt holes, and even, in extreme cases, dispenses with safety ropes. In this case the dangerous edge can be very close indeed—just the width of a finger tip between safety and "the sharp end of emptiness."[7] As one such climber put it, "Death is so close. You could let go and make the decision to die. It feels so good."[8] At the same time, to feel excitement rather than terror and panic, you have to be sure enough of yourself that you are convinced that you will not either let go or slip. As the previous climber also said: "You are probably pretty confident that you could walk from here to the door without trip-ping. Climbing is the same for me. It's an ordinary feeling to be sup-ported by finger tips, hanging on a rock wall. The possibility of falling feels very remote—like being struck by lightning."[9]

Another dangerous activity which involves playing with height is that of rappeling—that is, letting oneself down to the ground rapidly from a height, via ropes. (This is not to be confused with bungee-jumping.) An example of rappeling which I personally found particularly hair-raising was the exploit of five men who rap-peled from Toronto's CN Tower—which, at 1, 200 feet, is the tallest free-standing building in the world. "The group lowered them-selves through the windows at the base of the first observation level at the tower .... An anxious ground crew held the rope taut at the bottom. If a rappeler starts to sway, he could swing into the building and injure himself."[10] Since I had been in the building a few days before this money-raising event and had stood petrified in the observation level from which they set off, afraid even to go up to the edge and look over, I have to say that I admired the confidence that these men must have had in their equipment, and in each other, to launch themselves into space—and to enjoy it. "It felt great, it was fantastic," said one exuberant rappeler: "You could see for ever. I was going to ask if we could come back and do it again."[11]

The "dangerous edge" metaphor used throughout this book is of course not supposed to imply that there is always a literal physical edge, even though there is a sense in which the examples just given *do* involve such real edges. To generalize the concept, let us turn to a totally different area: medicine, and specifically surgery. Although surgeons tend to work long hours, take a great deal of responsibil-ity, and know that a mistake can be fatal to the patient, most of them appear to take a delight in their work, and to obtain particular joy from the challenges and emergencies which arise. A plastic surgeon explained to an interviewing journalist that he often got on an adrenaline high, and indeed felt strange if he was not rushing around. Another explained to the same journalist that "The worse the case, the more enjoyable it is." He went on to say that he never noticed the goriness or wondered whether the patient would make it or not. In other words, surgery was an absorbing technical challenge to him rather than a matter of life-or-death. Yet another admitted that surgery is "like a drug. It gives you the same kick, the same adrenaline feeling as hang-gliding. The riskier it is, the more we enjoy it." These feelings were echoed by the surgeon who added that after a 13-hour stint cutting out highly malignant bone tumors he felt "lifted, and ready for a game of squash or a good party ... ."[12]

Surgeons are not the only medical specialists who can enjoy risk. Robin Skynner, a British family therapist, has compared his feelings during some family interviews with his experience of flying Mosquito bombers on low-level attacks during the Second World War. In particular, he reports, there comes a critical moment in a family interview when the "feeling of being absolutely attentive and completely *there*" was the same as "I used to have when we were just going to drop a bomb. In both instances, I was dealing with something of an explosive nature. In therapy the aim is to defuse the bomb rather than try to escape from it or be blown up. It's very risky and exciting."[13]

Work, then, can provide as much risk and excitement as sporting activities can. This is more obviously true of a range of jobs, such as mining, offshore fishing, and deep-sea diving, than it is of surgery. And it is particularly obvious in such extremely risky professions as troubleshooting in oil fields, and bomb disposal. For people to be able to enjoy and continue to practice such occupations it must be possible for them to experience much of what they do in the excitement-seeking state, and to see their work for much of the time within a protective frame. For example, a Canadian troubleshooter who puts out fires in oil fields and caps pipeline blowouts told a reporter that there is "not a serious risk. It's no more risky that skydiving," and pointed out that he was protected by special clothing, by thinking every move through in advance, and by good communications. "You see dirt and shrapnel flying around and everybody running and looking to get out. And they're looking to you to go in." His work, he said, gave him not only a sense of accomplishment but also great excitement. As he succinctly put it, in a phrase which sums up the whole of this chapter, "Excitement is danger's reward."[14]

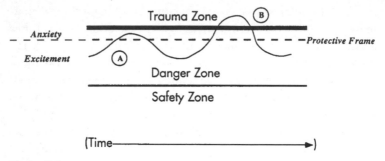

Figure 3.1

Of course being either at or on the dangerous edge is a volatile place to be, a kind of "knife edge," and many people who deliberately choose to play with danger actually switch back and forth between the excitement-seeking and anxiety-avoidance states when they do so. Since their arousal is high throughout, the result is that they switch to and fro between excitement and anxiety. That is, the protective frame comes and goes while they are in the vicinity of the edge. This phenomenon is depicted in figure 3.1 where the snaking line represents, from left to right, movement over time. Above the line which represents the protective frame, anxiety will be experienced, and below it excitement. At point A we see the protective frame being crossed, in which case anxiety will be felt. This is seen to be followed by a movement back to the "right" side of the frame, signifying a return to excitement. At point B we see not only the protective frame being breached but also the dangerous edge itself, so that injury or pain will be experienced, as well as anxiety. Subsequently we see a return to the feeling of protection, and the resumption of excitement.

Imagine skiing downhill. Point A would represent seeing a hazard, feeling anxiety, avoiding the hazard, and then feeling excitement. Point B would represent seeing a hazard, feeling anxiety, falling down and being hurt, getting up, continuing, and eventually feeling excitement again. The more aroused one is during such episodes, the greater will be both the anxiety and the excitement. The aim of course is to spend as much time as possible on the excitement side of the frame, and as little as possible on the anxiety side. People who indulge in risky activities must have continuing expectations that they will be able to achieve this, otherwise they would presumably not continue.

It is rather like listening to a concert on the radio which is interspersed with periods of interference. Turning up the volume may make the music pleasant to listen to, but it also makes the interference even more unpleasant. As Cus D'Amato, Mike Tyson's trainer at the time, once put it: "Fear is like fire. It can cook for you. It can heat your house. Or it can burn it down."[15] So arousal can be good or bad. The stronger it is, the better or worse it will be.

If we go back to figure 2.3, we see this illustrated graphically. As a person reverses from one state of mind to the other, so he or she switches between points on the two lines that are vertically above or below each other—for example, between points D and B on the graph. So, what happens is that real danger is perceived as such in the anxiety-avoidance state and produces great anxiety, but as it is avoided or overcome, so the switch to the excitement-seeking state that comes with this coping brings with it the reward of high excitement. We saw an example in the last chapter when talking about parachuting. The experienced danger of jumping out of an aircraft produces anxiety, but this anxiety is converted into euphoria when the parachute opens and everything suddenly becomes safe. This moment of switching from anxiety to excitement has been described by Mike Tyson as "like a snap, a little snap of light I get when I fight. I love that feeling. It makes me feel secure and confident, it suddenly makes everything explosive It's like: 'Here it comes again. Here's my buddy today'."[16] A similar metaphor has been used by a bank robber to describe how, although he feels nervous before starting on a job, "the minute it's on it's like the sun coming out from behind a cloud."[17]

In other words, one buys excitement with fear, and the greater the cost, the better the product. (In the context of this "purchase" the description by one climber of his activity as an "intense extravagance"[18] is particularly fitting.) Sir Chay Blyth, the yachtsman who—among other odd things—has rowed across the Atlantic with a companion (John Ridgway) and sailed non-stop around the world single-handedly, has described this kind of transaction during an incident on the solo voyage:

> The boat was lying over at 90 degrees with the mast parallel to the water and all I could do was hang on to the outside of the cockpit and talk myself into believing I'd come through the nightmare. 'Come on, wrap up.' I was saying to the storm, knowing that the boat would disintegrate at any moment. Then the pampero suddenly blew itself out and I felt the wonderful exhilaration once again. I was thinking to myself, 'That was really something—let's have another one.[19]

In the same interview he makes a comment which graphically summarizes the whole theme of this chapter.

> Most of the time there is a very thin line between fear and exhilaration and one very rapidly gives way to the other. It's like when you're driving out in the country and ... you fly around a corner and there is a tractor across the road in front of you. You're flooded with adrenaline and you see a gap, go for it and get through. When you have made it what you feel is sheer exhilaration.[20]

Interestingly (since Blyth uses a racing-driver metaphor), racing drivers themselves do indeed report exhilaration. As Stirling Moss, one of the greatest champions of the 1950s, once put it:

> You go through a corner absolutely flat out, *right on the ragged edge*, but absolutely in control, on your own line to an inch, the car just hanging there, the tires as good as geared to the road, locked to it, and yet you know that if you ask one more mile an hour of the car, if you put another five pounds of sidethrust on it, you'll lose the whole flaming vehicle as surely as if someone has smeared the road with grease. So you stay just this side of that fraction of extra weight that could ruin everything and perhaps kill you to boot, and you are on top of it all, and the exhilaration, the thrill, is tremendous.[21]

An autocross driver, while faced perhaps with less danger, reports some of the same feelings, her protective frame coming from wearing a helmet. "For the few minutes that my helmet was strapped to my head, my hands guiding the wheel, for those few minutes I could believe with the faith of a child that I was bullet-proof, mistress of my fate." The result is that she can enjoy the risk that she experiences, such as an occasion when she spun around one and a half revolutions. "I heard myself shout 'woo hoo!' into the gritty dust floating through the open windows. Don't skinny guys in loincloths spend entire lifetimes on mountaintops hoping to experience this?"[22]

It would seem that people involved in dangerous sports of all kinds—from parachuting to bungee-jumping—use this "brinkmanship" as a deliberate strategy. They take real risks, confront real danger, and hope for the unexpected challenge. In doing so they *know* that they will feel fear. But they *also* know that in coping with it in the danger zone they will be able to convert this base metal into the gold of excitement.

PLAYING WITH BULLS

Let us look at more length at just one source of danger, and how people play with it. This is the danger that comes from proximity to bulls bred for fighting.

The bullfighter literally turns the game of "going up to the edge" into a fine art, since he is expected to show courage by making his passes with cape or muleta (small cloth attached to a short stick) as close as he can to the bull. Hemingway, in his classic description of bullfighting, *Death in the Afternoon*, says of one matador:

> When he has a bull that charges straight enough so that the matador can put his feet together, he works closer to the bull, becomes more exalted, more excited, curving on himself so he thrusts his waistline at the horns, and with his amazing wrist controlling the muleta brings the bull around him in circles, again and again, passes him so close before his chest that the bull's shoulder sometimes jostles him and the horns so close to his belly that you can see welts on his abdomen afterwards at the hotel.[23]

As he says of the same matador, elsewhere in the book: "If there is no blood on his belly afterwards you ought to get your money back."[24]

In a similar vein Kenneth Tynan says of another matador, in his book *Bull Fever:* "No matter what the cost in grace or dignity, he will stay close to the bull; there he is in his element, with the horns tearing the braid from his thighs and the blood from the morrillo staining his stomach."[25] (The morrillo is the huge muscle on the back of the bull's neck.)

Going close to the bull and courting danger is the essence of bullfighting. The high point in this risk-taking, the so-called moment of truth, is the moment of the kill, or *estocada*. To accomplish this, the matador, who now only has a muleta to protect him, must thrust his sword into the back of the bull at a precise place. In order to do so he has to lean over the bull's horns, thus exposing himself to maximum danger—since his chest is completely "uncovered" to the bull at this moment. He simultaneously attempts to get the bull to lower its head and neck, by attracting its attention with the muleta held close to the ground. But if this distraction does not work, then there is nothing to prevent his being immediately tossed. In fact, the majority of deaths in the ring have occurred as the result of this moment of supreme risk.

Quite apart from the risks of the passes and the kill (of either participant), which are an integral part of the fight, a matador who is on form and feels he has the measure of the bull will take many other quite gratuitous risks. These may be relatively mild, and often indulged in—such as "passing" the bull from a kneeling position, or standing quite close to the bull and only swinging the muleta out to the side at the last moment when the bull charges. Other actions are considerably more risky, and indulged in only occasionally. An example would be the matador taking some passes with his back against the fence of the ring, so that if the bull swerves towards him the matador has no chance of shifting backwards out of the way. Another even more showy risk, the kind of thing the Spaniards call *tremendismo*, is to go up to the bull when it is subdued between charges, and do such things as stroke it on the forehead, fondle a horn, or kneel in front of it facing away.

It may be that, for this particular dangerous activity, the excitement comes after the danger has been faced and overcome, while the arousal level still remains high. One has the impression, for example, that most bullfighters experience it this way since, in talking about their art, most of them take pains to emphasize their fear, and the courage it takes to overcome this fear. Belmonte, one of the greatest matadors of all time, is reported to have said: "If we matadors had to sign the contracts one hour before the corrida [fight] was to start, there would be no bullfights."[26] And Manolete, perhaps the greatest bullfighter of them all, said: "My knees start to quake when I first see my name on the posters and they don't stop until the end of the season."[27] If this is true, then the excitement during the fight is entirely the spectator's (and I shall return to this point in chapter 5). But after the bullfight, if all has worked out well, what feelings of euphoria and triumph the matador must experience! He has been to the dangerous edge—over and over again—and come back each time. And he has shown no fear to others. As Barnaby Conrad, one of a small number of bullfighters from the United States, said after a fight: "They dragged the bull out of the ring with the mules, and the crowd kept applauding and yelling for me to take a lap around the ring while they threw hats and cigars down to me. It was the happiest moment of my life."[28]

In some towns in Spain it is possible for members of the public to take their own risks with bulls, when the bulls are run to the bullring from their corral outside town, through public streets. The aim is to get near the bulls without being caught and gored. In Pamplona, the San Fermin Festival every July has as its centerpiece the most celebrated of the "running of the bulls," or *encierro* (literally, "corraling"). This was made famous by Ernest Hemingway's 1926 novel *The Sun Also Rises*. On each morning of the week-long festival the six bulls that are to be fought that evening are run through the streets from their corral on the edge of town to the bullring in the center—a distance of nearly a kilometer (about two-thirds of a mile). Much of the route is bounded by the walls of houses and shops; elsewhere, temporary barricades are erected. From the balconies of the houses, and thronging behind (and *on*) the barricades, are many thousands of spectators, including photographers and television crews. The interest, of course, is not just in the bulls. Rather, it is in the hundreds of people—the *corredores*—who take the risk of running the course *with* the bulls.

The course itself is mainly uphill, especially in the early stages where the incline is steepest, sheer walls rising on either side of the street. At the top of the hill the course flattens out somewhat, veering left and through several plazas. Then there is a dangerously sharp turn to the right, and a long run up a shopping street. Finally, there is an alleyway, created by barricades, which crosses another plaza and up to the narrow entrance of the bullring itself. The last 50 yards or so being downhill, the bottleneck at the end of the run is reached in a rush.

Activities begin about seven in the morning, when bands start parading through the streets, and those who are going to run (mostly men, many of them wearing the traditional white shirt and trousers with scarlet beret, scarf, and sash) enter the streets in readiness. Spectators are already jostling for the best positions along the course, and the bullring itself is filling up with those who want to watch the final stages of the run as well as the activities that follow. At eight o'clock sharp the corral gates are opened, this being announced to the waiting crowds by the explosion of a rocket. Another such explosion a few seconds later announces that the bulls are actually in the street and (together with the team of oxen that accompany them) are on their way. A gasp of anticipation rises from the crowds lining the route, which has now become a danger zone.

What happens next takes place very rapidly. In fact, in the normal way of things the whole course is covered by the bulls in no more than a couple of minutes, and from any given vantage point the action to be observed by the spectators may be over in much less time than that. But sometimes one or more of the bulls will become distracted by runners or spectators, stop or turn around, and attack them. The run of course is then prolonged. Some runs take more like four or five minutes (the record being about ten minutes).

From the runners' point of view, there are three main strategies that can be followed during the run. The first—and the one adopted by the majority, many of whom are running for the first (and probably only) time—is just to run like mad as soon as they hear the first rocket explode. The sensible thing here is to start the run from a position a long way up the course and hope to arrive in the bullring long before the bulls do. The second strategy is to run in front of the bulls from early in the course and then, as they catch up, to step aside, flatten oneself against a wall or barricade, and (hopefully) let them pass. The course can then be completed at a jog. The third (and "correct") strategy, the one adopted by the more experienced locals, is to wait for a bull to arrive and, as it passes, run alongside it—ideally with one hand on its back—for as long as can be managed. This is the classical aim of the run, to run *with* the bulls (like surfing with a wave), and even the *experts* can achieve this for perhaps only 30 or 40 yards.

Of course, things often go wrong. The main danger is tripping, something which is easy to do with so many people running close to each other and with those behind often running into, and pushing, those in front. Sometimes an individual falls and is trampled by other runners—or, even worse, by a bull or an ox. Sometimes a sprawling tangle of people forms, none of whom can get out of the way of the bulls in time. Sometimes a bull will stumble and fall onto someone. The greatest danger, however, is generally acknowledged to arise when an individual bull slows down and becomes parted from the others. At this point the animal is likely to take an interest in, and charge, particular runners. This is when serious gorings can (and do) occur.

Eventually the whole mass of bodies—those running in front of the animals, the bulls and oxen themselves, and more people running behind—stream into the arena of the bullring. There is now a dangerous few moments, when the bulls have lost some of their forward momentum and have the space to run around at will. If this happens, it is not unusual for one or more *corredores* to be tossed before the animals are finally herded through a gate leading into the bullring corrals. At this point another rocket is exploded overhead as a signal that the *encierro* proper is over.

But the morning's festivities are far from finished, because now a wild cow is released into the ring, the tips of her horns sheathed. The arena is still milling with people, and the cow chases one after another, as her fancy takes her, running into this one and that, tossing people or knocking them down, and causing confusion, panic, and hilarity everywhere. The traditional aim of those taking part is to the hit the animal as it passes, using a rolled newspaper. It all seems light-hearted after what has gone before—but sometimes the animal seems to fix on a particularly hapless person, and tosses that human piñata again and again, to the screams of the crowd. (It should be said that although the cow's horns are sheathed, serious injuries can still occur.)

After about five minutes, the first cow is guided out of the ring and replaced by a fresh one (or even two at the same time). This process is repeated several times, each time the cows prancing around unpredictably, causing waves of movement in the ring. Meanwhile, the bands play, the spectators cheer and catcall, and the braver (or more foolhardy) of those in the ring court bovine attention. Putting themselves in as much danger as they can, they often either receive a severe bruising, and limp off—or strut around waving to friends outside the ring.

As with the examples of risky sports cited earlier in this chapter, the same psychological phenomenon occurs: danger is used to give rise to arousal that is experienced as excitement rather than anxiety.

Three people interviewed by reporters now tell essentially the same story. Here is a 40-year-old New Yorker: "I played three sports at university, but none gave me the thrill of waiting in the street for the *encierro* to start: the fantastic noise; the danger; the whole town watching us. And then the bulls came out; incredibly beautiful creatures. Just to run close to them is a sensation most people can't understand."[29] A 42-year-old lawyer from Dallas comments: "I feel the adrenaline flow when the bulls are close enough to hear their heavy breathing. They bear down on you, snorting, like a train."[30] And a 29-year-old Californian enthuses: "It's a tremendous adrenaline rush, a unique feeling, more than you've ever felt in your life except a war."[31]

In his book *Iberia,* James Michener reports a discussion with a confirmed runner who has shown him a horn scar across his chest:

"'Is it something mystical?' I asked.

Matt looked at me as if I were out of my mind. 'Christ, you miss the whole flaming point. It's fun! It's joy!'"

Later on, Michener asks: "Do you run to prove your bravery?" Matt replies: "When those rockets go off and the black shapes come tumbling at you ... Hell, you've already made your commitment and all it takes now is a sense of joy ... to be a part of the stampede."[32]

Since 1910 fifteen people have been killed in the encierro, usually by goring from bulls that have become parted from the others. (The last death was in 1995, when a young American was gored to death.) Furthermore, many scores of people every year are injured seriously enough to be taken to a hospital, mainly with broken bones and horn wounds. (Besides these injuries are of course numerous severe bruisings, cuts, and sprains which never reach a hospital.) In the run I saw at Pamplona there were two serious injuries, both of which I observed. A 42-year-old local man was tossed by a straggler from the herd, the horn entering his right knee. When he landed, he was gored again in the abdomen and in the neck. An 18-year-old Spaniard was also gored by a straggler, being thrown spectacularly into the air by a horn which went into his thigh. Both of them were rushed to hospital in serious condition.

When we consider running with the bulls, then, we are moving away from the kind of dangerous sport in which the danger is actually very small, given certain levels of technique and skill, and into an area where chance plays a larger part and where people's self-confidence may have little basis in reality. This means that once the protective frame is penetrated, it may be difficult to reconstruct for this activity. As one Englishman in Pamplona described it to me, he was in the thick of a crowd of runners, between two groups of bulls, and feeling great. But suddenly the people in front slowed down, so that he ran into the back of them. And then those in front started to fight their way backwards. Obviously one of the bulls in front had, for some reason, turned around. At the same time, those runners behind continued to push forward, away from the remaining bulls coming up. The result was that he was trapped between two groups of panicking people, with bulls on both sides. Fortunately, he was able to squeeze out of the melee and flatten himself against the wall until the crush of people and bulls sorted itself out and passed. But the moment was, for him, one of pure terror. Here we see a clear-cut example of the sudden removal of the shield provided by the protective frame, and a consequent transformation of excitement to fear. The fear was in fact *so* great that he decided as a result that he would never run with the bulls again. He had lost confidence in the protective frame in this context, once and for all.

At times, protective frames are misleading in that they imply a spurious safety. One might describe this as an example of the "pathology of excitement-seeking." This will be the topic of chapter 9. Meanwhile, we need to look at some types of protective frames which are rather different from the kind of frame that has been the focus of attention in this chapter. These other kinds of frames are ones that most of us are likely to experience far more frequently as we go about our everyday lives—not the type we have been looking at here, which provides a way of experiencing immediate dangers.

4

Into the Safety Zone

THREE KINDS OF PROTECTIVE FRAME

One of the most exciting things in life is making love. Equally (or more) exciting for some is playing a hard-fought game of tennis. In neither case is there usually danger. Of course, there may be danger if one is making love to someone else's wife, or playing tennis after recovering from a heart attack. But, in the normal course of things, the excitement does not in either activity come from danger, but from other sources.

In fact, when we come to look at the whole range of ways in which people attempt to achieve and enjoy high arousal we find that danger, experienced within the kind of protective frame described in the previous chapter, is only one way. Altogether there would appear to be three basic types of protective frame, of which the one that we have just looked at is the first. We shall look at the second of these in this chapter, and the third in the next chapter. All three have in common that they allow high arousal to be enjoyed—that is, they maintain the excitement-seeking state. But the *sources* of high arousal are typically different for both of the two new frames. And each is associated with a different zone of experience, different from the danger zone.

Let us call the kind of protective frame associated with the danger zone, as described previously, a *confidence frame*, since it derives from the confidence that the individual feels in facing danger—be the source of the confidence the individual's own ability, or that of his or her equipment, friends, or colleagues.

The second kind of protective frame I shall call a *safety-zone frame*, since it is experienced when the individual feels safely ensconced in the area I have called the safety zone. The third kind I shall refer to as a *detachment frame*, because the person in it feels effectively detached—in a zone I shall call the *detachment zone*—from the need for any immediate or meaningful action. These frames will shortly be explained in full, in the order presented here, so do not worry if these introductory descriptions do not make too much sense. For the present, all you need to know is that there are these three different types of frame, and that if *any one* of them is being experienced, the individual will both feel protected and be in the state in which stimulation and increasing arousal are pleasant.

THE SAFETY-ZONE FRAME

The kind of frame we shall look at in this chapter is one which can occur only when the person feels himself or herself to be in the safety zone—which, it will be recalled, is the zone in which individuals feel that they are not in the immediate presence of danger. We can imagine the safety-zone frame as extending along the inside of the edge that separates the danger zone from the safety zone (see figure 4.1). Its effect is that one feels protected not just from trauma, as with the confidence frame, but also from *feelings* of danger. In other words, one is removed one stage further again from trauma itself.

Experiencing this frame is not just feeling that you are in the safety zone, but rather that you are in this zone and *not* going to slip into the danger zone. What might be simply an area of experience is turned into an enclave—something encapsulated, demarcated as a special zone in which the threats and problems of the real world cannot, for the time being at least, impinge. It is not just

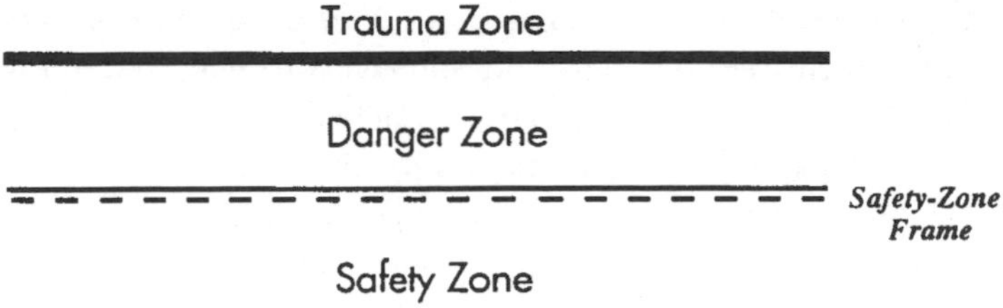

Trauma Zone

Danger Zone

Safety-Zone
Frame

Safety Zone

Figure 4.1

that there is no danger: it is that there is temporarily no danger *of* danger. Trauma is more than contained, as it is in the confidence frame—it is excluded. Where the confidence frame protects the individual in the danger zone from slipping into the trauma zone, the safety-zone frame protects the individual in the safety zone from slipping into the danger zone (compare figure 4.1 with figure 2.4).

Just as there is a difference between simply being in the danger zone, and being there in the presence of a confidence frame, so there is a difference between just being in the safety zone and being there in the presence of a safety-zone *frame*. Being in the safety zone without the frame means that (for reasons we have already examined) one will be in the anxiety-avoidance state, worried about being pushed or pulled into the danger zone. However, since the safety margin is large in this zone (one perceives oneself to be some distance from trauma), the chances are that one's arousal will be low, and one will feel relaxed. In any case, one will be somewhere on the relaxation-to-anxiety line on the graph.

For example: at your place of work, you probably are usually in a serious state of mind in which you realize that things could go wrong and you then could get into all kinds of trouble. Most of the time, however, you probably conceive of this sort of occurrence as remote, and feel fairly relaxed about things. For most people, the workplace is probably experienced as a safety zone much of the time, but not as one with a safety-zone frame which would guarantee immunity from serious problems or mishaps.

In contrast, if the safety-zone frame *is* in place, one will be in the excitement-seeking state and somewhere on the boredom-to-excitement curve. As a general principle, then, being in the excitement-seeking state depends on the presence of a protective frame, *not* on the zone one is in. One can be in the danger zone with or without a protective frame, and the same goes for the safety zone.

The prime safety zone for most people is likely to be their home, or some space within it, like the den, the bedroom, or even the bathroom. The home is not only a safety zone but one with a safety-zone frame—all those things that make it a home rather than just a house, a personal rather than a public space. The coziness and warmth of the home, made up from family pictures, knickknacks, memorabilia, and general clutter, produce a feeling of ease, comfort, and security. This represents a world removed from "*the* world," a world where the individual may more often than not be himself or herself in peace.[1]

The safety zone is not restricted to physical space. For example, it may be a time of the day: during the morning coffee break, when arriving home and pouring a "happy hour" drink, while putting the children to bed. The point is that it is a *psychological* space which represents secure freedom from the stresses and strains of the real world: somewhere where there is no threat of threat.

GAMES AND SPORTS

Besides these individual (and even idiosyncratic) enclaves there also are socially agreed-on areas in which the threats of "real life" are not allowed to enter, such as the park, the fairground, the betting shop, or the swimming pool. In particular, there are all those institutionalized spaces where games and sports are played. These are both literal spaces—the tennis court, the golf course, the baseball diamond, the football gridiron—and psychological spaces demarcated by special rules which put limits on what may or may not occur within them.

Sports are indeed the prime example of the institutional creation of safety-zone frames: in principle, nothing which happens on the playing field refers to anything in the real world outside itself. To be sure, certain aspects of the real world are *simulated* within the rules: the cooperation and competition model many human activities, from running a small business to bringing up a family. Nevertheless, it is clear that, in playing the game, one is dealing with a simplification, a stylization, and not with the real world itself. As one writer on sport has put it:

> Within each sport there is a bubble in which dwells the sacred ethos. The bubble encloses a world which is indeed separate because it is imaginary. The actual playing of sport takes place within the bubble, in a world of make-believe. Reality is suspended. The rules of life are replaced by artificial laws and conventions. A white line painted on the grass represents the boundary between life and death; the passing of a ball into a hole in the ground becomes the very purpose of life. Thou Shalt Not Pass the Ball Forwards is an inviolate commandment within the bubble; if you tried to live by that rule in everyday life they would throw a net over you and haul you off to the funny farm.[2] (American readers puzzled by this particular commandment may like to know that it relates to rugby football.)

In talking of a sport played within a safety-zone frame, then, we are dealing with one in which people pit their wits, skills, and determination against each other—not one of those dangerous sports in which they challenge the elements. As we saw in the previous chapter, in the latter case there is real danger, which may or may *not* be mastered. In the former case, there is no real danger at all. Naturally, there is the "danger" of losing. But this is hardly the same as the danger of such traumas of disfigurement, or as a terrifyingly rapid (or alternatively a horribly lingering) death. In the second instance we are talking about *real* life or *real* death, rather than what is essentially a simulation.

Of course, in no sport can danger be totally excluded. In particular, there is always some danger of injury. Even in playing chess one may fall out of one's chair, or during a game of bridge the roof may fall in; one is never actually free of danger in life. And of course in such vigorous sports as boxing and football the chances of injury are high. The point is that if one is aware of the risk factor while playing, then the safety-zone frame will, by definition, not be there, and anxiety may be experienced rather than excitement. Another ever-present source of danger in sport is danger to one's self-esteem. One may play so badly, as I have myself found on many an occasion, that one risks becoming a laughing stock. But, again, if one plays with this danger in mind, the protective frame will not be in position, and there will be no chance of the real enjoyment that comes with excitement. The fluctuations described in the previous chapter can occur, too. A person can start a game in an excitement-seeking state of mind, play so badly that he or she feels threatened, revert to the anxiety-avoidance state—and then perhaps recover sufficiently to save face and experience once more the pleasures of excitement-seeking.

Once the sporting situation has been set up, and the magic circle as it were completed, then the excitement-seeking state comes into being and can be fulfilled by all those arousing qualities of a good game: the antagonism and hostility and aggression; the unpredictability and uncertainty of both the outcome and the precise way in which the outcome will be reached; the physical strenuousness; the successes and failures; the hope and despair; the encouragement and jeering; the noise and silences. All of human life is here, but in a delightfully simplified and idealized form. When danger is no longer the source of arousal, then, excitement is achieved through a systematic use of a variety of other sources, called upon by the nature of the game itself. Taken together these can often, it seems, produce as much arousal as danger can.

One objection you might have at this point is to say that you can be both relaxed and excited at the same time, and furthermore that this is exactly how you have experienced playing sports. You might say, "I felt relaxed, so I went and played tennis." However, this is really only a problem of the use of language, because the world "relaxed" in everyday speech has *two distinct* meanings. On the one hand it means pleasurable low arousal—and this is the way it has been used so far in this book. But it also means "unthreatened," and in *this* sense it means essentially to be in the state of feeling protected by what I have been calling a protective frame—and in consequence to be in an excitement-seeking state. In this second sense of "relaxation" the objection is in fact something which exactly exemplifies the point being made.

So far I have been talking about playing for fun: real "play." But we should remember that for *professional* athletes, playing is in fact work; and how well they do has immense consequences for their finances, their careers, possibly their families, and certainly their colleagues and their colleagues' careers (if it is a team game). So the discussion of sports up to this point has really been about *amateur* sports, about playing a game *as* a game rather than a job. By contrast, the professional may not experience excitement, but only anxiety, during the course of playing. And sometimes the anxiety of professional sport can be extreme. For example, Bobby Jones, although one of the great golfers of all time, "was the victim of exceptional nervous tension, to the extent that he threw up before an important round of golf and afterwards had to cut his tie free because the sweat-soaked knot resisted all attempts to release it."[3] As one manager of a soccer team is supposed to have put it when asked if winning was a matter of life and death to him, "No, it's more serious than that."[4]

For the professional athlete, then, the game often is *not* encapsulated within a safety-zone frame. It relates to everything of real importance to the player, and each action throughout the game may have implications for his or her future. In terms of danger to self-esteem and financial security, alike, a player is fully exposed to risk. It is therefore likely that much of the time the average player will be in the anxiety-avoidance state even though, ostensibly, he or she is only playing a game. Of course it is quite possible that he or she will also spend long periods in which the game is so absorbing that there will be a lack of awareness of the dangers. During these periods a protective frame of the safety-zone type will be in existence— and then excitement may be experienced. (Conversely, as we have seen, the amateur may feel danger to self-esteem, and switch into the anxiety-avoidance frame of mind and feel anxiety.) But, by-and-large, we may suppose that playing within the safety-zone frame is less likely for the professional than for the amateur athlete.[5]

SERIOUSNESS AND PLAYFULNESS

There is of course a whole variety of other ways in which people set up safety-zone frames for themselves, other than through playing sports for fun. For instance, in taking a touring holiday abroad, one is cutting oneself off from one's normal, serious world of work, and doing so in such a way that makes it almost impossible to be contacted. The distance and the lack of a permanent address creates a psychological barrier between oneself and one's normal world of problems and duties. Going fishing usually is another classical form of such escape: after all, there normally is no telephone available on the bank of a body of water. Yet another example is the practice of nudism. Here, in abandoning one's clothes, one is symbolizing removal from the everyday world. One is, paradoxically, adding safety by removing a kind of protection—since the "protection" is really another link to the mundane and problematic world of suburbs, shops, and offices. For some, being naked may also symbolize a return to the security of babyhood; of being fed, washed, and protected; of being free of decisions and responsibilities.

Another human activity which normally requires a safety-zone frame is sexual behavior. Sexual intercourse usually takes place with no reference to anything outside itself. It does not relate to any threats or problems in the real world, but rather creates its own special world, a kind of universe which focuses down onto a bed (or sofa, or back seat, or wherever). Within this domain, all that matters are the pleasures of the moment—the powerful sensations, the feelings, the expressions of love and passion, the playful variations, the approaches and teasing withdrawals, the words of endearment.

But, you may say, sexual behavior *does* in fact have implications in the real world, and implications of the most serious possible kind.

After all, through sexual intercourse one may be creating one or more new human lives. Or one may be setting up a visit to an abortion clinic or a clinic for sexually transmitted infection. And, even if precautions have been taken, one might be in the process of developing a complex and relatively permanent human relationship—or making the break, when it comes, more upsetting than it would have been. All this is true. But it misses the point that at the time of intercourse itself such considerations are far from the minds of the two (or more) people concerned. It is only rarely that intercourse is engaged in *in order to* have a child; and if it is, this is unlikely to be what is in mind at the moment itself. Here, as elsewhere in this book, the point is a psychological rather than a biological or physical one. If there is no psychological safety-zone frame, then inevitably, according to this analysis, there will be no excitement (although there may be anxiety as arousal mounts). And since excitement is intrinsically bound up with the whole process of foreplay leading to intercourse leading to orgasm, there will not even be successful sexual behavior at all—and the result will be frigidity or impotence.[6] What is happening in these cases is not that anxiety is inhibiting sexual excitement (as it is usually put by sex researchers and therapists). Rather, the anxiety that leads to dysfunction *is* the excitement experienced in the wrong state of mind. The unfortunate and paradoxical result is that the more sexually aroused the individual is, the less well will he or she be able to perform.

One way of summarizing the argument in this chapter is to say that if one is in a *serious* frame of mind, then one sees one's activity as connected in a consequential way with the real world and cannot be at the same time protected from it. But if a person sees what he or she is doing as *playful*, then what this means is that it does *not* "connect up" in this way. Rather, it is cut off and protected in a safe psychological space behind a safety-zone barrier. The person's activity at the time is then enjoyed in and of itself. It is done for fun.[7]

Although props and scenery may be helpful in setting up such a safe psychological space, they are not always essential. Most of us will experience a safety-zone frame regularly even in the absence of physical barriers (like geographical distance) or external symbols (like nudity). Indeed, some people seem to experience their lives almost entirely in this way, as if they carry around with them their own portable frame, which they can put up at a moment's notice, under any conditions and however great the challenges. Consider a businessman like Donald Trump (who most people will know through the television series *The Apprentice* if not through having heard of his various larger-than-life business dealings). "Everything in life to me is a psychological game," he said in an interview, "a series of challenges you either meet or don't."[8] His comparison of himself with a friend makes clear the difference between someone like himself, for whom making deals is a kind of sport, and others (like most of the rest of us) who are totally unable to experience large transactions as games:

> I have a friend who is extraordinarily smart. But he never became successful, because he couldn't take pressure. He was buying a home and it was literally killing him—a man of forty with an I.Q. of probably a hundred and ninety. He called me one day for the umpteenth time, worrying about his mortgage, and I was sitting in my chair, thinking to myself, here I am, buying the shuttle, the Plaza Hotel, and I don't lose an ounce of sleep over any of it.[9]

In any case the point is that the safety-zone frame is not just something behind which games are played. Rather, it is where we *see ourselves* to be safe and able to play games. This may seem a subtle distinction, but it is important since it emphasizes again how protective frames are related to the way one sees what one is doing, not how what one is doing is conventionally classified from outside. Something may be labeled as play, but taken as deadly serious. Something else may be labeled a business transaction or a committee meeting, but if one is enjoying it as a game, as fun (whatever its long-term consequences might be), then a protective frame *is* in place and one *is* in the excitement-seeking state.

It should be clear that there are huge individual differences in the ways in which people experience safety-zone frames. At one extreme we see businessmen like Trump, with robust frames which allow them to carry out far-reaching actions without anxiety, or professional risk-takers like stuntmen. At the other extreme we see people suffering from a variety of anxiety disorders whose safety-zone frames are particularly weak and vulnerable. Take the agoraphobic person, for example. Often a housewife, this person sees the only safe space as the home. Outside the home there is no safety-zone frame, and therefore high anxiety is always possible in the outside world. These people therefore find it best to stay inside—and not go out, even for shopping, visiting friends, or picking up the children from school. This life-style therefore becomes desperately limited.

Or to take the victim of another kind of anxiety disorder: the person who feels it necessary to carry out obsessional-compulsive rituals in order to keep anxiety at bay. Such people can be seen as trying to establish rules so that, like the rules of a game, they will constitute a protective frame. Unfortunately, this strategy seems not to be effective in most cases, so that the individual falls back on the creation of ever more complex and bizarre rules which come to dominate his or her life. For example, he or she may spend hours in the morning getting dressed in a very precise way, or waste hours during the day in elaborate washing rituals.

One way of regarding what the psychiatrist does (albeit often unwittingly) for someone with an anxiety disorder is to see him or her as setting up a safe space, within the clinic or consulting-room, in which those things that would otherwise cause anxiety in the client can be faced up to.[10] Successful therapy then involves the joint exploration with the client of ways of setting up more general, flexible, effective, and "portable" safety-zone frames which will allow the client to lead a reasonably normal life again.

5

On the Sidelines

OBSERVATION, FANTASY, AND MEMORY

Having investigated at length two of the three different types of protective frames (the confidence frame and the safety-zone frame), let us look more closely now at the third type—which you will recall was referred to earlier on as the detachment frame. It is probably the frame of mind that you are in as you read these words.

If the safety-zone frame provides a greater degree of removal from the dangers and threats of the real world than does the confidence frame, then the detachment frame provides a yet further degree of removal. For in the confidence and safety-zone frames the individual is actually operating in the world, whether he or she perceive themselves to be in the danger zone or the safety zone. But in detachment, one is not behaving in the real world at all (or at least is doing so only in ways that are on the whole psychologically trivial—like sitting, breathing, or scratching). Basically, one is *observing*. So what happens in detachment is that the individual no longer interacts significantly with his or her environment at all, but instead merely takes in information from it. The real action takes place elsewhere.

If a dangerous sport can illustrate the confidence frame, and a 'regular sport' the safety-zone frame, then the involvement of the *spectator* might represent the detachment frame. After all, the spectator can feel excited, too, *without* being exposed to risk (unless he or she is a soccer fan in Britain—but that is a matter I shall hold for a later chapter). So the detachment frame involves a new dimension of safety; a kind of disconnection from the world of real threats, problems, and dangers that would require a response. If we think of the confidence frame as being like a line of railings and the safety-zone frame as being like a wall, then the detachment frame is like the gap between a free-floating hot-air balloon and the ground. Someone in the gondola would be in what we might think of a detachment zone, independent from the rest of the world, but able to observe it. It will be realized from this simile that the detachment zone automatically carries its own protective frame with it. So, whereas one can be in either the danger zone or the safety zone without a protective frame, this is not true of the detachment zone. In the detachment zone, from the very fact of being in that zone, one always feels oneself to be experiencing the world from the vantage point of complete safety.

Being at the ringside of a boxing match would be a good example, or being a spectator at some other dangerous activity like NASCAR racing, or bullfighting. A particularly dramatic example would be to observe cage fighting, otherwise known as ultimate fighting, in which fighters fight each other within a cage with few holds barred, and using kicking, stomping, punching, and other forms of aggression.[1] The cage is probably not required from the point of view of the sport itself, but it helps the spectator to maintain the detachment frame by clearly demarcating the area of action from the area of observation.

The radical way in which the detachment frame differs from the other two is shown in figure 5.1, which depicts the trauma, danger, and safety zones as perceived from outside the system by a detached observer (represented by an eye in the figure). "Detachment" here, of course, does not mean emotional detachment in the sense of not caring: one may be very much emotionally involved in what is going on. The "detachment" of the detachment frame simply means that one is removed from the part of the world in which things are actually happening.

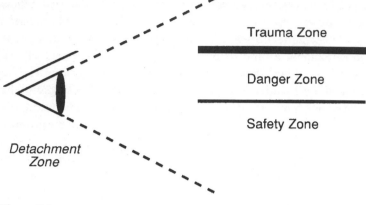

Figure 5.1

It is possible, on reflection, to discern three alternative types of psychological process which display detachment. Let us look at each of these in turn.

The first of these is *self-substitution*, and is involved in the example of detachment already given: that of being a spectator at a sporting event. Since ordinarily there is no personal threat to the spectator there usually is no reason for that party to feel threatened, and so he or she is likely to be in the excitement-seeking state. However, in order to gain arousal, he or she must normally empathize with the action, and identify with one or another of the protagonists. The same is true with another type of spectator event: the theater. Here one is invited by the playwright to enter into the magic world of the stage and identify with the hero or heroine. Indeed, fiction of all kinds—novels, films, plays, narrative poetry, opera, soap-opera—works on the principle that the spectator *will be in* the excitement-seeking state. Fiction can thus provide means of producing states of high arousal (for example, through the identification of the spectator with the actor). This strategy is called *self-substitution*, since what one is doing is putting someone else, to act as a surrogate for oneself, on the hot seat. Or—which comes to the same thing—one is temporarily losing one's own feelings of selfhood and allowing them to be taken over by another.

The spectator is often helped into the excitement-seeking state by first entering a special safety zone (the sports stadium, the theater, the cinema, and the like). Usually each of these venues has very distinctive features which act as signposts—not of danger but of the absence of danger. They tell people: "Here you can relax and enjoy your high arousal for a while: abandon fear, all ye who enter here!" Then, within each there is a "citadel of safety" in which the action occurs: the arena, screen, or stage.

By the time you reach your seat in the theater you have already encountered a number of special signposts which help you to set up a safety-zone frame: the foyer, with its ticket office and publicity displays; the coat-check room; the refreshment stand. You have been through the ritual of having your ticket torn in half at the door, acquiring a program, getting people to stand up so you can sit down, and finding that you do not have the right change to put into a machine to get the rental opera glasses out (if the place provides such a service). Also—to emphasize the special nature of the area—the colors, decor, and lighting within the theater are unlike anything you would see elsewhere, except perhaps in the caravan of a megalomaniac gypsy. So what happens here is that first of all we have a safety-zone frame set up, and this becomes a "way station" towards detachment, the latter occurring when the curtain finally rises (or parts) on the presentation itself. Self-substitution now occurs in the sense that one identifies with one or more of the characters in the "enchanted zone" of the stage, the drama occurring in a way which is detached from reality by, among other things, the literal frame of the proscenium arch.

In this self-substitution strategy we are faced with something of the same kind of paradox as occurs with the confidence frame, where the trick of obtaining excitement was to feel both threatened and safe at the same time. In the present case the paradox is that one must identify and empathize closely enough with one's "substitute self," or rather "selves," to be able to experience something of the latter's emotions yet remain detached enough to retain the protection of the frame.

The British theatre critic and columnist Bernard Levin, in his book *Enthusiasms*, describing his developing love of Shakespeare's plays, puts it like this:

> What was I responding to? I think it must have been the abrupt assault of emotion; more precisely of emotions I could feel in safety. Much later, when I discovered Wagner, the same thing happened, far more intensely, and it was not long before I realized consciously what was happening to me when I listened to *Tristan* or *The Ring* on the knowledge, simultaneously held and rejected, that this was not the real world but an opera house; for a few hours, no restraint on feeling was required, because for one thing it could be reimposed as soon as the performance ended, and for another and much more important thing it was too dark in the auditorium for anyone to see.[2]

This feeling that the action to be observed is cut off from the real world for a period of time occurs equally in relation to the cinema. Bruno Bettelheim, the psychoanalyst, described this detachment as follows:

> Watching the movies, one can be carried away to the degree that one feels part of the world of the moving picture. It is an experience that lifts one out of oneself into a world where one is not beholden to ordinary reality, at least for the length of the films. So it seems that what one feels and does while in the movies does not really count. But as soon as the lights are turned on, the spell is abruptly broken.[3]

Of course the same detachment from "real life" and attachment to fictional characters occurs, par excellence, in reading. The novelist Vladimir Nabokov described how "It is there that occurs the telltale tingle even though we must keep a little aloof, a little detached, when reading."[4] Fay Weldon, in her delightful *Letters to Alice*, writes; "Truly, Alice, books are wonderful things: to sit alone in a room and laugh and cry, because you are reading, and still be safe when you close the book."[5]

The second psychological process that can occur within the detachment frame is that of *make-believe* of the kind in which, unlike the passive experience of fiction, the individual produces his or her own imaginative material—as in daydreaming, fantasizing, and playful wish-fulfillment. The range of emotions conjured up through these personal images and narratives can of course be intensely gratifying. Included here would be the *aggressive* fantasies of children, the *power* fantasies of adolescents, and the *sexual* fantasies of adults. Being fantasies, they are not real—and so the detachment frame is inherent in the whole nature of the process. For those attracted to computer analogies, one could say that the individual has gone "off-line," like a computer which is no longer interacting with something outside itself but rather processing data already in store.

It is notable that many fantasies involve the contemplation of situations which would cause horror if they were to occur in reality. Many women, for example, report rape fantasies,[6] and children seem to enjoy the idea of confronting pirates, red "Indians," witches, dinosaurs, and mythical monsters of various kinds (at least this is suggested by the pattern of their make-believe play). None of this should seem surprising. Within the detachment frame one can with quiet confidence turn to whatever it is that causes the most arousal, however menacing, perverse, or sadistic it may seem to be—always provided, of course, that it does not bring with it enough realism to break down the detachment frame.

The third process is that of what we might call *retrospection*, which also, like make-believe, involves going off-line. Here the individual is not so much fantasizing as contemplating or reliving something which actually happened to him or her, and feeling at least some of the emotions of that episode. This is what Wordsworth called "emotion recollected in tranquility."[7] The event may have occurred only a few minutes before: the participant may be sitting in a roadside cafe, thinking of an accident he or she just avoided when crossing the road. Or it may have occurred rather longer ago—praise received from the boss two weeks back, or an argument with a romantic partner two months before that. It may even have occurred in the distant past—perhaps in early childhood. Since the danger or other circumstance is now completely in the past, however, then by definition it cannot be in the present to cause further concern. (If whatever it is *does* prove a continuing problem, then the process of thinking about it can no longer be interpreted as retrospection.) So, like make-believe, the detachment is intrinsic to the nature of the process itself.

Retrospection often involves more than just remembering, however. It can involve not only going over things, but also actively turning them into story-like forms which can fascinate in much the same way as fiction. It is epitomized by the sort of personal anecdotes that are traded back and forth at dinner parties. Here one takes some past incident and, in describing it, elaborates on and exaggerates it. Typically these accounts are about some misfortune which, in the telling, can be converted into an exciting account: how one was robbed while touring in Spain; the time one's back gave out at a most inappropriate moment; how one misunderstood what the surgeon said; the coughing fit he or she had while meeting his or her future mother-in-law for the first time; the promising financial transaction that went badly wrong. In the light of the analysis presented in this book, it can now be seen why "bad" things are so much more attractive as conversational topics than good ones: they can easily give rise to a range of arousing emotions which, however supposedly negative, can be enjoyed once they are sufficiently distanced by time. As in so many other cases delineated in this book, it is exactly those things that cause displeasure when confronted in reality that cause pleasure when experienced through a protective frame.

Both make-believe and retrospection, then, involve bringing material into consciousness which will cause increased arousal, be it in the form of ideas, images, memories, or narratives. Those readers familiar with the work of Sigmund Freud will know that he posited at different times a number of so-called defense mechanisms, the aim of which was to help in the avoidance of such anxiety as might derive from the conscious recognition of repressed unconscious ideas (e.g. shameful sexual urges, or memories of childhood traumas). Such mechanisms may well exist, functioning in association with the anxiety-avoidance state. But if this is in fact the case, then it is likely that the excitement-seeking state will have associated with it mental mechanisms which work in the *opposite* direction. In other words, the mechanisms associated with excitement-seeking will function in such a way as to make arousing unconscious materials available to consciousness, rather than to suppress them. These mechanisms will therefore *increase* the feelings of arousal that are experienced so that they can be enjoyed within the detachment frame. (Since the Freudian mechanisms are called *defense* mechanisms, I am tempted to call any opposite mechanisms which might exist *offense* mechanisms.)

You probably have already realized that these three detachment processes—self-substitution, make-believe, and retrospection—cannot always be clearly distinguished from each other, and that, because of this, an activity will often have elements of more than one of them at the same time. Thus in remembering some dramatic event in one's past (retrospection), one might start to fantasize about how things might have been different (make-believe). In watching a sportsman who is not performing well (self-substitution) one might fantasize about how he or she could perform better (make-believe). And, one might remember (retrospection) some event at which one was a spectator (self-substitution). The proliferations seem endless.

While we are noting some of these complexities it should also be born in mind that there is a dynamic by which it is possible to pass from one type of protective frame to another. We have already seen (in the illustration of going to the theater) the example of the safety-zone frame being used as a way station towards detachment. Similarly, a child playing with toys within the safety-zone frame of a playground may use them as the starting point for a fantasy. Although he or she continues to be active in the playground (running around for example), in psychological terms, make-believe detachment has taken over if the fantasy is dominating the experience—for instance if the child is pretending to be a cowboy. In the other direction, make-believe as a form of detachment can lead to action within the safety-zone frame. For example, sexual fantasy can lead to actual sexual activity within the safety-zone of the bedroom.

Returning specifically to detachment, it should be noted that in all three types of detachment things may go wrong, and anxiety-avoidance may be induced by actions aimed only at increasing the intensity of arousal. Thus, in relation to self-substitution, some people find pornography so threatening that it produces in them feelings of anxiety and disgust rather than the perhaps hoped for excitement. Some effects in films may be so threatening and realistic that they become genuinely unpleasant: think for example of the eyeball being cut open in Bunuel's famous film *Un Chien Andalou*. And of course some sports teams may play so badly that they induce real despair and grief in their supporters (I cannot help but think of years of watching unbelievably incompetent and unimaginative performances by the teams I support). Similarly, in the make-believe situation, arousing thoughts may lead on to thoughts which are worrisome and anxiety-causing. And in retrospection the memory of some previous trauma may be so painful that it is frightening; or thinking of some past problem, like a tiff with one's lover, may raise again an attempt to rethink what one should have done or said, and with it a host of worries, grievances, and annoyances.

PARAPATHIC EMOTIONS

A number of different emotions have been referred to in the past few pages, and this leads me to a conclusion which at first might seem to you rather startling and unlikely. It is that *all* emotions are enjoyed, even supposedly unpleasant ones like fear and anger and horror and grief and disgust, in the presence of detachment. After all, in fiction, one enjoys all the emotions that one experiences out of empathy with the characters, whether these emotions are positive ones like love, or negative ones like hate and terror. If we did not do this, we would be unlikely to expose ourselves to fiction in any of its many forms; or fiction would be just limp wish-fulfilment—which it generally is not. But just think of the enjoyment of terror in fairy stories, horror in that genre of films, rejected love in romantic novels, grief in "weepy" movies.

These emotions are not just passing "bad moments," but rather the very lifeblood of the fictional process. A horror film would be nothing without the vampires, the corpses coming to life, the ghouls, and the ghosts. After all, you would feel cheated if a horror film left you not horrified. And the most memorable moments, the ones we go over with pleasure afterwards and look forward to with pleasure on seeing the film again, are the moments of greatest horror—like the shower scene in Hichcock's original *Psycho*—which provide the sought-after *frisson*. This analysis answers the question of Stephen King, the writer of horror stories: "Why are people willing to pay good money to be made extremely uncomfortable?"[8] Of course, a piece of fiction *may* go all the way and actually produce the *real* form of the emotion; but if it does so it has failed in its task of producing emotions of all kinds within a protective framework which allows them to be enjoyed.

Even "anxiety" (notice the use of quote marks) can be experienced and enjoyed in this sense in the excitement-seeking state, but such anxiety is not the anxiety one would experience in the anxiety-avoidance state; rather, it is a special version of it fit for consumption within the special protective framework of detachment—for example the "anxiety" that one might experience while watching a thriller film. It is for this reason that I have put it in quotes, as I could have with the other supposedly negative emotions mentioned earlier, such as "anger" and "disgust."

I have assigned a special name to the "emotions in quotes" that are enjoyable forms of negative emotions. I call them *parapathic emotions.*[9] They are, of course, genuine emotions, not pretence (or "pretend") emotions. For instance, not only is one aroused when the heroine dies in a film, but there is a sense in which one is genuinely upset. Similarly, one is genuinely angry when in a Western the villain shoots an innocent farmer (or, even worse, the farmer's dog), and genuinely terrified when the hero clings to a cliff edge by his fingertips in a thriller. In fact, everything about the emotion is the same as in its "real-life" counterpart—except that there is an awareness that it is *not* "real-life." And in this unreal context the unpleasantness of the emotion is turned into something positive, and enjoyed. In fact, the more intense the emotion, the more it is enjoyed, rather than the converse. So anger, terror, and grief come to have a special, almost voluptuous, quality—the sort that was referred to in the eighteenth century as "sublime."[10]

As with the attainment of excitement, then, the "trick" of achieving parapathic emotions is to manage to contrive a situation that both induces the emotion *and* maintains the protective frame. If this can be done, then, as we have seen, the more arousing the source of the emotion, the more enjoyable the experience. Hence the enjoyment that can be derived from the fictional (or even documentary) treatment of those things we most fear or that most worry us: the threat of Islamic terrorism, of nuclear war, of major hurricanes, and the like. Indeed, television news, with its tales of killings, calamities, and catastrophes, can be the most entertaining program of the evening. In the detachment frame, sad to relate, little psychological distinction is made by most of us between fact and fiction. We enjoy the news of a train accident, or the destruction of someone's political career through scandal, as much as the sports news that is (significantly) included in the same news bulletin. And we are intrigued by the major television coups—such as the pictures of the assassination of President John F. Kennedy, or the Challenger spacecraft blowing up, or even the planes flying into the twin towers on 9/11. The television moguls understand this well, and find every excuse to show us these arousing snippets over and over again, so that we can wallow in our shocked "horror" and "outrage."

There is, though, a fine line to be drawn here, and the strongest and most graphic images, such as those of the destruction on 9/11, may break through the normal "television watching" protective frame and cause real distress and horror. Television producers try to stay as close as they can to this edge and not go over it. For example, it is a commonly agreed practice to avoid showing dead bodies unless they are those of foreigners in distant lands. They are also helped in not going over the edge by the fact that the more often a particular horrifying image is shown, the more it will, through familiarity, be dissipated and lose its effect. Nevertheless, fact and fiction, past and present, real and imaginary, are all mixed by TV into one big shaken and blended cocktail and served to us, in our detachment, as a form of home entertainment. And most of the time we seem to be pretty happy with the mix.[11]

There is another point here: in everyday life the situations that bring about such negative emotions as anger and contempt are often sufficiently serious to destroy the protective fame at the same time as inducing the emotion. But if for some reason the safety-zone frame, and with it the excitement-seeking state, can be maintained, then—according to this analysis—the emotion will be enjoyed even here, as if real life were a huge fiction. For example, one may derive pleasure from watching people shouting at each other in the street, or pulling over to dispute someone else's careless driving. Such public events may be experienced as a kind of street theater. Or, one may really enjoy, at least at some moments, a friend's tale of woe, as if it were something out of a novel. This is not to say that we are all cynics who hypocritically pretend to be concerned, while in fact callously disregarding others' feelings. The point is that as we come into contact with the problems of other people, the appearance and disappearance of the safety-zone frame is not always precisely coordinated with the way in which their dramas impinge on us. There are, therefore, times—of shorter *or* longer duration—when (as in watching a television news story) we can actually enjoy observing the conflicts, frustrations, and even tragedies of those around us.

This human propensity for enjoying "bad things" lends itself to commercial exploitation, and this is indeed happening through what is becoming known as "grief tourism" or "dark tourism."[12] This term is applied to the recreational visiting of sites associated with death and disaster. Such sites include the battlefields of World Wars One and Two, including Hiroshima, concentration camps like Auschwitz, the book depository in Dallas from where Lee Harvey Oswald supposedly shot John F. Kennedy, and the sites of nuclear accidents like Three Mile Island in Pennsylvania and Chernobyl in the Ukraine. Clearly dark tourism has always been with us, from pilgrimages to sites where saints have been martyred to the dungeons of the Tower of London. But they seem to have taken on new life in recent years. For example, the Ground Zero site in New York has been attracting more visitors per year than the World Trade Center did. Such sites also lend themselves to the most blatant and tasteless commercialization. At Ground Zero, along with guide books and other printed ephemera, one can buy Twin Tower tea shirts, and toilet tissue bearing the face of Osama bin Laden. At Hiroshima one can buy key rings and t-shirts from the Visitors Bureau. At Three Mile Island it is possible to buy, as well as the requisite key rings and t-shirts, such souvenirs as drinking mugs, bumper stickers, and belt buckles. The t-shirts say such things as "A Little Nukey Never Hurt Anyone" and "Hell No, I Don't Glow." In New Orleans, tourists are picked up from their hotels and taken on organized tours of the Lower 9th Ward devastated by Hurricane Katrina and its aftermath.

There could not be a better illustration than the phenomenon of dark tourism of the way in which people seek out and enjoy such emotions as grief and horror—when they can be experienced vicariously through a detachment frame. (Having myself visited a number of these sites, and driven around the flooded parts of New Orleans not long after the disaster, I am in no position to moralize about this phenomenon.)

This discussion of parapathic emotions has taken place in the context of the detachment frame. But the parapathic form of an emotion will also be felt if either of the other two types of protective frame (confidence or safety-zone) is in operation. So we can say that within *any* type of protective fame, i.e. when the excitement-seeking state is in operation for whatever reason, *any* arousing emotion will be pleasant—even supposedly negative emotions. For example, in playfully arguing with someone (a kind of intellectual game that may be played within the frame of the safety-zone), one may take pleasure in the anger or contempt one feels towards the other's claims and counterclaims. The point about parapathic emotions arises in connection with detachment because it is within this frame in particular that we happen to see—at least in our culture, and especially in connection with fiction—the greatest range of emotions being enjoyed.

The reason why *any* emotion is enjoyed in the excitement-seeking state is that emotions involve *arousal*. And, as we have seen, the higher the arousal, the more enjoyable it is felt to be in this state. The arousal-seeking state is the same as the excitement-seeking state, therefore, and the arousal-avoidance state is the same as the anxiety-avoidance state. The terms can be used interchangeably. One thing that this discussion attempts to make clear, however, is that danger is only *one* possible source of arousal. We shall look at others in a later chapter.

THE THREE FRAMES

This might be a good moment to pause and see where we are. We have now looked at three *general* types of protective frame (the confidence, the safety-zone, and the detachment), each associated with a particular zone of experience. And we have seen that there are three *particular* types of the third frame (self-substitution, make-believe, and retrospection). We are now in a position to be able to contrast these frames. (See the summary in table 5.1)

Table 5.1

Types of Protective Frame		Description
I.	Confidence	The individual feels confident that he or she will avoid trauma, despite an awareness of the immediate presence of danger.
II.	Safety-Zone	The individual feels that there is no immediate danger or possibility of slipping into danger.
III.	Detachment	
	Self-Substitution	Someone else is perceived to be in danger.
	Make-Believe	The danger is perceived to be imaginary.
	Retrospection	The danger is perceived to be in the past.

Suppose there is the danger of falling from a crumbling cliff edge. In the case of the confidence frame, the individual in potential peril might be actually walking on the edge, but see himself or herself to be *relatively* protected by railings or a fence. In the case of the safety-zone frame the individual might, in a *completely* safe area, be simulating walking along the cliff edge, perhaps with the imaginary edge delineated somehow (perhaps by chalk) on the stony ground. Finally, in the case of the detachment frame he or she might be fascinated while watching (from a safe distance) someone else walk the edge (self-substitution), or fantasizing about doing the walking (make-believe), or remembering some previous occasion of walking on such a dangerous edge (retrospection).

These different types of frame are in fact displayed clearly in sequence (but in reverse order to that employed here in describing the frames) during the running of the bulls at Pamplona. Here (as we saw earlier), the dangerous edge moves rapidly up the streets composing the course. You will recall that first of all, before the *encierro* starts, one may observe the spectators on the balconies and in the streets. They are in a festive frame of mind, removed from personal danger but anticipating, with great pleasure, the risks that will arise for others. These, then, are experiencing the run in the self-substitution version of the *detachment frame* of mind.

Now if one takes a particular position on the course and observes the runners as they go past, it is clear that the first runners feel themselves to be within a *safety-zone frame*. They are well away from the bulls and are therefore out of real danger. In consequence they are only playing at being *corredores*. They wave to the crowd or brandish their rolled newspapers, and laugh and jostle each other. Although they certainly do not just hang around, their mood is as festive as that of the spectators. Many of them (presumably those who have never participated before) look blissfully unaware of the serious danger that could overtake them if they did hang around.

Suddenly, as the runners continue to pass, one sees the tempo of the running change. A new wave of runners arrives, pushing into the backs of the others. They are agitated, but not panicking.

Presumably, for the most part, they are experienced and enjoying the closeness of danger from within a *confidence frame*.

Finally comes a group of runners scrambling desperately to get through the melee. They continually glance behind them, and some thrust themselves towards the barricades and attempt to climb clear. These are runners who see themselves to be not only in the danger zone, but with no protection. And for good reason: almost before one knows it, the bulls are there, a whole tidal wave of commotion passing up the street, leaving a debris of fallers. These fallers complete the sequence of stages, since we may safely assume that they have experienced trauma to some degree or another.

6

How People Differ

PATTERNS OF CHANGE

If *any* of the three types of protective frame is in place, then the individual will want to increase his or her feelings of arousal. If none is in place, then the individual will want to do the opposite. So as people pass through their everyday lives they switch back and forth between these different ways of being, sometimes seeking high arousal and sometimes low, as protective frames appear and disappear.

You can recognize this kind of changeability in your own life by observing yourself carefully over time. For example, if you drive to work, observe how some of the time you are likely to be bored, and looking for stimulation (perhaps turning on the radio to give yourself something interesting to listen to, or driving faster). At other times, however, even during the same drive, you may be anxious (perhaps because you are late), or angry (perhaps because you are frustrated by delays)—and at these times you would like to feel more tranquil.

It is difficult to study these kinds of changes in people when they occur in everyday life, because to find out what state of mind someone is in you have to stop and interview him or her, or administer a questionnaire. This sort of thing not only interrupts what they are doing, so that they have to change the course of their behavior, but the very fact of questioning may itself change their state of mind.

One study used an ingenious method to get around this.[1] There is evidence to show that, by-and-large, people find that hot colors (like red) raise their feelings of arousal, while cool colors (like blue) lower them. In other words, across the spectrum, colors of longer wavelengths tend to make people feel more aroused, and colors of shorter wavelengths to make people feel less aroused. Suppose that you show someone a set of colors selected from across the whole spectrum and ask which one that person finds most attractive at a given moment. Then their choice should be a good indicator of whether, and by how much, they want to be aroused at that moment. Now, asking someone for a color-preference choice at a certain moment is, if odd, only minimally disruptive—certainly in comparison with, for example, asking them to spend ten minutes or more filling in a questionnaire.

In this study, more than a hundred office workers were observed by a researcher individually in their places of work, over periods of time which varied (depending on where they were working and what type of permission had been obtained) from one to as many as eight working days. Each of them was regularly asked to choose, from among a set of colors covering the whole spectrum, the color that seemed most attractive to them at that exact moment. The researcher presented them with the color display, and asked for such a response, either every quarter of an hour or every half an hour (again, depending on where they were working), throughout the period of time concerned.

When each individual's results were analyzed, patterns emerged of just the kind that would be expected from the analysis given in this book. On the whole, subjects swung backwards and forwards in their choices between colors which for them were very arousing, and those that seemed very relaxing, choosing intermediate colors much less often. In other words they changed, over time, with respect to how much arousal they wanted. And when they changed they changed radically, jumping from one relative extreme to the other. In fact, the neutral arousal color (green, for most people) was hardly chosen at all throughout the whole study.

The picture that emerges of these people at their places of work is of people whose arousal needs are frequently and dramatically changing. These changes arise as they encounter the different situations and events that arise during their daily round of tasks, problems, crises, frustrations, distractions, phone calls, social niceties, gossip, break times, and the rest. (It should be emphasized that this data represents not how aroused people *were*, but how aroused they *wanted* to be: a color is assumed to be attractive if it helps to either increase or lower arousal.)

In looking at the results, one thing in particular quickly became apparent: people differ from one other considerably in their patterns of change. The most immediately obvious difference was that people vary in how *frequently* they change, some people being relatively stuck for long periods of time at a particular level of desired arousal, but others showing great instability in this respect. Said otherwise: some people tend to stay in either the arousal-seeking or the arousal-avoidance mode for some time before they switch; others tend to switch after only short periods of time. Inspection of the data showed that this difference between groups was largely related to age. The youngest group (17–19) reversed between states relatively infrequently, but frequency of reversals increased up to a peak for the 40–49-year-old age group, and then fell away again rapidly in the older groups (the oldest being 60–65).

The second obvious way in which people varied was in terms of their balance toward one or the other state. That is, some people spent relatively long periods of time in the arousal-*seeking* state, and others in the arousal-*avoidance* state. This important personality difference will be at the focus of the rest of this chapter. Let us call this balance or bias toward one state or the other *dominance*. Then we can say that whereas some people are arousal-*seeking* dominant to some degree or another, others are arousal-*avoidance* dominant in varying degrees. So, although people are generally inconsistent in the sense that they flip-flop back and forth between these different states, there would seem to be a kind of consistency within the inconsistency. Thus some people are consistently more likely, other things being equal, to be in the arousal-seeking state, while others are consistently more likely to be in its opposite.

At one extreme of dominance we have the happy-go-lucky, playful, adventurous kind of people, who are more often than not looking for stimulation. At the other extreme we have the nervous, serious, play-it-safe, cautious kind of people, who more often than not are looking for safety and for relief from problems and threats. And in between we have people representing every degree of bias in either direction. Psychometric scales are available to measure the degree of dominance that a person experiences.[2]

THE CAUSES OF AROUSAL-PREFERENCE

Where does an imbalance in one direction or the other come from? What causes it? Is it something which people learn from their experiences, or is it rather predetermined in their individual biological makeup? Unfortunately, there is no definite answer to these questions at present, although there are some clues that can be indicated here fairly briefly.

First of all, it must necessarily be the case that as we go through life we learn which particular situations are safe, in terms of one kind of protective frame or another, and which are not. As a child we learn that bath water is safe, but that flames are not. Later we learn such complexities as which subjects are safe to discuss with one's spouse without danger of upset or argument, and which are contentious. In general terms, we learn where we should feel confident and where we have no right to feel confident, which areas of space and time can be treated as being within safety-zone frames, and so on. There are issues for the psychology of learning here, about exactly what kind of learning this "frame learning" is. The important thing from the perspective of the present argument is that we *do* learn to frame our experiences in this respect, and also to experience some things through a protective frame, and some things without one.

So, as we move through our daily lives, the balance of arousal-seeking over arousal-avoidance will be a reflection of the balance of situations we encounter in which we have learned to feel safe, over situations in which we have learned to feel that we are exposed to some kind of danger or risk that we may not be able to handle. Some of us tend to run scared, some of us do not. If we followed two people through a similar set of situations, and found that one tended to experience them in an arousal-seeking kind of way, and the other to treat them in an arousal-avoiding style, then we could infer that the difference was due to their individual learning histories.

So far, so simple. Unfortunately, for this point of view, there is also evidence that, at least to some extent, a person can experience the *same* situation in either the arousal-seeking or arousal-avoiding states of mind at *different* times. This is difficult to explain in terms of learning. On one occasion, a person may take part in a commit-tee meeting in a worried, nervous state, yet on another be looking for stimulation and excitement. Taking the children to a park to play may be boring on one occasion, relaxing on another. Examples abound.

Now it may be that such situations are not really the same on different days, but change in subtle (or even not-so-subtle) ways that make a crucial difference for the protective frame. But what if we take the same situation on the same day, and find that we experience it in alternating ways? Several experiments have demonstrated precisely this tendency. In these experiments, each subject is placed in a room and given free access to materials that reflect either arousal-seeking or arousal-avoidance—for example, computer video games versus computer teaching materials. (Of course, which materials are which in terms of arousal-seeking and arousal-avoidance are checked out independently for each individual subject). Most subjects in fact alternate, albeit at different rates, between one kind of material and the other—but tend to spend *longer* with one than the other.[3]

This behavior implies two things. The first is that the reversal process, the movement between opposite states, has to some extent its own dynamic—it is not just instigated in a learned way by different situations as they arise. A good analogy here would be to sleeping and waking. There is a natural biological alternation between the two, although it can be overridden by environmental circumstances. An interesting film on television, or the possibility of erotic pleasure, may keep us awake longer than would otherwise have occurred. A telephone ringing, or a loud street noise, may wake us up sooner than we otherwise would have awakened. So environmental events may play a part in whether we are asleep or awake at a given moment. But, generally speaking, an innate biological rhythm is more important in determining how long we sleep and stay awake. And without specific events to keep us in the sleeping or the waking state, or to move us between these states, this innate process will eventually move us from the one to the other anyway.

The second point about these arousal-preference states is that this internal movement displays the individual's balance in one direction or the other, which is to say that the individual, when left to himself or herself in this way, tends to spend longer periods in one state than in the other. However, unlike the situation in the color study described earlier, the environment in the studies being referred to here is essentially unchanging. The balance therefore cannot be explained in terms of a balance of different situations evoking different states through their learned significance. It must, rather, reflect some other kind of unlearned bias, some kind of underlying personality factor which relates to a general innate tendency to see, or not to see, the world through protective frames, and which surfaces when the environment is kept relatively constant— as it was in these experiments.

It is still not impossible that this internal bias is itself learned in some way, in which case one might expect it to reflect something of the overall tone and atmosphere of the environment in which the individual has been brought up. That is, it might be that the time an individual spends in each state in the course of everyday life is not determined by the experience of specific events, but rather by some global orientation which is derived in a diffuse and general way from his or her background. Thus, one might expect that if someone is brought up in a casual, happy-go-lucky, easygoing, fun-loving family, then he or she might well become arousal-*seeking* dominant. And if that person is raised in a serious, disciplined, hard-working, punitive family, he or she might as easily become arousal-*avoidance* dominant. In the first case the person would learn to feel, on the whole, relatively unthreatened by his or her environment, and to look for the pleasures and excitements to be extracted from it. In the second the person would learn, again in a general way, to see all the serious implications of his or her actions, and be aware of the consequences of error. Unfortunately for this kind of explanation, evidence at this point shows no support for such a relationship between the upbringing style of parents and the dominance of their children.[4]

There may be some reason to suppose, therefore, that there is a biological underpinning to arousal-seeking/avoidance dominance. Evidence consistent with this has been provided by the Norwegian psychophysiologist Sven Svebak, who has shown in a series of interesting experiments that there are definite physiological differences between people who score high and low on personality tests which make this kind of distinction. In particular, people who are usually serious-minded, and therefore tend to be arousal-avoiding, show among other things, greater muscle tension, faster heart rates, and more rapid and deeper breathing, in response to various tasks, than do people who are more play-oriented, and therefore generally arousal-seeking.[5] He has also suggested that such differences extend to structural as well as functional features of the body. Specifically, he infers from evidence that the muscles of people who frequently are arousal-avoiders are made up of a different mix of fibers from those of people who frequently are arousal-seekers.[6] This is a highly technical area that we cannot go into in more detail here. Suffice it to say that there do appear to be some "prewired" and therefore unlearned differences between people who spend different periods of time in these two alternative states.[7]

If, in referring to such physiological differences, I now seem to be pushing matters in the direction of a biological explanation, there is a further factor on the environmental side of the equation that also needs to be considered. Not all environmental effects take place through learning (in the conventional sense of that term). Some take place through critical "one-off" incidents that change the manner in which people see things, sometimes in far-reaching and profound ways. These crucial experiences,[8] as they have been called, include such things as episodes of religious conversion, occurrences of love at first sight, and hearing a lecture that leads one to choose a particular career.

Now, it is possible that there are some kinds of crucial experiences that bear on the protective frame. For example, learning that someone loves you, having an astonishing piece of good luck, or overcoming some personal handicap may have reassuring effects that make it easier to see the world through a protective frame. Suffering from a painful and unexpected illness, being let down by someone you trusted, losing money in a business venture, and similar unfortunate events may, by the same token, make it more difficult to sustain a protective frame in situations where you would otherwise have been able to do so. For example, if you are injured while playing football, you may find it more difficult, for a period after you have recovered, to play the game with the abandon and enjoyment that you did before. In a study of the training of undercover police agents—an unpleasant and hazardous experience—it was found that the trainees were more serious and less arousal-seeking after this training than they had been before.[9]

At the extreme we have severe traumatic events like bereavement for a close family member, or being injured in an automobile accident. It would be strange if such demonstrations of personal vulnerability did not produce major difficulties in sustaining a protective frame. We shall return to this point later in the book when we discuss post-traumatic stress disorder.

Two other factors need to be taken into consideration. The first is that of age. There is evidence that, on average, people become more cautious and more likely to avoid arousal as they get older over the whole adult life span.[10] It is reasonable to suppose that this maturational effect is built into us, and that this is therefore another kind of biological influence on dominance. The second factor is that of gender. Here the data obtained so far do not support the idea that the sexes differ with respect to arousal-seeking or arousal-avoidance dominance.[11] This implies that if men and women are different, that difference is not in terms of how much time they spend in each state, but in terms of the specific things that they do to raise or lower arousal levels when they are in one state or the other.

Overall, our tentative conclusion here must be that each individual has a biologically-based bias, albeit one that changes over a lifetime, in favor of arousal-seeking or arousal-avoidance—but that both learning and crucial experiences may work to strengthen or weaken this innate predisposition.

GETTING INTO CONTROL

Given that we have *no* control over our underlying biological bias in one direction or the other, and that this bias has also been influenced by past learning and crucial experiences, do we not nevertheless have *some* control over how much time we spend in each state in the present? In other words, can we change our "effective" dominance to some degree by overriding these internal biases? The analysis here implies that we can indeed do this, should we want to, to the extent that we can deliberately set up or remove protective frames within our experience.

Thus if we wanted to spend less time in the arousal-seeking state, we could do this by avoiding those situations that tend to invoke protective frames—such as situations in which we are clearly playing games, or in which we are undeniably spectators. We could even deliberately spend more time in those places where we do serious things and where, therefore, it is more difficult to establish a protective frame, such as our place of work. Or we could commit ourselves to important and possibly long-term projects which we know will make, and continue to make, demands on us, and which it will be difficult to back out of. If we can make such commitments, then we know that there will be frequent occasions when the urgency or seriousness of the task will make the establishment of a protective frame all but impossible. (In an earlier chapter, I gave a personal example of the consequences of committing myself to give a paper at a conference, this leading inevitably to various anxiety-avoiding episodes such as the moment of starting to deliver the paper itself in front of a possibly critical audience.)

By contrast, if one wanted to get into the arousal-seeking state more frequently, there are a variety of means for introducing a protective frame into experience. As we have seen, there are many kinds of places which our culture sets up for us to feel safe in—areas demarcated for play in its broadest sense: parks, playing fields, concert halls, art galleries, and so on. For most of us, our home can also constitute a safety-zone frame. Just being present more frequently in such locations can help us to increase the periods of time we spend feeling unthreatened and looking for pleasurable stimulation. Being with people who are reassuring can have the same effect. This is perhaps why doing things with friends is so widespread: friends can create safety "auras" for each other to bask in. We can also make sure that, as far as possible, we avoid tasks and challenges which, over the longer term, are liable to tax us to the point that they break through any protective frame. In other words, the means used to increase the frequency of arousal-seeking are by-and-large the converse of those used to increase the frequency of arousal-avoidance.

It will be realized in all this that being in either the arousal-avoiding or the arousal-seeking state is not something which is under direct, voluntary control. To get into one state or the other is a matter of attempting to remove or set up frames. We cannot just decide to see the world through a protective frame, in the way that we might decide to stand up or sit down. Some intermediary is, it seems, always needed—be it a person, a place, or a situation. The most direct form of intermediary is a suitable thought or image, if it can be conjured up. If one can manage to think of something sufficiently threatening, and focus on it, this action should dissolve any kind of protective frame. Alternatively, if one can think of something that is fun, or even imagine that what one is doing at the time (arguing on a committee, let us say, or taking instructions from a client) is really some kind of game, or a piece of drama, this move should help to re-establish a protective frame. Another related technique is to associate each state with an image, or set of images, such that conjuring up the image is sufficient to induce the state. A technique that I use regularly in self-development workshops is to ask the participant to imagine rooms representing the arousal-avoiding and arousal-seeking states, and to furnish them in their mind's eye with things that they associate with each of these states. The serious arousal-avoiding room might, for example, contain an imposing desk, a planning calendar, some diplomas on the wall, a book-case with reference books, and so on. The more playful arousal-seeking room might contain a pool table, a drinks cabinet, a flat screen TV, a comfortable sofa, etc. If the individual wants to get into one or the other state, he or she imagines going into the corresponding room.

This raises the question of why one might want to get into control of the process of switching between states, or attempt to change one's dominance in one direction or the other. It should be remembered that neither kind of dominance is inherently better than the other. Each presents advantages and disadvantages in life. Thus, if you are strongly arousal-*seeking* dominant, you will by definition be more likely to enjoy some of the good things that life has to offer— sports, games, fiction, parties, and the like. But you may have difficulty taking seriously some of the serious things that have to be dealt with if you are to succeed in long-term projects, such as those associated with a successful career. On the other hand, if you are strongly arousal-*avoidance* dominant, you are more likely to be intensely aware of all the serious consequences of your actions, and not be distracted by passing diversions, or misled by spurious feelings of safety. But you may miss out on many of those things that are inherently enjoyable in themselves, but have no significance beyond themselves. In this respect you would not lead life to the full.

Indeed, the fullest life is probably led by people who are able to experience both states on a regular basis, and to switch between them at appropriate times: to face up to things which are genuinely threatening or important, as well as to have fun when it is time to have fun. So it may be best not to be too dominant in either direction. In this respect, paradoxically, it is the people who are unstable who are likely to be the most psychologically healthy. This does not mean that both sides of the personality need to be in perfect balance, but that both sides need adequate expression at appropriate times.

There may therefore be good reason for some people—those who spend almost all of their time in one state or the other—to want to gain an increased control over the state-switching process, so that they can bring the two states into somewhat greater equilibrium. Indeed, as you read this you may be asking yourself whether you are such a person. Are you missing out on the good things of life by being too serious all the time? Are you failing to achieve anything solid by never being serious enough? If you can answer yes to either of these questions, however tentatively, then you may want to think about ways in which you can change the status of the protective frame in your experience.

THRILL-SEEKERS

One of the themes of this book is that we are all thrill-seekers at certain times, and that in this respect there is nothing inherently different between ourselves and people who carry out obvious, dramatic and attention-capturing forms of risky behaviour—such as sky diving, car racing, or bull fighting. The mechanisms are the same in all people, but work themselves out in different ways in different individuals. In this respect, there is no special "type" that is fundamentally distinct from the rest of us. Now it may well be true that the person one might recognise as a "daredevil" is high in arousal-seeking dominance, but there may be many people who are equally arousal-seeking dominant but who obtain their arousal in a variety of less obvious and less public ways. In any case, arousal-seeking dominance appears to be a continuous dimension that does not have cut-off points.

So why do some people seem to go to extremes and to take enormous risks that the rest of us would avoid? Why do some people jump with parachutes from skyscrapers, or scramble into deep caves? The answer must be in the protective frame that they develop for the activity involved. That is, they initially undertake some risky activity, like mountain climbing, that they succeed in. This then makes them feel confident to undertake the activity again, with perhaps exposure to a little more risk. Step by step they build greater confidence by overcoming greater risk, and in this way build up an increasingly robust protective frame for this activity. They probably also need to take greater and greater risk in order to achieve the same level of excitement, given that what seemed dangerous before, as they become more expert, no longer seems to pose the same danger. In other words, these kinds of people are people whose protective frame for some activity is much tougher than the rest of us could imagine it being in ourselves.

Because they have a strong protective frame with respect to a particular activity, however, does not mean that they are equally willing to take risks on other activities. There may of course be some generalization of confidence from one kind of challenge to a related challenge—from parachuting to hang-gliding, for example. But generally speaking, if a person is a high risk-taker for one kind of risk, this does not necessarily mean that he or she will be a high risk-taker for other activities. Because someone races motorbikes, it does not mean that they would be willing to swim with sharks. Because someone has climbed a high mountain, it does not mean that he or she will cross a busy street without looking. In crossing the street, he or she will be likely to behave like the rest of us. Putting it in another way: a thrill-seeker is not a thrill-seeker all the time. In talking about excitement-seeking, we are not referring to an enduring personality trait that stays the same at all times.[9] The desire for excitement is something that comes and goes in everybody and is expressed in particular ways in particular situations. There is a great temptation to oversimplify in terms of traits and types—"this person is a thrill-seeker, this other person is not"—but it is a temptation that we must resist if we are going to understand the psychology of excitement in its full richness and complexity.

This book is in part about people who take certain things to extremes, and who as a result accomplish great things or who do crazy things or destructive things. But our attention to them is not only because they are interesting in themselves, which they are. It is also because by observing them we will come all the better to understand ourselves.

7

Getting Turned On

THE VARIED SOURCES OF AROUSAL

In previous chapters we have been looking more at the protective frame than at the sources of arousal that may be experienced within such a frame. In the metaphor of an earlier chapter, we have been more interested in the cage than in the tiger. Let us now turn our attention to the tiger.

Of the sources of arousal that we *have* looked at, danger and risk have figured most prominently. But we have also paid some attention to sexual stimulation, the competitiveness of sports, and the empathic enjoyment of other people's emotions. In fact, of course, there are many more kinds of stimulation and ways of becoming aroused than these, and one of the aims of this chapter is to explore some of these other sources of arousal. So our main interest here moves away from the protective frame and on to those stimulating situations and events that can be experienced within such a frame. We must not forget that the frame will be necessary for their enjoyment, and that whatever causes "good" arousal when it is present will cause "bad" arousal when it is not.

In changing the focus in this way, the first thing to strike one is just how amazingly varied are the different kinds of things that people do to "get turned on"—from smoking cigarettes to taking heroin, from collecting match boxes to breeding piranhas, from origami to orgasm. This range becomes amplified many times if we take into account different cultures and different periods of history. Fortunately for our purposes here, these different activities and sources of stimulation do seem to fall into a number of universal categories. In looking at these I will emphasize sources of stimulation which we have not already looked at.

These types of situations and activities touch on so many aspects of life that there is a sense in which we shall be looking at the whole of everyday experience in relation to this arousal theme. This is not to claim that excitement is the most important part of every pleasurable experience. (Many other psychological rewards may be more important at a given moment—such as feelings of power and control, or of being loved.) It is rather to emphasize the way in which the arousing quality of the stimulation can contribute significantly to the enjoyment of many situations, or detract from them if we are in the arousal-avoidance state of mind. And often it *is* the most important facet in our experience.

At the outset, two main overriding categories of stimulation can be identified. The first includes all those sources of arousal that are presented to us by the nature of the various environments in which we either find ourselves or place ourselves at different times. The second derives from how we act on these environments including, especially, how we interact with other people. In the first case we are in a sense relatively passive, simply opening ourselves up to stimulation. In the second we vigorously pursue active strategies of different kinds, the excitement coming from the action.

Admittedly there is something artificial about this distinction. After all, we can actively set out to discover situations that are, by their very nature, likely to raise arousal in us when we subject ourselves to them. For example, in building a record or CD collection the searching, choosing, and purchasing is active and exciting in itself. But listening to the music afterwards may produce excitement in a way that is (at least in the sense intended here) relatively passive. Similarly, the fact that one is actively pursuing some exciting course of action, like climbing a mountain, does not mean that excitement cannot also be derived simultaneously from the arousing properties of the environment (for instance, the perception of being high above the ground). All the same, it is useful to consider these sources of excitement separately.

BEING STIMULATED

The first main category, then, concerns something from which we can never escape for as long as we are alive and awake. This is the sensory and perceptual properties of the world around us: the colors, shapes, smells, tastes, and noises that, together with the meanings they hold for us, go to make up the fabric of our conscious experience. In fact, it is possible to identify *three* general properties of stimuli (things we perceive) that play a part in arousing or soothing us.[1]

The *first* of these consists of their simple, basic sensory qualities. For much of our life we may push this into the background by attending to other aspects of those things that impinge on us, such as how we can use them. But it is possible to experience very simple sensations with great intensity. Here, for example, is a writer talking about his enjoyment of books: "I am an incurable book-sniffer; when I open a new book I at once savour its scent, and I have had some odd looks from bookshop assistants in consequence, particularly since the next thing I do is to run my fingertip over the pages, for the sensuous pleasure to be had from touching fine book-paper is not to be underestimated."[2]

If we are sufficiently sensitive we can become excited by the most mundane aspects of our world of sensation and perception, and experience the fabric of consciousness as a rich tapestry indeed. Arguably, women may be better at this than men. But everyone seems to be able to develop this sensitive relationship to at least certain kinds of experience which are special to them—the gourmet to food, the gardener to plants (and even manure), the sun-lover to both the intense heat of the sun, together with the smells of sand, sweat, and suntan oil. If we are fortunate, we can derive such sensory excitement from *any* aspect of the world as it impinges on us during the course of our everyday lives.

Often we do not need to be especially sensitive to be not only aroused but overwhelmed by sensations. Rather, the world breaks in on us like the sea and, whether we like it or not, inundates us with waves of intense stimulation. Thus bright colors and loud rhythmic noises can be highly arousing, and both are deliberately made use of—at fairgrounds and in rock concerts, military tattoos, parades, discos, and the like—in order to get us worked up. Noisy motor-bikes, transistors played at full volume, brightly colored hair and clothes, all seem to be irritatingly attractive to (most especially) youngsters in search of fun. By contrast, many of us prefer to be overwhelmed by size and grandeur, as displayed by mountains or cathedrals, or by the more refined intensity of the art gallery or concert hall. But in *whatever* form intense sensory stimulation arrives at our eyes and ears, it has the power to lift us to new heights of arousal.

Conversely, of course, settings that reduce sensory stimulation to a minimum—like the quiet decor of many people's bedrooms, for example—allow arousal to fall back to low levels. Similarly, the use of stimuli which are de-arousing, such as soft colors, can also have this effect and so tend to be used in situations, like hospital waiting rooms, where people do not wish to be aroused more than they already are.

The *second* general propensity of stimuli is that they may act as *signs* of impending pleasure or pain, or remind us in some way of joy or misery: the fire alarm going off, the dinner bell sounding, the arrival in the mail of a scented pink envelope (or a brown manila one), the tuning-up of the orchestra, the sound of the dentist's drill. These may all play some part in determining whether we experience the *arrival* or *removal* of a safety frame, and therefore whether we are in the arousal-*seeking* or arousal-*avoidance* state. But, more to the point in terms of the present argument, they are also likely to produce marked surges of arousal. (Other signs, of course, may lower arousal: seeing one's house after a long drive, the final whistle of a football game, and so on.)

Third, there are the rather abstract properties that have to do with the "structure" of the situations that confront us. Thus something very hard to make sense of (like a tax form) is likely to be more arousing, other things being equal, than something relatively simple and straightforward (such as a menu in a British restaurant). Similarly, something ambiguous (a vague shape seen in the street at night) may be more arousing than the same everyday object with its ambiguity removed.

One particularly important structural aspect of situations is the degree of surprise or novelty that they hold for us. Routine, predictable, or monotonous situations will certainly not raise arousal, and indeed may induce torpor. But unexpected events will be likely to jolt us into alertness. An example that we are all familiar with is a sudden loud noise. But just about anything we had not anticipated can be arousing: seeing a friend in unfamiliar surroundings, the delivery of an unexpected parcel, bumping into one's daughter in town when one thought she was at school.

Some situations are deliberately designed to keep the level of unpredictability and uncertainty as high as possible for as long as possible. Examples might include the thriller novel, the football game between roughly equal sides, and the beauty contest. And part of the reason we enjoy such contrived situations (if in fact we do) is that they keep us in suspense about the outcome—and even from time to time provide us with some unexpected twist or turn. The piece of music to which we return time and time again (to the exasperation of others) often is one that is complex enough to be continually surprising. So although we already know its general structure, we seem to hear it fresh on each occasion, becoming aware of seemingly previously unheard details and nuances which throw new light on the whole work. To quote again from the writer cited earlier:

> In all these instances [of thrilling moments in music] the shock of the unexpected is as great, and as exciting, as when I first heard the works, and I will go so far as to say that the fact that I now know in advance what is going to happen makes the experience more

thrilling, not less; it would ruin the enjoyment of a visit to *The Mousetrap* to enter the theatre knowing the identity of the murderers, but the same cannot be said about *Hamlet*.[3]

This is presumably because Hamlet is too complex to be completely 'mastered' and so always retains the power to surprise and even shock us.

COGNITIVE SYNERGY

Another aspect of the structure of situations that relates to arousal is what I have defined as "cognitive synergy."[4] A cognitive synergy occurs when one experiences something—a person, say, or an object—in opposite ways, either at the same time or in quick succession. For example, a man dressed as a woman would be a cognitive synergy because, in looking at him, one would simultaneously experience both masculinity and femininity. Equally, a woman dressed as a man, and particularly if wearing a moustache, would create a synergy. A child acting like a grown-up (e.g. pretending to be a doctor), an animal doing something human (e.g. a chimpanzee's tea party), an inanimate object appearing to be alive (e.g. a puppet), someone clever seeming very stupid (e.g. the absent-minded professor)—all of these, when observed, involve opposite qualities brought together in experience at the same moment. Of course, *logically* something *cannot* be both itself and something else at the same time, but *psychologically*, as these examples testify, there is a sense in which exactly this *can* happen. And it tends to produce fascination, and at least a mildly heightened arousal.

Experiencing things as changing quickly into other things is also synergic if the transformation is so rapid that for a moment one sees the object in both ways: the transformation of the conjurer's cane into a scarf, or the flat picture into a solid model in the child's pop-up book. Here is an example from my own experience of such a quick-change synergy, and one that impressed me greatly. The fortress of Saint-Marie-Among-the-Hurons (in Midland, Ontario) is a meticulous reconstruction of a frontier post that had been over-run by local Native Americans and largely destroyed. Visitors to the post start their tour in a lecture theatre. Here they see a film that pre-sents the background story of the fortress, and finishes with a pic-ture of it in ruins. Suddenly the screen rises, to disclose immediately behind it an open doorway of the same size as the screen. Through the doorway one sees exactly the same view as one had seen on the screen—except that now there is a perfect fortress (the reconstruc-tion) instead of the ruin. The effect is dramatic and breathtaking, not only because of this unexpectedness but also because of the syn-ergies involved: the almost instantaneous transformation of a screen into a doorway, representation into reality, and ruin into reconstruction.

Here is another synergic experience I had in a museum, this time in Australia. In an exhibition room on the life of the Abelam people of Papua New Guinea, in the Australian Museum in Sydney, there is a viewing-hole in the wall. On looking through, you see yourself reflected back, but with your head as part of a cut-out of a typical modern Western costume. You have become part of the exhibition, and an anthropological specimen as alien and bizarre as the Abelam tribesman. Here the set of synergies include the bringing together of self and other, civilized and primitive, usual and unusual, normal and alien. A similar synergic effect was achieved at London Zoo when they opened an enclosure exhibiting the human animal as a new primate exhibit. Eight men and women volunteers sunned themselves on a rock ledge, barely clothed, and spent their time waving at visitors and exercising. A signboard informed visitors about the species' diet, habitat, and other characteristics.[5]

It would appear that all such experiences of synergy raise arousal, at least momentarily. Perhaps, because cognitive synergies do not seem to make logical sense, there is an effect of surprise and puzzle-ment. And the fact that opposites are being brought together may make the experience of both of the characteristics concerned more striking than they otherwise would have been by themselves. In this, the effect may be essentially the same as that of seeing com-plementary colors (such as red and green) next to each other: both colors seem more vivid than when on their own. But in any case there is a fascination about synergies which makes one's whole experience seem more alive while contemplating them.

The word "synergy" is used because it means "working together"—in this case the working together of opposite qualities within experience to produce effects of an intensity and type which neither could have done alone. This is, in fact, the way the word is used in other areas of science. For example, in pharmacology it refers to the way in which some drugs, when administered together, give more powerful, and/or different, effects from those they would have given if administered separately. In developmental biology it refers to the way in which two tissues growing next to each other interact so as to change each other's course of development in ways necessary to the normal healthy formation of the organs concerned.

Now, in the arousal-avoidance state of mind, cognitive synergies tend to be disliked because of these very same arousing properties. In fact, words like "ambiguity," "incongruity," "inconsistency," "contradiction," and other negatively valued expressions are used in this state to describe synergies. In the arousal-*seeking* state, by contrast, they are actively sought, or created. Part of the child's enjoyment of pretence is that which comes from seeing things in two ways at the same time—the haystack as a house, the cardboard box as a car.

Representational works of art, just like toys and other "pretend" objects, also make use of this, albeit in more sophisticated, interesting, and surprising ways. After all, a landscape painting is simultaneously experienced both as a flat, stationary, limited area of canvas with paint on it, and as a three-dimensional, moving, unlimited scene; and this is part of its fascination. The more that one is aware of both these aspects at the same time (the flatness and the depth, the movement and the stillness, the artificiality and the reality), the more synergic the effect of the painting will be in experience. In a related way, metaphor in poetry involves bringing together opposites—a ship being talked about as if it were a swan, a woman as if she were a flower, and so on.

Humor is also based on synergy, although this synergy is of a special kind. Every joke, comic situation, and figure of fun involves at least one synergy—and often many; and we enjoy the sudden surge of arousal that comes with our laughter. The rugby player flouncing around in exaggerated feminine attire at a fancy-dress party, Laurel and Hardy being knocked about like balls in a pinball machine, the entertainer impersonating a well-known politician, are all making use of synergies. Even the humble pun involves a word having two incompatible meanings.[6]

Cognitive synergy is a huge and complicated topic, the detailed discussion of which would take us far from our main theme here. But it has to be recognized as a frequently occurring aspect of experience, and one that we tend to make great use of in everyday life when we want increased arousal.

LOOKING FOR CHALLENGES

We can now turn to the second main category indicated at the beginning of this chapter, that of generating arousal through acting on the world in various specifiable ways, rather than simply by responding to it.

The *first* active strategy (of four to be discussed here) is that of *exploration*. The point is that the activity of exploration itself, quite apart from what one might discover, is itself a source of excitement. Whether or not one is actually confronted at any stage with novel or surprising information or experiences, the very anticipation that one might be, the fact that what one is doing has not been done before, exposure to the unknown, the asking of new questions, and trying out new techniques—all these things can be highly arousing. The explorer entering some uncharted area of Amazonian jungle, the artist attempting a new graphic technique, the physicist setting up a new experiment: all such "adventurers" are not only exposing themselves to unknown risks, physical and/or intellectual, or to new kinds of experience, but also, by the very fact of doing so, are becoming passionately engaged in the process of exploration.

The importance of the search for intellectual excitement, for new understanding and insight, for seeing old things in new ways, for discovering new patterns, cannot be underestimated in the lives of many—especially artists and scientists. As E. O. Wilson, the founder of a new branch of science called *sociobiology*, has put it: "Newly discovered truths, and not truth in some abstract sense alone, are the ultimate goal and yardstick of the scientific culture. Scientists do not discover in order to know, they know in order to discover.... Scientists therefore spend their productive lives struggling to reach the edge of knowledge in order to make discoveries."[7]

We can also, perhaps, under this general heading of exploration, include a very different kind of exploration—one not primarily intellectual at all. This is the mutual exploration involved in a developing intimate relationship. After all, the other person is a kind of unknown territory. In exploring this physical and psychological landscape, one does not know what surprises—what ambushes and quick sands—may be in store. And in the process one exposes oneself too—one's fragilities, sensitivities, hopes, and illusions—and becomes particularly vulnerable. But what more exciting voyage of discovery could there possibly be?

The *second* type of active strategy that brings its own excitement with it is *confronting frustration* of different kinds, since frustration can have the effect of making one become more "alive" and engaged in order to overcome the barrier which frustration represents. This is a very general strategy, since it enters into so many human activities. In the arousal-*avoidance* state, of course, such frustration causes irritation and worry, but in the arousal-*seeking* state it is exactly this same feature of frustration that is turned to positive effect.

Not that just any frustration will do to increase arousal: frustration that seems to be impossible to overcome is more likely to lead to despair and depression. But delays, puzzles, and challenges in some activity may well—*if* the individual sees them as essentially surmountable—lead that person to raise his or her arousal level in order to succeed. Imagine a rock-climber coming up against an overhang, a scientist discovering something intriguingly anomalous in the data, an artist finding a technical difficulty that must be resolved to achieve the desired effect. It could be said that the whole of sport is based on frustration, since in competition each player systematically attempts to frustrate his or her opponent. And pleasurable frustration enters life in all kinds of ways: the pleasure of the frustrating delay in taking the wrapping paper off a present, or waiting for the curtain to go up on a show; the way frustration is played on in striptease or manipulated in sexual foreplay. In all such cases one sees the frustration as essentially temporary, the reward looming on the horizon. One will of course shortly win the game, climb the overhang, solve the puzzle, see the play, satisfy the curiosity, obtain the gratification. In this way, confronting oneself with the right kind of frustration can be seen as a second type of excitement-seeking strategy, and one which is bound up intrinsically with activities of many different kinds.

The opposite of frustration—the moment of success on reaching a goal *despite* frustration—can also produce a surge of exultant arousal. But the elation of achieving a goal is so bound up with *every* purposeful activity that one can hardly count it as an arousal-seeking strategy as such. However, there is one kind of "success" behavior special enough to be worth counting as an arousal-seeking strategy in its own right—our *third* active strategy. This is the one that involves *overcoming* (or at least seeming to overcome) one or another of our *basic physical limitations*. Indeed, it is interesting to see just how many arousal-seeking activities there are of this kind. Think, for example, of how many types of fun involve toying with, and overcoming, one's overwhelming tendency of falling to the ground if unsupported. From children's activities like playing on swings, seesaws, and trampolines, to such highly equipment-oriented adult activities as flying planes, ballooning, gliding, hang-gliding, parachuting, free-falling, mountaineering, bungee-jumping, rappeling and all the different kinds of extreme sports, we see how this limitation is turned constructively into an exciting form of release. Many hobbies and small pleasures likewise involve empathizing with objects which, to some extent at least, *do* escape from gravity: kites, model airplanes, rockets, and spinning tops.[8]

In a similar way also, many activities involve going at greater speeds than the human body could naturally achieve without assistance. Rollerskating, skateboarding, go-karting, biking, hot-rodding, motorcycling, skiing, water-skiing, and power boating all attest to the pleasure of rapid movement. In all these cases of overcoming gravity or inertia, the exhilaration comes not only from the intensity of the sensation, and the risks involved, but also from the feeling that one is doing something which is, as it were, physically impossible.

Not only do we enjoy overcoming such inherent biological limitations of movement in vertical and horizontal space, but also our unaided limitations of contact with people and things which are far away from us. Put another way: we like to take on the challenge of distance. Modest examples include target sports like archery, shooting, and golf, in which we make contact with distant objects (like the hole, or "cup," in golf). More technologically sophisticated examples involve the hobbies of star-gazing, and the use of short-wave radio. And if we can overcome space, why not time? The more fantastic, but for some people exciting, phenomena of horoscopy, astrology, palmistry, precognition, and fortune-telling derive some of their fascination from their seeming ability to overcome the limitations of linear time.

The *fourth* (and final) active strategy is one that can be referred to succinctly as *negativism*.[9] By this is meant a desire to do the opposite of that which is required or expected in a given situation. (Perhaps here one is overcoming another kind of limitation, that of social rules.) Satisfying such a desire can lead to a thrill of malicious glee. Remember how much more exciting it was even to *think* of smoking or drinking in school, given that such practices were not allowed, than to smoke or drink elsewhere? And who has not enjoyed, at least momentarily, saying something provocative or risqué at a party, walking on forbidden grass, trespassing in a private field, going through the traffic lights on red, parking where it is forbidden, arguing just for argument's sake, pretending not to hear an order, wearing the wrong clothes, smuggling something through customs, swearing in public, complaining in a restaurant, or generally raising hell? Of course, there may be many reasons for such enjoyment—not the least of which is the sheer joy itself that being cussed, difficult, rebellious, or awkward can cause. But an important part of the pleasure of troublemaking surely comes from the surge of arousal that goes with the defiant act.

Negativism may be no more than a mild strategy designed to gain excitement: the child deliberately talking in class or being rude at the dinner table, or the adult keeping an argument going longer than is strictly necessary. But it may also involve more serious breaches of convention or law, like smoking pot, or breaking the speed limit in a residential zone, or streaking at some public event. And in turn it may enter into extremely serious infringements of the rights of others—or even of the criminal law, such as the violence of vandalism and the aggression of mugging.

Whether trivial or serious, negativistic behavior would appear to be widespread. Here is a simple everyday example from my own experience: during a visit to the zoo in Stanley Park, Vancouver, I noticed with some puzzlement that the bottom of the alligator pool was littered with coins. Then I saw a sign asking visitors *not* to throw coins into the pool because the metal discs might choke or otherwise distress the animals—and with this my puzzlement was much reduced. The sign has in effect acted to focus people's negativism onto a particular negativistic act. Indeed, during the several minutes that I stood by the pool, three more people tossed coins in.

Continuing my visit, I was not at all surprised, therefore, on seeing a notice requesting visitors *not* to feed peanuts to the otters, to observe that the surface of the pool was littered with peanut shells. Presumably any of the other animals in the zoo could have been fed peanuts, but people chose to feed them to the very ones which were specifically excluded.

Not that negativism is necessarily harmful: much that is creative and original in human behavior seems to have its origin in this arousal-seeking strategy. Much of the joy of philosophy involves denying generally accepted common sense ideas—for example, the concept that it is obvious that there is a real world outside us, and that we know something about it. At least some of the excitement of scientific research comes from such acts as overthrowing accepted theories in a given area, or rejecting previous approaches to a problem. And avant-garde painting throughout the previous century has shown how art moves creatively forward by attempting to destroy the validity of what came before. (We shall return to this theme in the final chapter.)

At its best, negativism represents people's refusal to be less than they could be, their obstinate commitment to freedom and self-determination, their unwillingness to be mere ciphers. "Few sensations can compare with the ecstasy of resistance. Anyone who has faced a wall of policemen at midnight or stood vigil at a barricade or toppled buses when rumors spread that the tanks are rolling has known the rare elation of righteous rage," wrote one political commentator following the toppling of the Russian reactionary coup in August, 1991.[10]

You may have noticed that there is a certain similarity about all these "active" strategies and techniques that have as their primary (or incidental) purpose that of obtaining high arousal. What they have in common is that all of them are ways that involve the individual in gratuitous problems, difficulties, and challenges. The person behaving in this way is leaving the tried and tested paths and exposing himself or herself to unknown danger (exploration); is confronting himself or herself with temporary extra difficulties and barriers on the way to goals (frustration); is playing at doing things which have previously seemed difficult or impossible (overcoming human limitations); or is looking for trouble (negativism).

There is a sense then in which all of these are different aspects of the same underlying strategy—a strategy of defiance of nature and others, of not leaving well enough alone. Dividing up this strategy in the way that has been done here is therefore artificial in some respects. However, by listing these different versions separately we have been reminded again of just how varied and complex arousal-seeking behavior can be, and how many aspects of life it enters into. This is especially the case if we add the "passive" sources of arousal discussed earlier in this chapter to the "active" ones discussed here.

Those who want a quiet life will of course avoid *all* of these active strategies. They will refuse to take unnecessary risks or otherwise go outside the normal way of doing things. They will not look for gratuitous difficulties and problems. They will be happy to accept and work within their physical limitations. And they will be willing to conform to the rules of the situations they find themselves in, and to the expectations of others.

THE USES AND ABUSES OF AROUSAL

Recognition that people in the arousal-seeking state may search for challenges because of the increased arousal that attempting to overcome them can produce, goes a long way toward explaining many kinds of human behavior and attitudes which would otherwise seem paradoxical. Why, for example, do some businessmen go on and on, risking everything they already have in ever new enterprises, when what they already possess is more than they could spend in a lifetime of high living? Aristotle Onassis put it like this: "Money becomes unimportant. What matters is success. The sensible thing would be for me to stop, but I can't. I have to keep aiming higher and higher—just for the thrill."[11]

Why do youngsters from well-off, secure backgrounds sometimes get involved in revolutionary political movements? The novelist Doris Lessing has suggested this:

> A great deal of political action, I now think, has little to do with aims, but more with means—in short, people get sharp, excited, satisfying sensations from it all, and that is the real motivation. There are hundreds of thousands of people, mostly young people, who judge political events by the emotions they feel about them which of course makes them easy prey for any demagogue.[12]

A Polish acquaintance said to me, when the country was still communist, that she preferred to live with the shortages and restrictions of this regime. She went on to explain that she enjoyed the challenges and difficulties, because there was a special pleasure in finding ways of beating the system. In the West, she said, life would surely lose much of its spice without this daily challenge.

The seeming paradoxes here are very similar to those discussed in chapter 3 on danger, and especially the paradox of putting oneself unnecessarily at risk. And the explanation is essentially the same. It can now be seen that deliberate risk-taking and exposure to danger—balancing on the dangerous edge—is another "active" strategy that can be listed along with the four other strategies outlined in the present chapter. And, like the other four, it also involves the search for, and attempt to overcome, challenges. What in the arousal-avoidance state may seem like an unwanted duty, a form of stress, a worrying task, can become in the arousal-seeking state a glorious challenge, an invitation to adventure.

Before finishing this discussion of the different kinds of strategy available for increasing arousal I should, for the sake of completeness, add one further strategy. This is a strategy which does not easily fit into the category of either "active" *or* "passive"—and which is in fact not really a psychological strategy at all but rather a physiological one. This is drug-taking. Most of us have probably taken prescription drugs at one time or another, simply to tranquilize or sedate us for a while. But a minority of people use drugs (less legitimately) for *raising* arousal. The self-administration of stimulants of different kinds, such as "poppers," "speed," and "crack" can of course be an extremely effective device—at least in the short term. But even this sense of arousal needs to be experienced within a protective frame to be enjoyed. As one writer has put it: "Drugs become the medium for mastering anxiety. To let go and be high is to play at dissolution and yet, through self-administration, maintain control .... A drug patient commented, 'I have my hand on the switch. It is safe to have feelings.'"[13] On the other hand, without this feeling of safety, a drug-induced high can become frightening rather than exciting. As one marijuana user put it in describing why he initially gave up after his first attempt: "It wasn't a moral thing; it was because I'd gotten so frightened, bein' so high. An' I didn't want to go through that again."[14] And as another put it about his first experience of marijuana: "I walked around the room trying to get off, you know; it just scared me at first, you know I wasn't used to that kind of feeling."[15]

In concentrating on arousal-seeking we should not lose sight of the fact that, as we have just seen in relation to drugs, all those activities and features of the environment that help to generate *pleasant* high arousal in the arousal-*seeking* state will, by the same token, produce equally *unpleasant* high arousal in the arousal-*avoidance* state. So in the latter state one will generally avoid intense stimulation, cognitive synergy, exploration, frustration, and the like, all of which may cause at least irritation, and possibly acute anxiety. For example: if one is at a job interview, one is likely to prefer a setting with subdued colors and soft voices to a garish and noisy office; easy, unambiguous, and expected questions to difficult, ambiguous, and novel ones; and so on. And one will certainly avoid being provocative, wearing loud clothes, challenging the questioner, answering questions in novel and risky ways, making jokes with sexual overtones, indulging in caustic asides, or deliberately raising topics likely to cause problems for oneself. By contrast, one might do *all* these things at a dinner party with friends, when one is in an arousal-*seeking* state of mind.

Let me emphasize again that seeking high or low arousal is only one aspect of human motivation, and that there may be other, more important or salient, needs at any given time. Indeed, these may even override the need for a given level of arousal. So the mountaineer may be willing to tolerate long periods of boredom, especially during the early period of a climb, because the increasing feelings of mastery that he or she is experiencing may be more important at that time than excitement (even though he or she is in the arousal-seeking state). Conversely, a businessman negotiating an agreement, although in the arousal-avoidance state and experiencing anxiety, may be willing to tolerate this feeling for a time in order to clinch the deal. Arousal-seeking or arousal-avoidance may indeed enter into everything we do. But we should remember that they do not necessarily represent psychological priorities or always override other considerations.

In this chapter we have looked at the different ways in which people may increase their levels of arousal, and have seen an astonishing variety of sources and methods of stimulation that can be used. We have also found that some of these are subtly bound up in a whole variety of activities that may simultaneously have other purposes and potential rewards, so that the arousal-seeking involved may not be evident until it is exposed. There are, then, many aspects of our physical and social environments that can be productive of pleasantly enhanced arousal in the arousal-seeking state. We should not, of course, mistake all pleasure and happiness and joy for excitement. But clearly excitement plays an important role in people's lives, contributing to that strange feeling that most of us seem to experience from time to time—that, after all, life really is worth living.

8

Fueling the Flames

COMBINING AROUSAL SOURCES

The Japanese have a strange custom of eating a blowfish called *fugu* that dwells in the waters off their coasts. The custom is strange for the simple reason that the *fugu* is poisonous. It should be said straight away that most of the poison is supposed to be extracted from the poison gland before cooking. But the aim is to leave just enough in to make your lips tingle after you have eaten it. Unfortunately, it is not possible to be sure exactly how much poison has been left until it has been eaten. If too much remains, there is nothing you can do about it except pay the bill (quickly): there is no known antidote.

Not that many people die from eating *fugu*, but it does happen from time to time—and the knowledge of it is enough to add an element of risk to the other stimulating pleasures of a good meal. This bizarre culinary practice can act as a symbol for the present chapter, since we shall now look at the way in which different sources of arousal can be *added* to each other. The effect of this is to produce even more intensely enjoyable experiences in the arousal-seeking state than would have been possible if one source of arousal alone had been used. (Up until now in this book, for clarity of exposition, I have tended to discuss things as if people used only one kind of stimulation at a time.)

A number of researchers have provided evidence for this kind of additive effect. A typical experimental design here involves participants being exposed to one source of arousal and then to a second, totally different, source. Participants are tested physiologically, or through questionnaires, or in some other way, to see if the arousal or intensity of the emotion experienced after the *second* stimulation is greater than it would have been after the *first* stimulation alone. Thus subjects might first be shown a film clip to induce one arousing emotion (let us say distress, following a short documentary showing the results of a car accident), and then a clip to induce another emotion (for example sexual excitement, following a short piece of pornography). The question is whether the second emotion is more intense than it would have been if the first emotion had not been aroused. That is, is there greater sexual excitement than there otherwise would have been?

Actually, many of the experimental designs are much more complicated than this one, and there are many variations on this design, but the basic idea remains essentially the same. The results of such research show that, generally speaking, there are indeed strong carry over effects. Arousal from the first emotion does indeed carry over to the second emotion, making it more intense than it otherwise would have been. In the experiment cited, the sexual excitement was found to be stronger than it would have been without the earlier stimulation. In other words, arousal is indeed additive. The general phenomenon has aptly been referred to by one notable researcher in this field, Dolf Zillmann, as "excitation transfer."[1]

An ingenious demonstration of this effect is the "Capilano Suspension Bridge experiment." The suspension bridge in question stands near Vancouver, in British Columbia, spanning a deep canyon with rapids. Not only is the bridge high and narrow, but it is the kind that is slung together from slats of wood—and, as a result, it tilts and wobbles as one passes over it. As a consequence, we may suppose that it produces some degree of fear in most people (and terror in someone like the present writer). In the experiment an attractive female participant approached unaccompanied males on the bridge and, in the guise of doing research on people's reactions to the beauties of British Columbia, asked them to say what they saw in an ambiguous drawing she showed them. (This is an example of what is called a *projective test*—a stimulus so vague or indefinite that, in responding, subjects tend to project their own feelings and desires into it.) The subjects' responses to this test were compared with those of unaccompanied male subjects interviewed by an attractive female on a bridge nearby, but one that was low and solidly built, and spanned a quiet tributary to the main river. It was found that the subjects interviewed on the high suspension bridge showed a great deal more sexual imagery in their responses than those interviewed on the lower bridge.

The conclusion was that the arousal produced by the bridge had become transferred into sexual excitement by the presence of the pretty interviewer, and that this excitement was much higher than it was in the low-bridge subjects because the latter had no arousal to "add in" from the bridge experience. (When, as a check, the experiment was repeated with a male interviewer interviewing the male subjects on the high bridge, very little sexual imagery was found.) Interestingly, the female interviewers gave their telephone number to subjects, suggesting that they call if they wanted to talk further. Far more of the men interviewed on the high bridge than on the low bridge followed through.[2]

The implication of all this for the analysis in this book is that if the protective frame is in place, then everything which increases arousal will be felt as good (provided it does not destroy the frame). Even if only one source of arousal is at the focus of experience (for example, if the arousal comes from competing in a sport, or it is sexual arousal), other kinds of stimulation can be added to enhance the overall experience and make one feel even *more* worked up and alive. This bonfire can burn many different types of fuel, and these can even be added to each other in any combination—surprise to danger, danger to sexual stimulation, sexual stimulation to negativistic defiance, and so on. So we should not be surprised when we look around to find that when people are in the arousal-seeking state, they are liable to make use of whatever arousing agents are available, and to draw them into whatever constitutes their main activity at that moment. This is true whether the setting is the boardroom or the bedroom.

This notion that arousal has a unitary character also implies that no one particular "flavor" of arousal (such as risky, sexual, or competitive) is more central or primary than any other. This is in contradiction to the views of Freud, who saw sexual arousal as the most fundamental kind to which all others could, in some sense, be reduced. Although many exciting events can be described in sexual terms (for example, the bullfight has been described as representing the phases of sexual intercourse[3]), this does not mean that the arousal in such cases *is* sexual. Arousal from our perspective is rather like brightness—which can be experienced in many different colors but cannot be reduced to any one color. From this point of view any theory, such as Freud's, which attempts as it were to collapse the color spectrum into a single hue, will necessarily be inadequate in attempting to understand the full range and diversity of human experience.

We should also remember that arousal-seeking is not the only motivational factor at work in determining behavior, even when arousal *is* being pursued. The individual will typically have other needs to satisfy at the same time that may even be *more* important. So if (for example) a person is thirsty when in the arousal-seeking state of mind, he or she may well go to a bar and, while satisfying the need for something to drink, do so in surroundings that are also likely to be stimulating. In other words, when thirsty he or she chooses the particular sources of arousal available at the bar. These might include the animated conversation, the chance of meeting new people, and the music. The point is that there would be a preference for the bar rather than any one of the many other sources of arousal that are (at least in principle) available elsewhere (such as the movies, the swimming pool, or the shopping mall). This is because in the bar both needs—the biological need to drink and the psychological need for stimulation—can be satisfied together.

Generally speaking, there are many different things one can do in almost any setting, simultaneously or successively, to "turn up the brightness" and increase feelings of arousal. And there are myriad aspects of the environment, interacting together, which may be stimulating or soothing to some degree or another. Of course, people themselves differ vastly in relation to which aspects of the environment they are most sensitive to and which are their preferred strategies (e.g. exposure to danger, negativism, search for cognitive synergies) when they are in the arousal-seeking state. We should not lose sight of such differences between people when discussing those aspects of arousal-seeking that are universal. Indeed, in the next two chapters in particular this individual aspect will come more to the fore, because we shall be looking at people who take things to abnormal extremes in different ways, and who therefore display their individuality in a more striking manner than other people do. In this respect, human perversity is an exaggeration of human diversity.

SOME EXAMPLES OF MULTIPLE AROUSAL

The different sources of arousal and of strategies available are therefore not a simple slot-machine-like system in which, having paid your money, you are allowed one—and only one—strategy or source of arousal. Strategies tend to evolve and become inextricably intertwined with each other. As a result, a vast and complex array of different combinations becomes possible.

Think of the variety of different sources of arousal that are available at the swimming pool, and the way that people are able to combine them simultaneously, or in quick succession. First of all, there are sources of stimulation deriving from the sensations of the water itself—its coolness, and the feeling of its flow over the skin. Then, at least if the pool is outdoors, there may also be intense heat from the sun, the feelings of hot and cold being strongly contrasted as one moves in and out of the water. The diving board may add some feeling of danger, too, especially if it is high. Then, as you dive, there is the multiple experience in quick succession of being free in the clear rushing air and then enveloped in a suddenly murky and soundless underworld of water—until you burst through the surface again to a welcome explosion of noise and color.

All these swift contrasts can make for an intense, even overwhelming, experience. Also, the water *itself* may for some people have a dangerous "feel" about it which adds to its arousing qualities. Furthermore, mastering this alien environment may produce the thrill that comes with overcoming seemingly normal human limitations—in this case being in an unnatural environment, free of the normal effects of gravity. As if all this were not enough, one can observe people adding to it the spice of frustration by racing each other, the excitement of negativism by pushing each other in and shouting and splashing, and the stimulation of cognitive synergy by pretending to be fish or monsters or frogmen. (You will remember from chapter 7 that a synergy, in the sense used here, occurs when something is perceived as possessing opposite qualities either at the same time or in quick succession.) Quite apart from all this there is (for men) the sexual stimulation of seeing women in bathing suits, and (for women) the excitement of possibly meeting an interesting man. And for many of both sexes, I might dare to suggest, there is perhaps the pleasure of showing off their bodies.

Here is another, deliberately dissimilar, example of a situation in which different arousal-inducing agents may be brought together to enhance overall levels of arousal: the college football game in the U.S. The central source of arousal, which is enjoyed through the detachment frame, is of course that provided by the game itself. As in all games, the arousal comes from the competition: the way each side systematically attempts to frustrate the other. But excitement also comes from the fact that the outcome is unknown until at or towards the end, leaving room for the unexpected to occur. Surprises may also enter through novel plays, or the sudden twists and turns of the game itself—for example, when there is an interception. In turn, the spectator can empathically share, in parapathic form, the emotions of the players: the hope and despair, triumph and humiliation, as the game takes its course.

To its great glory, however, college football is more than just a game. It is an occasion—an event shared and celebrated by the players, students, faculty, and alumni who take part in it—and usually a very colorful one. It is therefore not surprising that, as an institution, it has evolved a whole set of activities whose purpose is, at least in part, to add new sources of arousal to those provided by the game alone. In this way excitement may be achieved before the game even starts, brought to an even higher pitch during the game, and maintained for a period after the game is over. At the sensory level the bright colors worn by the teams add gaiety to the proceedings, and these colors are reflected in the dress of the spectators, in their scarves, caps, T-shirts, and the like. In consequence, the stimulation of the colors of the two teams starts from the moment of arrival in the vicinity of the stadium, and lasts until one is well away from the area afterwards.

The tradition of tailgating adds in the stimulation of taste and smell to those who are cooking and eating the food they have brought, and of aroma to those who are passing by. In the stadium the stirring music of the marching band, and the announcements on the public address system, add their own form of excitement. Even sexual stimulation is brought into the equation, with scantily-clad cheerleaders being brought on to dance and gesture provocatively. Nor are cognitive synergies overlooked. The teams typically represent something other than themselves—tigers, Trojans, hurricanes, and so on. And then the synergy is usually developed, often in a humorous way, in the team mascot.

To take one further example of this "multiple-arouser" theme, consider all the different sources of arousal that can contribute to the enjoyment of a hobby like antique collecting. First of all there is the excitement of the chase if one is searching for a particular item, and the fascination of exploration if one has no preset idea of what one is looking for. There is a special thrill in entering an antique shop which all collectors will recognize: a moment of anticipation, almost an expectation of discovering something unexpected and unexpectedly good. (It must also be added that, these days, this expectation is much diminished—but it is still a force). Then there is the momentary surge of arousal as one recognizes something desired, the uncertainty involved in deciding whether or not it is genuine and undamaged, the tension of waiting to hear the price, and possibly the gambler's thrill of taking a chance by putting money down on it. Alternatively, if one is sure of what one is buying and the price is low, there is the thief's thrill of getting something for nothing. (I have heard one collector describe a purchase of this kind as "legalized burglary".)

If one is purchasing at auction, of course, the excitement of the contest in the presence of an audience is added to that of the risk-taking, and also to that of the outcome (which is unknown until the last moment). But there can also be an element of contest in the purchase of a piece of furniture or an *objet d'art* in an antique shop, and the collector may make use of a number of ploys here. Thus he or she may spot the object wanted but, disguising growing excitement, look at everything else in the shop, returning only occasionally to this desirable piece. In this way he or she avoids signaling any special interest to the dealer, and thereby risking paying more for it than otherwise.

Eventually, in asking prices, the collector will slip in a passing query about this object, perhaps denigrating it slightly in some way. If despite this the price is still too high, the game may then change, and open bargaining be entered into—another arousing form of contest. Of course the excitement generated by such a duel may also change to anxiety at various points, but on the whole the seasoned collector will expect to experience more pleasant anticipation than unpleasant apprehension. After all, the worst that can happen is that he or she will be unable to afford the desired object, or pay more for it than can be realistically afforded. Other things being equal, of course, the more expensive and desirable the item, the more we may expect the collector to experience arousal—pleasant *or* unpleasant.

Not only can the search for, and acquisition of, an antique present various sources of pleasant arousal, but the owning of an antique may be exciting, too. There may be the elation of successfully completing a set of some kind, and of showing the collection to other collectors (and empathically enjoying their envy as a form of parapathic emotion), as well as of being stimulated by the sensuous esthetic properties that the object may display.

An antique may also create arousal through the contemplation of the synergies that enter into it. The *main* synergy perhaps arises from the realization that although an antique is a real object it is also glamorously unreal, in that it comes from a different world: it *exists* in the present, but it is *of* the past. It belongs to you and is therefore part of your own mundane, everyday world, and yet at the same time it belonged to other people in other settings at some other, more romantic-seeming, period of history. There is also an exactly opposite synergy, a kind of mirror image of the first, which can arise. This is that it may well be an object which was commonplace and unremarkable in its time (a jug, a candlestick, a wine label) but which, because of its present-day rarity, is now valuable and sought-after. These kinds of paradoxes of past and present, commonness and rarity, worthlessness and value, are what lend antiques some of their special fascination.[4]

HEIGHTENING SEXUAL AROUSAL

To make more manageable the enormous topic of the way in which different sources of arousal can be combined to increase excitement, let us focus on one area: human sexuality. Sexual behavior itself involves only one way of achieving high arousal. But let us explore some of the ways in which it can be combined with other sources of arousal in order to achieve even more intense, and intensely pleasurable, arousal than is possible from sexual stimulation alone.

An obvious example of such heightening would be the way in which some people use such stimulants as amphetamines or cannabis, not to mention other, more prevalent, drugs (like alcohol) in order to enhance sexual experience. Another approach is to make use of novelty by making love in unusual places (over the kitchen sink, in the park at night), with unusual and inventive positions and, in the case of the promiscuous, with new partners. Frustration can be made to play a part by one partner or the other teasingly withdrawing and approaching, holding back and giving. Some people even find that anger, with the arousal it involves, is a stimulating preliminary to making love. As one woman put it, anger makes her orgasms "more intense, more sensual and magnificent."[5] And the prevalence of fantasy during sexual intercourse is becoming increasingly recognized.[6]

Perhaps one of the main strategies used in combination with sexual behavior to increase excitement is that of negativism. By negativism (you will recall from chapter 7) is meant the strategy of defying pressures, rules, or expectations. In relation to sexual behavior, then, it means knowingly and deliberately indulging in acts which are immoral or illegal, or which break one or another of society's taboos or conventions—or any mix of these. Here is an extract from a letter to an advice columnist from a middle-aged law-enforcement officer in Nevada: "I live in a county where prostitution is legal. My problem is that I get no thrill when I'm with a legal prostitute, so I find myself drifting over to the big city across the county line where prostitution is against the law. I realize that this is illegal and probably unsafe, but it seems to be the only way I can get any satisfaction."[7]

There can be little doubt that breaking laws or rules can add a special spice to one's sexual experience, both through the thrill of the defiance itself and through the added charge that comes from the feelings of guilt at the time and afterwards. An obvious example would be the thrill some people seem to derive from making love to someone who is prohibited to them in some way. Examples would be committing adultery, having intercourse with a lover's friend, or (much worse) engaging in sexual activity with a close relative or a person below the legal age of consent. The fact that a sexual act is also a sin can undoubtedly make it wickedly attractive to some people.

An interesting point here is that some taboos are so widely broken that they may almost be regarded as fictional taboos (or what I have in an earlier book called *convenient myths*[8]) whose sole purpose seems to be to provide people with the additional sexual arousal and glee that come from breaking them. A good example would be the "taboo" against oral contact with the genitals (the technical terms for these practices, *fellatio* and *cunnilingus*, even make them *sound* like diseases). Since surveys show that this practice is generally widespread, obviously there exists a sense in which such a taboo is one which—if the reader will forgive my putting it in this way—is paid no more than lip service.

More serious and genuine taboos are involved in various perversions and deviant behaviors such as voyeurism, exhibitionism, and in the most serious cases sodomy, rape, bestiality, masochism, and necrophilia. This is not to claim that all of these are always undertaken in a spirit of negativism. But clearly the knowledge that what one is doing involves the serious breaking of some social or moral rule is likely to raise arousal considerably, and may play an important part in the development of deviant sexual behavior—especially that of an aggressive kind. To paraphrase what one rapist is reported to have said, if rape were legalized he would not rape but have to do something else.[9]

Consider exhibitionism. Clearly, much of the excitement that the exhibitionist derives from the situation comes from shocking, frightening, or even disgusting the victim. And in the mirror image form of this deviation, voyeurism, the point is that the voyeur is seeing what he (and it is almost invariably a man) is not supposed to see. After all, there is not much problem today in seeing the naked female form in socially acceptable ways—in magazines, for example, or in striptease clubs. Indeed, one could argue that it is almost impossible nowadays to *avoid* seeing the naked, or at the very least scantily-clad, female form in magazines and newspapers, via videocassettes and cable TV, in connection with publicity releases, at the beach—even on network television. So the aim of the voyeur is to go beyond such allowable forms of sexual stimulation, and to look at those *who do not wish* to be looked at. (Now, if there is negativism in such relatively mild forms of sexual deviation as exhibitionism and voyeurism, it is that much clearer and more obvious—and indeed is involved almost by definition—in acts of sexual sadism. (But I shall save our look-in-depth at the related topic of rape for a later chapter.)

Turning now from negativism: another major strategy which is used to add arousal to the sexual situation is that of exposing oneself to risks and danger. Examples might be: the danger of discovery through making love in relatively public places; the risk of pregnancy through deliberately refraining from taking the necessary precautions; and the danger of injury from an accident—for example, mutual masturbation while one of the partners is driving. Here we can note in passing that there is a sense in which the advent of HIV makes *all* sexual intimacy more dangerous. If the argument of the present book is correct this should, paradoxically, make intercourse even more pleasurable for some people, and especially intercourse with members of such high-risk groups as prostitutes and drug addicts. Whatever the source of danger, of course, it must *not* be so great as to dominate the sexual situation and induce a reversal to the arousal-avoiding state. But if the arousal-seeking state can be maintained, through the presence of a protective frame (for example of the "It couldn't happen to me" variety), then the danger can boost the excitement being experienced.

An extremely hazardous way of combining sex and danger is the practice known in the vernacular as "scarfing" and in the psychiatric literature as *autoerotic asphyxiation*. It has been called the "most dangerous sex game in the world."[11] What happens here is that the individual (usually a male) hangs himself by the neck during masturbation in order to intensify his sexual excitement. Naturally, the person doing this attempts to control the situation so that he does not actually kill himself but rather can release himself once orgasm has been achieved. Unfortunately, during the excitement it is easy to make a mistake and go too far. This results in loss of consciousness and then inevitably, since control has been lost along with consciousness, death. If this death-defying stunt is pulled off successfully, heightened sensations deriving from giddiness and light-headedness (which go with a reduction in the supply of oxygen) will have been experienced, as well as increased arousal due to the risk-taking. As one surviving patient told his psychiatrist: "My pleasure is closely connected with fear, the fear of strangling, chaining, the fear of actual choking. In a state of fear, life and lust are compressed into a narrow space. The more pressure is exerted by fear, the more vivid the pleasure inside."[12] But if it goes wrong, the result is a bizarre and shameful death. A mother who found her sixteen-year-old son hanging by his belt in their bathroom reported:

It was like a Goya painting. All the lights were on, blazing. The fans were whirring. And there were mirrors set up, so there was an actual glare against the tiles. I remember thinking, there is too much light. He was hanging nude by his belt from a frame bar holding the sliding shower door. There was some semen on the floor below him, and a lighted cosmetic mirror positioned so he could see himself. He had a terrycloth towel around his neck to prevent the belt from cutting.[13]

It is difficult to know just how prevalent this practice is, since it only comes to light when it goes wrong. And even then it is usually judged to be (or given out to be) suicide, in order to avoid unnecessary humiliation for the victims' families. The practice has therefore been called one of the world's best-kept secrets.[14]

Should there be any doubt about the way in which the danger and pain increase sexual arousal, there follows an extract from a note left by a victim in which he describes, on the basis of previous experiences, what he expects to feel. (Unusually, this is a suicide note, and the victim in this case did indeed die as a result of his actions.) Having detailed a fearsomely complex preparatory ritual, including putting on women's clothes and pulling a stocking down over his head, he stands on a chair and puts his neck into a chain connected to a padlock.

The first time he attaches the chain to other parts of his body as well, so that he will not hang by his neck: "It is totally black and my blood pounds fiercely. Carefully I work my feet to the edge of the chair and ever so slowly let my feet slide off. The effect is thrilling. I can't tell where the keys are. I can't find the chair. I can't call for help, and I'm hanging controlled. I can free my hands this time and pull myself up on the chair again."[15] The next time the weight of his body will be taken by his neck, and he will also set fire to himself:

Quivering with excitement, I just stand and swish the lovely skirts about my legs. I know what I'm going to do next. I'm really terrified by a sadistic thrill. It is 9:35 Sunday night and in three minutes I will be dead. I strike a match, reach down and set fire to the gossamer edge of the black nylon slip. Quickly I wrap the chain around my wrists and snap the padlock firmly. In a frenzy of passion, I kick the chair over and my body is spasming at the end of the chain noose. I come wildly, madly.[16]

It is hardly surprising that sex and violence tend to be associated in the public mind. (Indeed, it is interesting that the word "violence" has the same root in French as the word for rape—"le viol.") Certainly sex and violence are frequently used together for titillation. This is true not only in parts of the film industry and in pornography, but also (in a playful "pretend" way) by many normal people, as part of their loving sexual relationships. As always, we see that there is a continuity to the use of one or another arousal-seeking strategy—from a mild, playful form up to its involvement in bizarre, immoral, and unhealthy practices. But we can understand the latter as a development of the former, and in this respect this development exemplifies the way in which "sick" behavior can have its roots in the banal and mundane world of everyday life, and grow seemingly naturally out of it.

In the last part of this chapter we have begun entering the realm of what might be termed "the pathology of excitement-seeking." That is, we have started to look at how the ways in which people seek high arousal can become an intrinsic part of disordered, self-defeating, or dangerous behavior. This general theme will be the focus of the next two chapters.

9

The Fallacious Frame

MISCONCEIVED CONFIDENCE

There is no doubt that arousal-seeking can go badly wrong. After the momentary thrill of exhibitionism, the individual may face the prolonged pain of prosecution. Instead of the "kick" that the voyeur had hoped for from his precarious position on the drainpipe, he may suffer the trauma of a broken leg. After the "ultimate" orgasm derived by masturbating while hanging may come the even more ultimate experience of asphyxiation.

Why do people engage in such short sighted and foolhardy behaviors? Part of the answer, of course, is that some appear to have the need for far higher levels of arousal than others do before they can feel excited and satisfied, and therefore need to take higher risks. But to give a fuller answer we also have to take into account the different ways in which people experience the protective frame. Now, I have emphasized that since this frame is subjective it may correspond more or less well with the reality of the situation at different times. This being so, errors and mismatches are always possible. What seems to happen with people who suffer severe trauma instead of excitement—or instead of some other pleasant high-arousal emotion—is not only that their arousal-seeking takes an extreme form, but also that they misperceive the nature or robustness of the protective frame that they are experiencing. An example would be war photographers who think of their camera as being what they call an "invisible shield" protecting them from bullets and explosions. Without this feeling it might be difficult for them to do their job but, as we know especially from the war in Iraq, photographers and journalists are as vulnerable as everyone else. The invisible shield is like the emperor's new clothes. Combatants also can have this feeling of invisible protection, as shown from the following quotation from a pilot who fought during the Vietnam era:

> Somebody in the present time, in this living instant from the ground below, was trying to kill me ... But wasn't there a bubble of protection around the airplane? ... They wouldn't hit us, would they? Didn't I also have a protective shield of some kind around my body, an outline of invisible light?[1]

In chapter 3 we looked at people who, in undertaking dangerous sports, or other equally risky activities, were fully aware of just how chancy these were. For the most part they were also realistically confident of their ability to avoid going over the by-now-familiar dangerous edge, from the danger zone into trauma. From time to time they may have made mistakes, of course, and miscalculated. But in general they were able to play around the edge, and as a result experience intense excitement (usually interspersed with occasional and unavoidable periods of anxiety). In contrast, what we shall be looking at in the present chapter are people who are unrealistic in their assessment of their ability to handle the dangers they confront themselves with; or who play foolish games which they conceive to be in the safety zone when in fact they are in the danger zone; or who, as seemingly detached spectators, fail to realize that they are getting drawn into the action. We shall not be looking at how people can face up to danger with courage and skill, and turn it into something that makes them feel more alive. Rather, we shall be looking at those who unwisely think that their lives are charmed, and that for this reason no harm can come to them, even when they confront themselves or others with outrageous risks. For example, many American soldiers who survive Afghanistan and Iraq, when they get back to the States, drive dangerously—presumably because they have a sense of invincibility. The result is that there has been a huge increase in the deaths of these servicemen on the roads. "Many were fresh from the battlefield, determined to have fun, live fast and sustain the rush of survival, army experts said."[2]

Turning to a very different and particularly dramatic example, consider those people who have lost their lives flirting with the dangers of Niagara Falls and the river below. The history of these foolhardy folk seems to have started with one Sam Patch, who in 1829 was killed when he leaped from a height of over 100 feet into the river beneath the falls. Others who have died include Charles Stephens, who tied his feet to a 100lb. anvil in the bottom of a barrel, and his arms to straps in the top. The barrel broke—and the only part of his body ever recovered was one arm, still strapped inside what remained of the top of the barrel.

In fact, to date fifteen people are recorded as having been over this literal dangerous edge in containers of one kind or another, and five of them have died. Presumably all were confident that they would succeed. The amazing thing is the strength of the confidence frame that must be required for such an exploit. Perhaps one of the most harebrained was the attempt of William "Red" Hill, who went over the falls in a contraption consisting of nothing more than thirteen inner tubes held together with fishnets and canvas straps— with the expected result. Equally crazy was one of the most recent fatal attempts, this one by Jessie Sharp, who in 1990 went over in nothing but a canoe.[3]

A number of dangerous sports regularly produce fatalities where the protective frame turns out to be illusory. An example is BASE jumping, where people jump with parachutes from high buildings or bridges.[4] For example, to celebrate his country's Independence Day, a Norwegian leaped from the second level of the Eiffel Tower (a height of about 380 feet), watched by his girlfriend and two others who were going to jump after him. His parachute became detached from his body and he crashed into the beams of the first level. He died instantly. In this case the feeling of confidence provided by the parachute turned out to have been misplaced.[5]

If these examples seem a bit far-fetched, consider this example, which most people will feel hits nearer home. Three schoolboys were playing around the base of an electric pylon. They had a catapult made from a wire coat hanger and elastic bands, and were taking turns using it to shoot stones at some tin cans. Eventually they decided to climb up the metal rungs of the pylon, as they had done a few times before—in the course of which they had cut through the protective barbed wire, which they could now just brush aside. But on this occasion one of them, the oldest (age sixteen), decided to go up higher than before, taking with him the sling. When he got to the top he started firing stones at the wires. Finally he put out his hand and touched one of the wires. This was, in fact, a 132,000-volt electric cable.

At the inquest, one of the other boys described how they had pleaded with him not to touch the wire, but how he had gone ahead anyway and taken hold of a wire that was hanging down. They had seen a bright orange flash, and then his body falling to the ground. The coroner seemed unable to make much sense of such voluntary risk-taking. Referring to all three youngsters he said: "It strikes me as being quite the most insane activity to climb such pylons and to put themselves at risk of electrocution when they knew perfectly well the risk they were running. I hope this will dissuade anyone from doing anything like this again."[6] To which one might add: "Some hope!"

The confidence frame, therefore, may in some circumstances be more like a confidence trick. What seems like a bit of fun in which nothing serious can really happen turns into tragedy. Here is an example of a kind that one can read about in the newspapers on almost any day. Two cars filled with teenagers were racing each other along a road at Patuxent, near Washington, D.C. on a sunny January afternoon. They overtook each other multiple times. Eventually, one of them overtook the other, and got back to his own lane, but then lost control, veered back into the wrong lane, and hit an oncoming truck head on. He died in the collision, along with his stepsister and his girlfriend. The truck driver was critically injured.[7]

Here are two other examples involving cars. At the Portuguese Rally, some spectators took to gambling with death by standing in the center of the track, only jumping out of the way of the cars at the last second. As a result, a number of the foolhardy were knocked down when local hero Joachim Santos ran into them. Three were killed. At the Indianapolis Motor Speedway, a man sneaked his pickup truck onto the track and drove several fast laps before he crashed and killed himself. "Witnesses said he appeared to be having a very good time. They saw him laughing and waving his arms."[8]

One thing that all these deliberately varied examples have in common is that in each the victim was, in some sense, performing before an audience. The degree of premeditation varied considerably from drunken spontaneity to long-term planning. But in all instances the victim appeared to lose his life through wanting to show off in front of others—that is, through one or another kind of bravado. It seems that the strength of the confidence frame can be boosted to highly unrealistic levels by the presence of spectators.

There are several different ways in which this might be brought about. First of all, in some cases the admiration directed towards the victim, or which the victim supposes is directed towards him or her, may be misconstrued to be a vindication of that person's own estimates of his or her ability to carry off the "stunt." We probably all have memories of this kind of thing from our own childhood; I certainly remember falling off my bicycle not long after I had learned to ride it, because I was showing off in front of a group of friends. In such instances the confidence frame is based on the perceived judgment of other people. "I didn't pray to God to help me make it," said Robbie Knievel, the son of Evel Knievel, about a motorbike stunt he was about to attempt: "I just asked him to watch."[9]

But there is a second, and more subtle, way in which such an unrealistic frame may arise. This is that the presence of spectators turns the situation into what seems like a game or performance, so that the victim temporarily has the impression that he or she is in the safety zone. The victim may even identify with the spectators, so that the frame becomes a kind of vicarious detachment frame. That is, such risk-takers observe themselves as if from outside, so that they have the impression that the risk is being taken by someone else. As a Jewish woman who had been prosecuted for high treason in a Nazi court put it many years later, it was "romantic and thrilling" and she felt "like an actress before an audience." But "I hardly visualized what lay before me."[10] We shall now turn, in fact, first to a consideration of the ways in which the safety-zone frame, and then the detachment frame, may also turn out to be fallacious.

JUST WHEN YOU THINK YOU ARE SAFE

Not only can the protective frame of the confidence type, then, be seriously misjudged and lead to injury or death: the same is true of the safety-zone frame. What can happen here is that the individual will see himself or herself as encapsulated securely within the safety zone, a kind of psychological womb, when he or she is really in the danger zone and exposed to trauma.

Let us start with a large-scale example. New Orleans sits below sea-level within a very obvious earth and concrete safety-zone frame—the system of levees that protect it from the Mississippi to the south, Lake Pontchartrain to the north, and various canals that impinge on it. This protection is one of the features of this unusual and uniquely colorful city that helps to make people who live there feel detached from the rest of the country and invulnerable to threat. One might argue that this encapsulation is one of the things that has created the "big easy" as a party town in which everything is about the glorious pleasures and excitements of the moment, especially food, drink, jazz, and sex. Many warnings were made over the years about the fragility of the physical protection, but little was done to shore it up. When Hurricane Katrina hit in the summer of 2005, the result was a catastrophic failure that, as is well known, led to large parts of the city being flooded, producing huge tracts of destruction and many deaths. The feeling of safety that the inhabitants experienced turned out to be ill-founded. Indeed it is difficult to think of a better example of the way in which a protective frame, being subjective, may totally fail to match the objective realities of a situation. Another interesting aspect of all this is that many people could not be persuaded to leave their homes and evacuate when the hurricane threatened. Many commentators have been puzzled by this, but it makes sense once one realizes that for most people, their safest safety-zone is their own home. When these inhabitants of New Orleans felt threatened their natural response, however unrealistic, was to stay where they felt safest. (We see the same phenomenon in Nazi Germany when many Jewish families stayed at home rather than emigrate—because this is where they felt protected.)

A generic kind of physical encapsulation is provided by casinos, which are typically constructed so as to cut the individual off from the outside world completely. Once inside a casino, all that exists are the gaming tables—which seem to emerge, spotlighted, out of the darkness. The outside world has disappeared completely since there are no windows, no clocks, and (because of air conditioning), no weather. It could be any time of the day or night, any weather, any season, anywhere. Even more to the point, one does not seem to be playing with real money, because chips are substituted for cash. So one actually gambles with a kind of Monopoly™ money, which further reduces any psychological danger. In these circumstances it is difficult to believe that one is playing with real money, that one's losses are serious, and that there will be real and often long-lasting implications for life afterwards in the world outside. One seems simply to be playing an exciting game with no real repercussions. As one gambler has said: "I never think about money when I'm playin'. If I thought I was bettin' my car and my house on a card, I couldn't do it. To me, it's just chips, just poker chips."[11] As is well known, the result of this is that some people take tremendous risks, with far more money than they can afford, and finish up by severely damaging themselves and their families.

A milder, if more far-reaching, kind of architectural safety zone is furnished by the modern shopping mall, which does its best to create a vacation atmosphere, where the trials and tribulations of the real world can be suspended. As with casinos, there is often an attempt to cut everything off from the outside world. One typical way of doing this is to point all the shops inwards, towards an interior set of spaces, and to make sure that none of the shops has windows facing the outside. Artificial lighting and soft background music also help to mark the space off, and create a special enchanted world which has little to do with reality. In some cases, various facilities are added to increase the appearance and qualities of make-believe and fantasy. In the enormous West Edmonton Mall in Canada, which is an outstanding example of the genre, there is even a swimming pool with artificially created waves, a fairground, a zoo, a lake with submarines, and a host of other attractions.

The point of all this otherworldly atmosphere is to make people feel "on holiday". After all, it is quite normal for people to spend money more freely during vacation trips than they would if they were simply shopping for things they needed. Partly, this may be because people are inclined to be self-indulgent when temporarily free of routine and restraint. But, more to the point, if on such an occasion people do not feel threatened then, much as when in a casino, they are more likely to take risks. In this case they buy a variety of merchandise they might otherwise consider more carefully.

The safety-zone frame, of course, does not have to be physical: as we saw in an earlier chapter (chapter 4), it can also be provided by a system of rules and procedures, as it is in sports. Problems can arise here if these rules are not codified or written down, but are simply conventions and understandings which may be misunderstood by some of those taking part, as well as by outside observers. A classic example is that of soccer hooliganism, especially as it occurs in Britain. According to the research of Peter Marsh and others,[12] soccer hooligans are spectators who for the most part are really playing their own elaborate "team game"—one in which *some* aggression almost invariably occurs, but aggression that is limited and regulated by *unwritten* rules understood by most of those involved. These researchers, on the basis of actual observation of such behavior, and detailed interviews with large numbers of the involved youngsters themselves (basing their research on Oxford United Football Club), have uncovered a complex structure of such "rules."

The "game" itself has as its dual objective: that of making the supporters of the opposition club lose face—and, by the same token, that of therefore feeling "big". It is won by the rival supporters either making clear signals of backing down (e.g. ceasing hostile gestures, looking away) or—even better because more visible—actually running away. Such confrontations may occur at the individual face-to-face level, or between small groups of supporters on each side. They may occur not only on the terraces (the large standing-only spectator areas), but also in the immediate vicinity of the stands and also on the way to and from the match, especially the route between the ground and the nearest railway station.

Confrontation may take place during the course of the match itself, between large bodies of spectators on the terraces. One set of "rules" governs when attacks on rival supporters may be made. At the large-group level, attacks may be initiated when a foul occurs on the playing field, or when there is an incursion of rival fans into one's own territory. At the individual and small-group levels, attacks may only be made on rival supporters (not on other spectators), and only when they are clearly displaying their sympathies, for example, by wearing their team scarves.

The nature of the attacks themselves is also governed by "rules." In particular, the harm caused should be minimal—no more than two or three blows on an opponent in an individual confrontation, and aimed so as to cause relatively little damage. In other words, the aggression itself, on those few occasions when it does actually occur, is largely ritualized and symbolic. And there also are "rules" governing how a fight should be terminated. In particular, gestures of submission should be immediately honored by the attacker, and flight should be not pursued further than is necessary to establish complete dominance and victory.

So it turns out that the events involved in soccer hooliganism involve a game of threat and counterthreat, display and counterdisplay. Occasional and minimal violence is needed to validate the whole proceedings. But, on the whole, it is all more or less like a game of poker—in which one can win without one's hand necessarily being called.

Unfortunately, things do sometimes go wrong, and supporters get themselves badly hurt (as happens to participants in almost all sports from time to time). There are a number of ways in which this can arise. One is that an unintended escalation of violence can occur, when someone gets momentarily carried away and goes too far. A second is that one or more of those taking part cannot understand the rules of the game. Such deviants are well recognized by those taking part as constituting a genuine risk. In fact, among the Oxford United supporters there was a name for them: "nutters." This is the sort who will pull a knife, or break a bottle, to use in their attacks. Most supporters will do their best to isolate and disown such misfits.

Thirdly, there can be accidents—injury caused unintentionally, of which the 39 deaths at the Heysel Stadium in Brussels in 1985, before the start of the European Cup Final, are a particularly tragic example. Certainly these deaths would not have occurred without the aggressive actions of some of the supporters of the Liverpool Football Club (Liverpool was playing the Italian Club Juventus). But it is clear that there was no intention on the part of the Liverpool fans that anyone should be seriously hurt, and certainly not that they should be killed. (The deaths arose as a consequence of the unforeseen collapse of a wall under the weight of Juventus supporters trying, *en masse*, to escape from an attack.) A fourth way in which the situation can become more serious is through confrontation with the police—since the police do not appreciate the nature of "the game," and therefore take the aggression at face value. In this respect it is ironic that the police do not rush on field to arrest rugby players when they tackle each other—but would certainly arrest soccer supporters doing the same thing on the fringes of the real game.

Of striking interest from our point of view is the observation of Marsh and his co-workers that there seem to be *two* kinds of language which the fans use to describe what they are up to. On the one hand there is the language of real aggression and violence, of "booting" people and "smashing them up." This is the language that they will use to each other in the pub afterwards, and which the mass media are so willing to pick up and broadcast, thus producing an ugly image of mayhem and chaos. On the other hand there is the language that emerges during the course of careful interview, in which the accounts bring out more clearly the rule-governed, artificial, and (to at least some extent) theatrical aspect of what is really going on—these accounts emphasizing the order and playfulness of it all. In these terms, the use of the rhetoric of violence (the first language) is part of the game and helps to generate excitement (as admitted in the second language). The researchers go on to argue that: "Football fans construct not a single reality but two distinct realities. On the one hand they view events on the terraces as being bloody and dangerous, and on the other hand they see the same events as orderly and safe."[13] So here we have it again: the need for both safety and danger if excitement is to be experienced; the need for danger to be perceived within the context of a protective safety frame. As Kerr has pointed out,[14] the structure provided by the implicit rules induces the arousal-seeking state and in this state the hooligans do everything they can to achieve excitement. Unfortunately, as we have also seen, the protection afforded by the rules of "the game" may be insufficient and illusory, so that injury and even death can occur.

Let us now turn to a topic that might, at first glance, appear remote from both gambling and soccer hooliganism: the topic of risky sexual practices. With the spread of HIV it has become clear that all sexual behavior is potentially risky from the health perspective. And it is widely agreed that, apart from monogamy or total abstinence, the best method of protection against this and other sexually transmitted diseases is the condom. For this reason, a great deal of publicity has been given to this matter, both in the mass media and elsewhere. And yet, the effect of it all has been less than it should have been. For example, one piece of research followed up a ten-week university course on human sexuality. This course had emphasized the importance of condom use, and it was found that the lectures had in fact had no effect whatever on the actual use of condoms by the students.[15] This kind of reaction (or non-reaction) has been deeply puzzling to sexologists, sociologists, and others. In terms of the analysis given here, however, it does make sense.

It will be remembered that in chapter 4, sexual behavior was cited as a kind of activity that requires the safety-zone frame if it is to be enjoyed. In other words, erotic behavior is a kind of game which needs to be perceived as being cut off from the real world, with all its problems and threats. It has to be experienced as a kind of playful fun. Without this, any sexual arousal would be experienced instead as a form of anxiety. In turn, this would serve to inhibit the successful performance of the behavior, making the male temporarily impotent and the female frigid. This means that, to the degree to which two people are in fact interacting in a sexually functional way, they are by the same token, and necessarily, unaware of the dangers of consequences of their actions. The last thing they will think of at that time is taking precautions. It is perfectly natural, therefore, for condoms not to come to mind at the critical moment.[16]

Unlike what happens with the Pill, the decision to use a condom usually is not made well before the very moment its desirability is realized, but rather when that topic is the least likely to be thought of—by which time it is most often too late. In these terms, it is hardly surprising that condoms are not used more frequently. The best solution might be the invention of a condom that could be put on before any kind of sexual interaction has started. This would have to be tight enough to hold in place over a totally unerect penis, comfortable enough to wear for a period of time, and flexible enough to expand sufficiently during erection.[17] Since this does not seem technically feasible at the present time, the alternative is to attempt to eroticize the condom and make it in itself an attractive part of foreplay. This approach has been developed by some companies manufacturing "fun" condoms in a variety of colors and shapes. How effective this will be remains to be seen.

Some other potentially unhealthy behaviors seem to have a similar dynamic. When the individual is acting within what appears to him or her to be a safety-zone frame, then behaviors which are fun and have no immediate health consequences can be enjoyed, their potentially cumulative and long-term damaging effects disregarded. One thinks here particularly of drinking and smoking. In one series of studies, people who were attempting to quit smoking were investigated concerning the situations in which they had been tempted to smoke again. Giving in to the temptation was found to relate strongly to the state of mind in which the search for excitement is a main feature, the act of smoking seeming to have little long-term significance in that state. "It was only one little cigarette" was a constant refrain, even though it is well known that often only one little cigarette is all that is needed to restart the whole big smoking habit.[18]

DANGEROUS DETACHMENT

The third type of protective frame, the detachment frame, can also mislead the individual into behaving in such a way that severe trauma results. Take the self-substitution situation, for example. It is quite possible for people to feel themselves to be spectators at some event when in fact they are participants, and to empathize with and applaud some person or event that is in fact a very real threat to themselves. History is full of examples of power-seekers who are first applauded as heroes but later feared as tyrants—from Caligula through Robespierre to Hitler.

Here is a dramatic and concrete example of the way in which people can misperceive their relationship to what is happening. In 1954, on the banks of the Rio Grande (the river that forms the frontier between the United States and Mexico), crowds watched and cheered the rising floodwater that would later destroy some of their homes.

> On the eve of a flood of the Rio Grande, as torrents of the swollen river rushed and seethed, people in festive mood crowded the river banks and the bridge to watch the "Bravo" acting up. Instead of engaging in precautionary activity, such as removing their belongings to high ground, people here regarded the danger source as a fine spectacle.[19]

In the event, hundreds were killed and thousands made homeless.[20]

Another such example was the way in which, in the great Chicago fire of the last century, people in the better part of town gathered in an excited mood to watch the progress of the fire from across the river. They little suspected that it would spread to their own district.[21] I certainly cannot sneer at such short-sightedness and naïveté, having, with my wife, settled down expectantly in our deckchairs, with drinks in hand, to watch a passing tornado in Toronto. We had no conception of what would have happened if it had passed closer to us than in fact it did, and only realized the real danger when we read the news reports the next day about the swath it had cut through the nearby town of Barry. Meanwhile, we had enjoyed the spectacle of the clouds scudding across the dark skies, much as in a film made by time-lapse photography. Like the psychologist William James experiencing the great San Francisco earthquake, we "felt no trace of fear; it was pure delight and welcome. 'Go to it,' I almost cried aloud, and go it stronger!"[22]

Similar feelings were experienced by the 24 residents of the Richelieu apartment complex at Pass Christian on the Gulf coastline of the Mississippi when they heard, on 17 August 1969, that a hurricane named Camille was heading in their direction. Most of them decided that it would be a good excuse for a party. In the words of one of them, Mrs. Mary Ann Gerlach: "The first thing that popped into my mind was party time! We all got together and decided we were going to have a hurricane party on the third floor .... I went out and got all kinds of stuff to fix, you know, sandwiches, and hors d'oeuvres and got a bunch of stuff to drink."[23] When the 200-mph hurricane hit, with its more than 30-foot waves, her apartment was torn to pieces. As she was washed out of the window, Mrs. Gerlach looked up and saw that "They were having the hurricane party up at the girl's apartment. I saw the lanterns and all up there. You couldn't see the people in there, but you could see the lights, and as it was washing me away, it was washing those. It went slowly down, and you could see the apartment, and you could see the lights and everything go under the water."[24] Everyone died except Mrs. Gerlach.

In all these cases, the festive mood of those involved tells us not only that there was not the fear that there should have been, but that there was strong excitement. People were aware that something unusual and powerful was taking place. But they felt that they were going to be spectators, not participants, so that they could view things through a detachment frame, and enjoy their arousal. In a similar way, the retrospective type of protective frame can also be an illusion, causing the individual to drop his or her guard before the danger is over—for example, the driver who fails to attend to the road just after avoiding an accident.

Surely the make-believe frame cannot lead to trouble for the person who adopts it. Certainly this is true as long as everything takes place in imagination. But often make-believe is acted out in some form, and then *real* dangers can arise. One way in which this happens occurs when some game so enthralls its participants that they create versions of it back in the real world that originally the game detached them from. This is particularly the case with role-playing games like *Assassin* and *Dungeons and Dragons*.

In *Assassin*, each player has a harmless plastic dart gun and is given an assignment to murder one of the other players. These assignments are secret and given out at the beginning of the game. A kill is achieved by hitting the victim with one of the plastic darts. Having done so, the killer takes over his victim's murder assignment, attempting to build up a string of assassinations—while making sure of not being murdered in turn. The winner is the only player left at the end of the game, which normally takes a few hours to play. The ideal setting for the game is a big house with a large garden.

In some areas, when the game was at its height of popularity, it came to be played by teenagers in such a way that there were *no* boundaries and no time-limits. And then for some players the game became an obsession, taking over the youngsters' lives. Nowhere was safe, not even the home or the classroom. Everywhere the player had to be on guard against possible ambush and assassination, and could not let his or her attention lapse. In Palo Alto, where the game became a cult among the pupils at Palo Alto High School, one player was even "killed" at home in bed. Parents and teachers naturally became seriously concerned at the effect the game was having on the children's lives, distracting them from their schoolwork and other occupations and encouraging an atmosphere of suspicion and aggression in the community.[25] How dangerous all this was to normal, healthy development is a matter of opinion. But the physical danger became real when a player of *Assassin* was shot by campus police at California State University at Long Beach. They mistook the fake gun he was using for a real one.

Dungeons and Dragons is a far more elaborate game than *Assassin*, and one which continues to have cult status especially among teenagers and students in many countries. Like *Assassin*, this game was at its most popular in the eighties, but it is still played by millions of people around the world, even though video games are now more popular than role-play games. It is set in the medieval period and peopled with a variety of such fantasy characters as wizards, swordsmen, elves, monks, clerics, goblins, and demons. Each player assumes one of these characters and rolls dice at the start in order to establish things like the character's level of bravery and intelligence. Different characters also have different types of powers, like swordsmanship or the ability to cast spells, as well as different limitations and kinds of vulnerability. These are all determined in the published rules of the game, which are fearsomely complex. The game is one of both chance, being based on the roll of the dice, and foresight and planning.

Just as with *Assassin*, some groups of teenagers and students came to act out the game in real environments and real time, sometimes with serious consequences. In 1979 a sixteen-year-old boy disappeared from the campus of Michigan State University. The investigator sent to trace him, who later wrote a book about the experience,[26] eventually found him, still alive, through the lead that he had been playing in a real-life version of *Dungeons and Dragons* with other students, in a maze of tunnels that ran for miles under the campus. These tunnels, conduits for heating-pipes, were extremely hot, dark, dirty, and slimy, and often so narrow that they could be traversed only by crawling: a dangerously real version of medieval dungeons.

In 1984 two brothers were murdered in Orangeville, Ontario, by a boy who was obsessed with the game. It was supposed that the killings occurred as a result of the youngster's inability to distinguish fantasy and reality.[27] In 1985 in Oakland, California, a teenager shot and killed his brother with a .32-caliber pistol while playing the game, because the character whose role his brother had taken was supposedly clothed in a protective cloak which made him invisible. Again, make-believe and reality were confused, with disastrous consequences.[28]

It is possible to carry such fictions over into real life in a way which makes them part of one's adult life-style—for example, by becoming a real-life spy in the spirit of playing games. When Hugh Hambleton, a Canadian professor of economics, was interviewed by intelligence officers on arrival in England, he not only admitted his spying activities for the Russians over many years, but also that he did not do so for money, because of political conviction, or out of fear. As *The Times* newspaper put it: "The Canadian academic dabbled in espionage for the fun of it. He rifled top secret NATO files, travelled the world as Moscow's eyes and ears, and ended his career as an important 'conduit' for spies in North America because he enjoyed the glamour and excitement." Describing some of his activities, *The Times* continued:

> Hambleton was now spending part of his life in a world which gives fact to the fictions of John le Carré and Graham Greene. In Vienna he met for discussions about his future with a KGB officer. The password would be 'Do you have any etchings of Paris?' to which Hambleton would reply: 'Not in Paris but in London.' The meeting was set up after a signal chalked in the street of a Vienna suburb.[29]

WHEN THE FRAME IS UNAVAILABLE OR DAMAGED

We have looked here at a variety of kinds of recklessness in which the dangerous games that the individual is playing are seen by him or her to be no more than fictions or fantasies, with little more substance or reality than the game on a video machine in an amusement arcade. There are of course huge individual differences. Some people treat the whole of life as like a game or a piece of fiction; others treat only small and particular parts of it in this way. And among the former there are individual preferences for an enormous range of different kinds of stimulation within different kinds of frames. The problems arise, as we have seen, from going to extremes in the search for stimulation, and misinterpreting the real nature of the dangers involved.

There is, however, an opposite kind of problem that afflicts many people. This is the problem of going to extremes to *avoid* stimulation, and seeing danger and threat where it cannot really be said to exist—which is another way of saying having difficulty in adopting a protective frame within experience, and therefore feeling exposed on the dangerous edge. It is striking that in everyday language we talk about feeling "on the edge" and "edgy." In some cases people treat the whole of life as if it were spent unprotected on the dangerous edge. Here the illusion is of danger rather than of safety. An example of this type of sufferer was the moody Norwegian painter Edvard Munch, who wrote in one of his journals, echoing the central metaphor of this book:

> My whole life has been spent walking by the side of a bottomless chasm, jumping from stone to stone. Sometimes I try to leave my narrow path and join the swirling mainstreams of life, but I always find myself drawn inexorably back towards the chasm's edge, and there I shall walk until the day I finally fall into the abyss. For as long as I can remember I have suffered from a deep feeling of anxiety which I have tried to express in my art.[30]

There are technical clinical terms for the different ways in which unrealistic fears can overwhelm the individual. Munch would probably be diagnosed now as suffering from chronic anxiety. Others whose fears and terrors arise only intermittently are classified as acute anxiety cases. And those whose fears relate to particular specifiable objects and situations are called phobics: the agoraphobic person fears going out of the home, the claustrophobic person fears confined spaces, and so on.

According to the terms I have adopted in this book we can say that in all clinical cases of anxiety, of whatever type, the individual has problems seeing the world from within a protective framework. The frame, for some reason, is not available to the victim at times when it would be for other people. So, whereas others would experience excitement (as in going to parties, traveling to new places, meeting strangers, or being spectators at sporting events), this individual, who cannot adopt a protective frame, will experience anxiety instead—even panic. And, whereas others would experience pleasantly intense parapathic emotions, the person with an anxiety problem may well experience the original *unpleasant* form of the emotions concerned. In such cases the individual may even be led into a cramped and anguished life-style, and come to lead a psychologically impoverished existence, in order to avoid the possibility of stimulation from almost any source.

The typical way in which anxiety, in any of its forms, is dealt with by psychiatrists and clinical psychologists is through techniques designed to reduce arousal levels. The most widespread method is the administration of tranquilizing drugs, but other techniques have been developed, including biofeedback (a kind of self-conditioning), muscular relaxation training, and meditation. From the perspective of this book, however, all of these miss the point. The problem with anxiety is that the individual is in a state in which high arousal is felt as unpleasant instead of pleasant. The solution should therefore be to find ways of reinstating the protective frame, at least at times when the frame is appropriate to the situation at hand, rather than to fiddle around with arousal levels.[31]

There is one other, rather different, kind of anxiety problem that the present analysis bears on. This is the kind that arises when someone has been subject to a severe trauma, like seeing a friend or relative die, being raped, being taken hostage, or nearly dying in an accident. Often there is a delayed reaction for many months, and then a variety of symptoms start to occur: nightmares, outbursts of anger, unwanted intrusion of memories of the traumatic event, and so on. This is known as post-traumatic stress disorder. At the heart of this seems to be a feeling of crushing vulnerability.

In contrast to most of us who seem to be protected by a "benefi-cent veil of denial,"[32] the victim of this disorder sees only too clearly how, in the last analysis, nothing can protect us. It is as if one of the necessary components of *any* kind of protective frame has become so damaged that, at least until it mends, the individual experiences a sense of nakedness in the face of the world's threats. As a result, he or she overreacts to any kind of provocation, sign of danger, or reminder of the original trauma.

Furthermore, unlike chronic anxiety or phobia, there is a sense in which the condition is realistic rather than unrealistic. The individ-ual has temporarily shed a certain irrational belief that we all seem to need if we are to live normal, happy lives and experience things regu-larly from within an undamaged protective frame. This is not the belief that death and suffering probably do not exist for us but that if they do, they exist so far in the future that we do not need to take them into account for the present.[33] The person suffering from post-traumatic stress disorder, in contrast, knows the truth, and knows it not as an abstraction but in its concrete immediacy. And the truth is that illness, pain, suffering, and even death can be visited on us at any time, and that ultimately we are powerless to do anything about it.

In this chapter we have looked at a number of different kinds of illusion that derive from misperceiving the protective frame. In rela-tion to the confidence frame we have seen the illusion that danger is guarded against, when in fact the actual protection is inadequate. In relation to the safety-zone frame we have seen that the illusion that there is *no* danger of danger leads the individual into situations where the danger is very real. And in relation to the detachment frame we have seen the illusion that the danger is fictional, or exists only in imagination or memory, when in fact real danger is still there, or is just coming into being. In all these ways the protective frame may be as helpful as a tiger's cage with the door open. We have also seen that there is an opposite kind of illusion—namely, that there is danger when, in reality, the particular danger is nonexistent or minimal. Finally, we have noticed that the protective frame itself must always contain an illusory component: the illusion that our own invulnerability is in some way guaranteed forever.

10

Crime and its Pleasures

ANTISOCIAL ANTIDOTES TO BOREDOM

As we have now seen, the protective frame can be illusory in the sense that it provides less protection than it appears to—or even no protection at all. This helps to explain why the quest for excitement sometimes ends in tragedy. The kind of tragedy we have looked at so far is that in which the instigator is the one to suffer. But there is another variety: the kind in which the victim may be someone else. And this is the sort that we shall look at now.

In these cases the person seeking excitement may well be successful in achieving a kick or a thrill, and in this sense the behavior involved is fully appropriate to its end. But the excitement is achieved either by putting *other* people at risk or by actually causing them deliberate harm. To call up the "dangerous edge" metaphor once again, it is as if some people gain excitement by placing others on the very edge of the cliff and watching them teeter around, or even by pushing them over and observing their fall. The frame may be illusory in these cases too, so that the person causing the harm may do so in a way that, while no doubt reckless, is actually accidental. At the same time it may also be deliberate and cynical, as we shall see. Of course the outcome is not always tragedy; it may simply be inconvenience or irritation. But the principle remains the same, whether the result is minor disruption or serious harm.

Typically, people using this excitement-seeking strategy will be simultaneously putting themselves at risk as well as others. Threatening or hurting someone is quite liable to provoke a violent response. And of course breaking the law may very well result in being arrested. Indeed, sometimes in the examples that follow, it will be difficult to tell whether the thrill comes primarily from the trauma caused to others, or from the risk of being caught. But in all the cases to be considered in this chapter, the desired high arousal comes through some kind of antisocial act in which other people either suffer or are put at risk. Here are two blatant examples of what I am talking about.

> Police Officers carried out an extensive search for a bomb ... after a 'bored' youth made a hoax emergency 999 call, it was alleged at the City Magistrates Court. [The youth], aged 17, rang a telephone operator saying there was a bomb in the market, after being left alone in his workplace to answer the phone. ... Asked why he did it, [he] is alleged to have replied: 'I don't know. I had nothing to do, I supposed I was bored.'[1]

> [A] signalman ... decided to liven up his work when he found it boring—he crashed trains. He laid concrete blocks across the line and watched as the trains smashed into them at up to 40 mph. From his box he had a 'grandstand view'. ... The 18-year-old railman was finally caught after seven trains, including one on which his father was a guard, had been forced to stop outside his lonely signal box. ... He told railway police: 'I don't know why I did these things. I suppose that sitting in the box I got bored.'[2]

This second example is a member of a category that is, unfortunately, widespread: vandalism. It is reasonable to suppose that at least part of the reason for the graffiti on buildings, the wrecking of telephone booths, the removal of locks from the doors of public toilets, and the rest of such nuisances, is a desperate need by some people to overcome monotony and boredom. Some of the excitement generated may come from the small risk involved in being caught, but more of it is likely to be due to the negativism, the defiance, the knowledge of the irritation that will be caused to others. To the vandal the whole world becomes, at least temporarily, a kind of high-adventure playground, a safety zone which prevails everywhere and in which the most outrageous behavior has no more long-term significance than a foul in football. One has only to observe (as I have) the egging-on and the laughter that can accompany the damage being caused to a telephone booth, to appreciate the mood of fun in which such an activity is undertaken. So although the exasperation caused to others may be central to the behavior, it is not necessarily seen by the vandal as being particularly serious.

Often there is no intrinsic difference between the way these (for the most part) youngsters experience what they are doing, and the way that student pranks are experienced by their perpetrators. But in the former instance the behavior is seen by outside observers as a vicious attack on society, and in the latter as a sign of high spirits or youthful exuberance. In the students' case the playfulness and excitement-seeking are recognized; in that of the vandals it is only the stupidity and the damage. Society can put up with student pranks because they are usually for a limited time, sometimes are in a (more or less) good cause, and often are witty, involving amusing practical jokes. Students also typically know where to draw the line and what constitutes going too far. Unfortunately, the young uneducated vandal has none of these advantages. This is neither to condone vandalism in any form, nor to deny that some acts of vandalism are performed more out of anger, resentment, or spite than in a spirit of—or at least a desperate search for—fun. Rather, it is an attempt to say something about the psychology of the young destroyer of property, who, like the soccer hooligan, may often see his or her involvement as simply playing a special game. What to others may seem like senseless destruction may to this individual appear to be no more senseless than participating in the sanctioned violence of a sports contest, such as tackling an opponent in football.

This negativistic excitement-seeking can sometimes also be seen in riots. (It is interesting that the word *riot* comes from the French *rioter*, meaning "to have a good time"—a sense which is maintained in the English phrase "riotous living".) For example, the inner-city riots that sweep Britain from time to time have been variously attributed to poverty, unemployment, racial tension, and insensitive policing. No doubt these factors have all played a part in bringing them about, but less widely recognized has been an aspect which throws a different light on the phenomenon: "The mobs of youths who surged through the shattered windows of ... stores, stripping shelves like locusts, were fired by a sense of excitement and bravado. There was much laughter and merriment. The tragic blunder which sparked this inner city violence had become an irrelevance."[3] Here we see the riot as a kind of carnival, a celebration of the joys of defiance, which in many rioters is not so much a political act as a godsent release from impotent boredom. They have been called, with reason, "leisure riots."[4] Likewise, in the riots that took place in the suburbs of Paris in the summer of 2005, although they were no doubt initially an expression of resentment at such problems as levels of unemployment and poor living conditions, many of the rioters, in the words of the Mayor of one of the areas affected, "just came along for the fun."[5]

Typically, those who take part in vandalism and rioting are youngsters, many of whom will finish up being classified for these or other reasons as juvenile delinquents. It is consistent with the argument being presented here that juvenile delinquency has been described by researchers as involving, among other things, a high need for excitement.[6] Two social scientists, on the basis of interviews with male delinquents, report that:

> What middle class adults call delinquency, the boys themselves see as fun. ... Many of the means that enable other children to have fun— holidays, large suburban gardens and playrooms—are often not available to those who end up in the delinquency statistics; and other forms of fun, such as youth clubs, are frequently not seen by them as viable options. For them, the excitement and variety of the street is the most accessible avenue for having fun; this means playing with public property and with private property belonging to strangers, and it means playing with or at the cost of members of the public"[7]

Particularly interesting, in light of the present argument, is the mutual incomprehension between these boys and the staff of the detention center in which they found themselves following conviction. "Whereas for those like the police and the social workers 'trouble' is the fun that the kid was up to, for the kid 'trouble' is getting caught and sent away. Whereas for the social worker his intervention in the case is the start of a solution to the young person's problem, for the kid this intervention *is* the problem."[8] In other words, the delinquent sees no reason for counseling or therapy—everything was just fine as it was. The social worker, on the other hand, as a serious-minded adult, may try to impose his or her arousal-avoidance strategies on the youngster, and produce bafflement and resentment in the process. The implication is that counseling these youngsters should be about helping them to find ways of achieving excitement which are not antisocial, rather than about trying to stop them from searching for excitement at all—a search which all healthy young people may, as one might imagine, be expected to experience frequently.

THE THRILL OF CRIME

We now come to the topic of adult crime. I should say at the outset that it is certainly not my intention to argue that all criminal actions are forms of excitement-seeking. Clearly, many different needs (including the need for money, status, power, and revenge) enter into different crimes. It would be naive, to say the least, to attempt to explain all crime in terms of one of these needs alone. What I do want to argue is that the need for high levels of excitement is a need that does on occasion, perhaps even frequently, play the major part in the commission of crime. I also want to say that excitement-seeking through risk-taking and causing trauma in others may enter into crime even when it is not itself the major factor. In other words, any attempt to understand the full range of crime will be unsuccessful if no reference is made to the phenomenon of excitement-seeking. Of course, it will not be possible to look at all types of crime here. Instead, let us at least take three representative kinds—shoplifting, rape, and murder—in each of which excitement-seeking may be discerned in many offenders.

Let us start with the relatively minor offence of shoplifting. A great deal of media attention has been paid to this with the conviction of film star Winona Ryder of having stolen goods worth over five thousand dollars from a Beverly Hill department store.[9] She was observed by a surveillance camera stuffing various luxury items into a bag, sometimes cutting the security tags off the handbags, hair accessories, and other merchandise that she took. The fact that she is well-off (reputedly earning five million dollars a film), and had no desperate need of the stolen items, underlines the fact that her shoplifting was not about material necessity. Rather it must have been undertaken to satisfy some psychological need. The same can be said of the various other celebrities who have, over the years, been convicted of this offence. These include tennis star Jennifer Capriati, film star Hedy Lamarr, television presenter Stuart Hall, and 1950s UK television celebrity Lady Isabel Barnett. Judging by what other people convicted of this crime have said, it seems that the primary need is often for excitement. Thus one woman caught shoplifting, later writing to the newspapers about her experience, said: "I had a nice home, money was not short, I had a loving husband and two fine children. Yet I risked their happiness for small items of clothing and food. I can only say that it became as much of an obsession to me as drink and smoking become to other people. The thrill of getting away with it was the drug, not the actual things I stole."[10] Likewise, shoplifters in France quoted in the newspaper *Le Monde* gave a number of reasons for their exploits. But the theme of playing an exciting game was an important one:

> For some, stealing satisfies their taste for playing games and for risk. They find in it ... the sharp pleasure of feeling themselves to be on a tightrope, at the mercy of an unfortunate gesture or a mistaken impression. The danger run allows them to escape from an over-conformist life which, after the age of thirty, grips them in a vice of monotony.[11]

A French civil servant in an important post, reported that he had been stealing from shops for eight years to prove to himself that he was not just a middle-aged, "respectable" bourgeois: "I do it in full knowledge of what I am doing, just as one might practise a dangerous sport knowing full well that one might kill oneself or be left crippled. All the same, it adds a little salt to my life. Like the feeling of passing another car dangerously."[12]

As the author of a book on shoplifting has put it:

> Shoplifting for many may well offer excitement, and be an exciting game, rather than an offence, as viewed from the offender's viewpoint. ... Predatory shoplifting is a gamble, and it may also be thrilling for those who engage in it. It may also be that, caught up in the excitement of trying to evade detection and capture, perpetrators forget the seriousness of what they are actually doing, and temporarily at least do not realize it. The 'game' of shoplifting from the offender's point of view consists in controlling the delirious excitement that he realizes he will feel as he removes the tantalizing object and escapes with it, and if he does outwit the shopkeeper and avoid capture, recollecting that excitement in tranquility.[13]

There could hardly be a clearer statement of the delight and ease with which people can perform risky and antisocial actions when they view the world through a protective frame. As one writer has put it, shoplifters can be seen to be "running along the edge of shame for its exciting reverberations."[14]

Let us look next at a much more serious crime, one in which the trauma caused to others is considerably greater than that of shoplifting: namely the crime of rape. (And let us limit the discussion to males as the rapists and females as the victims, and exclude acquaintance rape.) Now, obviously there must normally be some component of sexual excitement involved here, otherwise the full act of rape would not be physically possible. So in this trivial sense the crime, of necessity, involves excitement-seeking. But rape typically involves more than just sexual behavior. Often there are attempts to humiliate the victim—for example, by defecating or urinating on her. There also may be some violence, even over and above what is necessary to secure intercourse. Robbery may also be involved. And sometimes the victim is not someone whom one would expect to be treated as a sexual object. For example, she may be elderly. So the question arises as to whether these other aspects of rape are also to enhance excitement—in other words, whether *all* the different kinds of behavior that enter into the typical act of rape have to do with excitement-seeking, or whether only the actual act of sexual intercourse does. Rape can in fact clearly involve an attempt to satisfy a number of different needs; including that for power, for revenge against women (for real or imagined wrongs), for expressions of resentment against society, and as a confirmation of masculinity. For example, here is one rapist describing his feelings:

> I obtained the same basic emotional pleasure from rapes, robbery and voyeurism that healthy people derive from various acceptable contacts with others and sharing of feelings or competing with one another. A rape was like a daring businessman pulling off a successful business coup. This was some of the feeling before and during the act. High excitement, boldness, masculine images at stake, putting it over on someone. At times during criminal acts, such as rape and all the rest, I even felt I belonged with other people.[15]

Here we see a number of needs being expressed, including the need for mastery, for masculinity, and for contact with others, over and above the need for excitement.

However, all these different needs could be satisfied in a variety of ways, and the overall impression one gets from studying the subject is that rape is a generalized search for excitement, of which the sexual act is the central component. Other needs may be satisfied as well, the particulars differing from one rapist to another. But one of the main things that rapists appear to have in common is their need for exceptionally high excitement. As the ex-wife of a notorious British rapist said: "We always had a perfectly healthy sex life—but he always seemed to need that little bit of extra excitement, like a racing driver."[16] In this case one may suppose that rape was his way of obtaining it.

A prison psychiatrist who has interviewed many rapists over the years has built up a kind of composite portrait of the typical rape sequence which, while not representing any particular rapist or act of rape, gives a general pattern to which most rapes (in his opinion) more or less conform.[17] Each stage represents a different source of excitement, and will be utilized to different degrees by different offenders—depending on their tastes, abilities, and opportunities.[18]

(i) The initial thought or impulse, and with it a "buzz" of excited anticipation.

(ii) Preparation: assembling the "gear," which may include special clothes, perhaps even a mask, and possibly a weapon of some kind.

(iii) Initial activity such as finding somewhere to hide and wait in ambush, or peering in bedroom windows.

(iv) Hiding, or climbing into position.

(v) Fantasizing about the victim and the act: what will she be like; how will she resist; will she scream?

(vi) The sudden arrival of a potential victim, and the decision to attack.

(vii) The attack itself, accompanied by threats and the terror of the victim.

(viii) The stimulation of the continuing distress and anguish caused, and the struggle needed to exert control.

(ix) The sexual act itself, and the thrill of using sex as a form of aggression (a kind of cognitive synergy between love and hate, cherishing and destroying, valuing and despising).

(x) Continuing to hurt, wound, or humiliate. Possibility of robbery or removing "souvenirs."

(xi) The danger of discovery. Has anyone heard or noticed anything? Is there anyone in the vicinity?

(xii) Making good the escape, with the thrills of the chase.

(xiii) Later: the general consternation caused in the community, the media reports, and the feeling of being the successful cause of all the interest.

(xiv) Taunting the police, giving false clues, and laying false trails.

The sources of excitement in the complete act may therefore include fantasizing, breaking taboos, dressing up and play acting, doing things which are surprising and shocking, empathizing with someone in a state of high emotion, sexual stimulation, risk-taking, hunting and chasing, competing, experiencing synergies, and being the center of attention. If rape is more than just sexual intercourse, this is at least in part because it is a general pursuit of excitement which makes use of a large range of different possible ways of generating arousal. Naturally, once the resulting excitement wears off, the only way to produce it again is to restart the whole sequence once more. Hence the series of attacks that sometimes occur.

THE MURDEROUS PSYCHOPATH

Let us turn finally to the most serious crime of all: murder. It is obvious that this crime, too, may occur for a variety of psychological reasons, and may be performed in the arousal-avoidance state of mind so that high arousal will be experienced as intense anxiety rather than as excitement. In fact, this may be the typical way in which arousal is experienced during murder. Nevertheless, at least one type of severely disturbed person would appear to be able to enjoy and gain excitement from killing: the psychopathic murderer.

The pure psychopath can be seen as someone who spends most of life in the arousal-seeking state, needs particularly high levels of arousal in order to enjoy it, and tends to use negativistic tactics to achieve these high levels. In other words, this person seems to carry around his or her own protective frame, seeing the whole of life as one big game—even those aspects that would be taken seriously by most people (for instance, threat to themselves of injury or death). Whatever the source of danger or arousal, the frame is maintained. And, if there is no danger or other form of stimulation within this frame, he or she will set out to find it or create it, especially through violent or risky means.

This is therefore a dangerous person, using other people as disposable objects and tending to leave behind a trail of despair and destruction—feeling no more remorse or compassion for those harmed than a boxer would for a punching bag. We see here the clearest example of the person who enjoys pushing others over the dangerous edge. If the result for those pushed is the ultimate trauma of death, so be it. Furthermore, what happens to the psychopath may be of little more concern to him or her than what happens to others; the important thing is the immediate thrill.

In order to present a clear picture, I shall now describe what might be taken to be the most extreme type of psychopath. There are others who approximate this "ideal" version, or in whom the picture is complicated in various ways. Unfortunately, the extreme type exists as more than a mere abstraction. Take, for example, Jessie Bishop, a criminal of long standing and a heroin addict, who was condemned to death for killing a young honeymooner who tried to stop him from robbing a casino in Las Vegas. "He once said death 'would be an experience, like jumping out of an aeroplane. And maybe it'll be a bigger thrill than a woman. I hope it is.'"[19] Apparently he faced his execution by cyanide poisoning in Nevada's Carson City Prison without showing any signs of fear. His last gesture was to turn his thumb down and smile.

For those not particularly familiar with psychopathy, let us look in a little more detail at a particular case. A classic illustration is provided by Neville Heath, who in 1946, at the age of 29, was found guilty at the Old Bailey in London of murdering two women under particularly horrifying circumstances.[20] In one case the naked body was found in a hotel bedroom, covered with lash marks on the back and chest from a whip with a hard tip, widespread bruising, and bite marks (with both nipples having been nearly bitten off). The vagina was torn along seven inches of its interior walls by some blunt instrument. Death had been by asphyxiation. In the other case the naked body was found in bushes, the throat cut and with extensive mutilation to the breasts and vagina (this time one of the nipples had been bitten right off). There was also severe bruising, broken ribs, and cuts to the hands, with which the young woman had evidently attempted to fend off the knife thrusts. These were obviously not quick, cool killings but intensely hot-blooded, sadistic sexual orgies.

One would expect the person who could do such things to have every appearance of being a brute or monster (whatever these types are supposed to look like). In fact, Heath was a good-looking young man with blue eyes and fair hair, well-dressed and neat, a pipe-smoking and charming ladies' man. He was described to me by someone who knew him in South Africa during the Second World War as having an easy, outgoing personality and an engaging smile that made him generally popular with men as well as women.[21]

However, the more that one knows about Heath's life, the more one realizes that the two murders were not some kind of bizarre aberration, but rather the culmination of a career of deceit, selfishness, improvidence, and excitement-seeking. That he was a true psychopath there can be little doubt. That he was able to get away with as much as he did for as long as he did is testimony to his social skills and his capacity (as with so many psychopaths) for convincing play-acting and being otherwise highly plausible.

Heath's whole life was a catalogue of misdeeds: burglary, fraud, and confidence trickery were all in his repertoire. As a result, he spent a period in a juvenile detention center, was fined on a number of occasions, and was court-martialed and dismissed from no less than three services (the R.A.F. in 1937, the Royal Army Service Corps in 1941, and the South African Air Force in 1945). The streak of cruelty kept showing through, too. As a child he tortured animals, and engaged in a great deal of bullying of younger children. At a later stage he was caught attacking a girl in a fashionable London hotel. Her screams brought help to the bedroom, where she was found bound to the bed, being thrashed by him. For reasons of her own she declined to prosecute. Surprisingly, Heath did get married (to the daughter of a prominent South African family, in 1942), and had a son. Not surprisingly, and despite entreaties, he deserted them.

In the process of moving from place to place and service to service, Heath was continually changing his name in order to make fresh starts. And here we begin to see something of the playfulness and provocativeness of his approach to life—because some of the names he chose seemed to be designed to draw attention to himself, as it were to tempt the Fates. Thus at one time he passed himself off as Group Captain Rupert Brooke, naming himself after the famous poet. At another he assumed the name Major Armstrong, the latter being someone who had been hanged in 1922 for murder.

It was not that Heath was living in a fantasy world. There is no reason to suppose that he believed in the roles that he played. Rather, he chose to treat his life as a kind of game of charades, enjoying dressing up in uniforms and giving himself titles. At different times he called himself, apart from the two names just mentioned, Captain Selway, Lord Dudley, and Lord Nevill. He also often wore unearned decorations on his uniforms (specifically, Britain's coveted D.F.C., and—eventually—O.B.E.,). When out of uniform he frequently wore an Old Harrovian tie, or a perhaps equally prestigious Cambridge University tie. Among yarns he spun at different times were that he had played rugby for the University of Cambridge, that he had fought in the battle of El Alamein, that he had been a fighter pilot on special strafing missions, that he was a friend of various R.A.F. aces, that he was chief test pilot for the Auster Aircraft Company, that he was buying aircraft for the South African government, and that he was in disguise on a special secret service mission.

Within this safety frame (or detachment frame—often it is difficult to tell which, in his case), Heath was able to enjoy the arousal he experienced. This is presumably why he took so many quite unnecessary risks, seeming to challenge fate—or other people—to find him out. Let us look at some examples of this: he robbed a friend's house when he knew the friend was away on vacation, taking cash, jewelry, and other items. Later he commiserated with his friend over the burglary, and in doing so offered him a cigar—one of those that he had stolen from him. On one of the occasions on which he wore a military uniform, and also decorations to which he was not entitled, he did this in the very place where he would be most likely to be found out: his home town of Wimbledon. That is where his parents lived, where he had been brought up, and where he still had many friends. He got away with it, of course.

After the first of his two murders, Heath registered in a hotel, using the most unlikely and attention-getting of his aforementioned pseudonyms, Group Captain Rupert Brooke. Then, after the second murder, which occurred while he was staying at this hotel, he voluntarily offered himself for questioning at the local police station, knowing that a nationwide search was on for him in connection with the first murder. During the course of the interview he complained of feeling cold, and asked if he could get his jacket from the hotel. Instead, a police constable was sent for it. On searching the pockets, the officer found various pieces of incriminating evidence. Heath seemed determined to play a kind of Russian roulette. In the end, after one too many spins of the chamber, he lost.

Like Jesse Bishop (whom I referred to earlier), Neville Heath while in prison faced his execution with equanimity. If life was a game, then this was merely the final whistle. It is said that before he was led to the scaffold for hanging, the prison warden offered him a whiskey. "You might make that a double," he replied.

The case of Neville Heath is a particularly fascinating one because of his complex, flamboyant, and imaginative psychopathic personality. It should not be supposed that all psychopaths are like him. Indeed, in recent years the world seems to have been increasingly confronted with a more brutally efficient and machine-like type of psychopathic murderer—especially the serial killer who, having found a formula for success, repeats it over and over again. One thinks of the Yorkshire Ripper and the Stockwell Strangler in the U.K., and in America the likes of John Gacy (who killed 33 men in Chicago), Ted Bundy (who killed 38 across the U.S.), Jeffrey Dahmer (who killed 15 men in Milwaukee) and most recently Dennis Rader the "BTK" ("Bind, torture, kill" murderer) who was found guilty of 10 murders. Some have used the term "recreational violence" to refer to the activities of such callous murderers. In the reported view of the head of the Criminal Intelligence Bureau at the Department of Justice in California: "There are people who love to kill. ... We like to tack some deep psychological meaning on it, but really they're just killing for fun. Just plain fun."[22]

CRIME AS RECREATION AND ENTERTAINMENT

We have now looked at three different types of crime (shoplifting, rape, and murder), and have seen that excitement-seeking may be involved in each. We could have reached the same conclusion with other types of crime, including commercial fraud, arson, and burglary. But the point is made: excitement-seeking in association with one or another type of protective frame may be critical to the commission of a crime. This does not mean that the search for excitement necessarily enters into every type of crime, or every instance of a given type. Far from it. The argument is rather that excitement-seeking can, and does, enter into the arena of crime, as into so many other areas of human activity, and can play a central role when it does so. In the words of one repeat offender:

> There's no doubt about it, every part of the criminal lifestyle is a tremendous adrenaline buzz. Coming home with twenty thousand pounds in the car. The excitement of reliving what you've done. Also, the fear itself which is part of it. Then having a shower, putting on a smart suit, nice jewellery, going out, talking to other criminals, it never ends. Then next morning it all starts again. Sometimes you don't go, and you try to find other ways of substituting the adrenaline. Gambling comes close, but it isn't the same.[23]

Why some people get their kicks from serious crime, and others do it in other ways, including gambling, is still far from clear. But, as Jack Katz argues in his book *Seductions of Crime*,[24] simple economic and materialistic explanations of the kind that have been popular for many years among sociologists just will not do. Their general idea is that an individual is forced into crime by a lack of legitimate opportunity to make money in any other way. If, however, one looks at what criminals themselves say about crime, as Katz does, one finds that the satisfaction of economic needs does *not* generally play a prominent part. Consistent with the argument in this chapter, he finds that crimes are much more likely to be committed for immediate emotional gratification such as thrills, although other psychological needs—like the need to overcome feelings of humiliation, and the need to give purpose and meaning to life—may also play important parts. Thus, a successful crime can give rise to feelings of almost godlike power, and the reputation of being a tough guy can provide a role that helps to make sense of life. This cannot be reduced to simple monetary terms.

Just how much crime is about excitement-seeking specifically, or involves some degree of it, is a matter for present conjecture and future research. The American psychologist Stanton Samenow, in his book *Inside the Criminal Mind*,[25] is among those who are inclined to see excitement-seeking as one of the most prevalent motives in crime. Basing his conclusions on lengthy studies among antisocial youth at a hospital near Detroit, and adult offenders at a hospital in Washington, D.C., he argues that the criminal should be seen not so much as a passive victim of society (with its broken homes, unemployment, violence on TV, and so on). Rather, that person should be seen more often as someone who deliberately sets out from early childhood to defy society, manipulate other people, and avoid the tedium of everyday work through the excitement of illegal activity. Thus, whether or not he or she is actually classified as a delinquent, the child who later becomes a criminal almost invariably finds school boring, is contemptuous of children who work hard, and stirs up excitement whenever possible, through disruptive behavior.

Outside of school the criminal-in-the-making may start experimenting with drugs and join with others, for kicks, in shoplifting and vandalism. Following school, this kind of youngster is likely to drift—and, if finding employment, to work in a lackadaisical way, perhaps taking drugs while at work in order to make the monotony bearable. He or she rejects parental values and cannot see what satisfaction lies in working loyally for other people and putting in long hours for perhaps low pay. Instead, he or she has a philosophy that stresses having a good time and having it now. In this respect crime is experienced as not only bringing immediate financial reward for little work, but providing the thrills which are craved. "There is excitement in thinking about crime, bragging about crime, executing the crime, making the getaway, and celebrating the triumph.

Even if the offender is caught, there is excitement in dealing with the police, in trying to beat the rap, in receiving notoriety, and, if it gets that far, in the trial proceedings."[26]

It may be the case that crime which involves excitement-seeking is on the increase. Such violence as sport is gratuitous and difficult to understand if one is looking for a rational explanation, but it makes sense if one sees it simply as recreational. Fashions in such "unmotivated" violence come and go, implying a copycat mentality in those who perpetrate them. A current example that has spread around the U.K. is that of "happy slapping." Here groups of teenagers run up to other children, or unsuspecting passers-by, and slap or mug them. They record the event on the cameras of their mobile phones and upload onto the web for later enjoyment. Victims are chosen more or less at random and part of the fun is recording their surprise and distress. Typically little actual harm is experienced, although occasionally matters have become more serious, with real injury being experienced and even rape.[27] Another fashion in the U.K. recently has been for attacking firemen who are carrying out their duty. Attacks include throwing bricks and bottles, breaking the windscreens of fire engines, stealing or urinating on equipment, and directly physically attacking firemen. According to some estimates something like 100 attacks a month take place in England and Wales.[28]

There are also some disturbing signs that violence as sport has been reaching ever younger age levels. For instance, the number of juveniles arrested for murder even in sunny California has been rising steadily. And the "thrill kill"—the apparently motiveless murder by youngsters—is becoming a matter of serious concern. The horrifying nature of this kind of crime is captured in an entry in the diary of a 14-year-old living near San Francisco: "Today Cindy and I ran away and killed an old lady. It was lots of fun."[29] It will be remembered that the gang members involved in the Central Park jogger rape were aged only 14 to 17. When asked why they had done it, one replied: "It was something to do. It was fun."[30] Two fourteen-year-old boys who bludgeoned a drunken man to death bragged about it at school saying "We had a mad day—we murdered someone."[31] The 1993 kidnapping, torture and murder of two-year old James Bulger by two ten-year-old children sent a wave of shock and revulsion around the United Kingdom.

Why do people do such dreadful things as those described in this chapter, and do them for fun? How can someone rape an innocent young girl, or murder a passer-by for kicks? It is easy to throw up one's hands in horror and disassociate oneself entirely from such things. But you should now be aware, having read this far, of the connections between some of your own inner thoughts and every-day activities, and such bizarre extremes of human behavior as rape and murder. Only if you have never felt the least twinge of pleasure in reading about murder, for example, do you have the right to be mystified by the psychopathic murderer's behavior. This is not to say that we are all potential mass murderers; but we can all, by look-ing inwards, find within ourselves at least traces of one of the essen-tial ingredients of many kinds of brutal crime.

There is no mystery in people enjoying violence. For example, many of us enjoy playing highly aggressive sports that involve a real element of violence.[32] And most of us read novels and newspapers, and/or watch films and television, and these are full of violence. In fact, the mass media give us a perfect view of people who are slip-ping on, or have fallen over, the dangerous edge. We can easily be turned from viewers into voyeurs. Switch on the T.V. news and there will be film clips and interviews and still pictures concerning ter-rorist bombings, civil war, murder, accidents, disasters, and people in various other kinds of distress. To one degree or another, virtu-ally all of us are strongly attracted to violence. And some of us seem to love it enough to watch it practically all day.

It cannot reasonably be said that the difference between psy-chopaths and ourselves is that they always enjoy the excitement of violence but the rest of us never do. It is that they actually practise it. This is a pretty big difference, to be sure! But some of the basic psy-chological promptings are the same. As Katz has put it: "The reason we so insistently refuse to look closely at how street criminals destroy others ... is the piercing reflection we catch when we steady our glance at those evil men."[33] Lucky Luciano, the gangster, put the same idea in his own more direct and inimitable way: "Everybody's got larceny in 'em, only most of 'em don't have the guts to do nothin' about it."[34]

Nor can we be utterly sure that, by subjecting ourselves to these kinds of news stories in the mass media, we are not in some indirect way playing a part in pushing others into the trauma of loss, bodily harm, or even death. After all, terrorists need the publicity they get, otherwise there would be little point in their atrocities. They are in the public relations business. And young thugs are encouraged by the presence of cameras. The moral of all this is surely that none of us can afford to be smug about our own personal lack of violence or aggression towards others. If we live in a violent society, this may at least in part be because the observation of violence is something which most of us undeniably enjoy.

11

The Glamor of War

WAR AS A SPECTATOR SPORT

There can be little doubt that people find (and have always found) wars, battles, and other military encounters of all kinds to be matters of the greatest fascination. From Homer onward, many of the greatest works of fiction have been about the heroics and glories of war. And today people still spend large amounts of time watching war movies, reading war novels, watching war reports on television, reading about war in the newspapers. War is, among other things, a great spectator sport—perhaps the greatest of them all. The spirit of this notion is caught in the lines from the libretto of Verdi's opera *La Forza del Destino*:[1]

> *The drums gaily beating, the bright banners flying,*
> *The bugles give greeting as guns make reply,*
> *The enemy retreating, rejoice every eye!*
> *Oh war is exciting, yes, war is exciting.*
> *Hurrah for the thrilling glories of war.*

"War is exciting" is the theme of this chapter, and it is a theme large enough to bring together many of the different aspects of excitement-seeking discussed in previous chapters—and also to allow us to reach some conclusions which many people may find surprising, and even upsetting. To start with, we can notice that this consuming passion for war (or rather for observing war and its effects) is yet another example of the enjoyment of danger by proxy. In more prosaic terms, it involves the enjoyment of arousal within the context of the type of safety frame that I have labeled the detachment frame. The onlooker watches with great relish as others go into battle and expose themselves to danger. A good clear-cut war, with movement and counter-movement, can be even more exciting than a football game.

An outstanding example of this excitement is what occurred at the start of the First World War. It is beautifully captured by Vera Brittain in her diary of the period. On 3 August 1914, she writes, breathlessly: "Today has been far too exciting to enable me to feel at all like sleep—in fact it is one of the most thrilling I have ever lived through, though without doubt there are many more to come. That which has been so long anticipated by some and scoffed at by others has come to pass at last—Armageddon in Europe!"[2]

Then on August 4, the day the war was actually declared, she is quite 'beside herself':

> Late as it is and almost too excited to write as I am, I must make some effort to chronicle the stupendous events of this remarkable day. The situation is absolutely unparalleled in the history of the world. Never before has the war strength of each individual nation been of such great extent, even though all the nations of Europe, the dominant continent, have been armed before. It is estimated that when the war begins *14 millions* of men will be engaged in the conflict. Attack is possibly by earth, water and air, and the destruction attainable by the modern war machines used by the armies is unthinkable and past imagination.[3]

The story of her gradually wakening understanding of the reality of the war, her loss of this innocent detachment frame, and her increasing personal involvement, all of which is so absorbingly displayed in these diaries, stands for the experience of an entire generation.

For our own generation, when wars come along we are not just spectators, but, telespectators. In the main, the excitement of war comes, when it does come, through watching newscasts and programs on television. We cannot, of course, blame television for this. It is a natural human tendency to take the things which are most feared at a given time, and to turn them into entertainment by converting the anxiety into excitement through the use of a protective frame. And the television screen is an excellent means for establishing this experiential frame. But television tends to present war news in its own special way. As a number of commentators have pointed out, the television genre into which war tends to become absorbed, especially in America, is above all, that of the football game. For the Gulf War in 1991, each network had its own logo and signature tune for the war's programs, just as it does for the Super Bowl. The action, such as a Scud being blown out of the sky by a Patriot, was subject to instant reply. During any lull in the proceedings, experts were called on for their comments, and visually attractive diagrams were often used to clarify tactics and explain game plans (real and imagined). The scores—e.g. Scuds launched, Scuds destroyed—were given regularly. And then there were the interviews: "A few days ago there was an interview with a young bomber pilot who had just returned from a mission. He was talking enthusiastically about how great it felt when he dropped his bombs right on the target. For a moment I thought I was listening to a star quarterback describing a long pass completion that won a game."[4] Another commentator put it all this way: "As I sat on the couch, crunching Doritos and cheering—literally cheering—as the Patriot missiles took out a pair of Scuds, I had this eerie sense that something was very wrong. One just shouldn't be munching Doritos watching a real war—that's for the Super Bowl."[5]

This use of war to simulate sport seems to have been less true for the Iraq war. The reason is interesting. This is because, since the fall of Baghdad, the Iraq conflict has not been a war in the conventional and traditional sense. It was not declared by a country, and it cannot be won—there will be no formal surrender. The enemy does not wear a uniform. It is difficult even to tell who is winning or losing, since this cannot be represented in terms of territory lost or gained. Nor are there any particular events that could conceivably be cheered. In other words, describing what is happening in Iraq as a "war" is to use a metaphor. It is *like* a war. This being the case, it becomes more difficult to use the sport metaphor, because it is difficult to have a metaphor of something that is already a metaphor.

In general, though, war is a natural raw material for manufacturing entertainment, and already the first movies about the Iraq experience are hitting our screens. People may no longer quite glorify war in the way they once did in poetry and paintings, and modern warfare may be rather messy. But the modern mass media are adept at using all the means at their disposal to create compelling narratives that capture and hold our attention

PLAYING AT WAR

You will recall that another way of experiencing arousal within the detachment frame is through memory and retrospection: one is detached from an experience by the passage of time, and can then enjoy it in tranquillity. So it is that often those who have suffered the grim realities of combat are able to actually enjoy their memories in later years, and to reminisce about their most dangerous experiences.

As a Spaniard who had been imprisoned in the Civil War reported of a visit much later to where he had been incarcerated:

I was arrested by the Reds and I was put into prison. I was condemned to death. I saw my friends, some of the good people in this town, taken off to be shot. Good—Well! I went last year back to the place where we were imprisoned. I went to the very room, the very corner where I used to be. It wasn't horrible. It was marvelous. 'Here,' I said, 'is where I lay. Here so-and-so died beside me, and from here many were taken out and seen no more.' And I was happy, I was not sad. I wasn't happy because I had escaped, but because I lived it all again. I felt ecstasy.[6]

Another detachment strategy, as we have seen, is that of make-believe and fantasy. We can observe this particularly clearly in many children's games, and most pertinently in the popularity of toy guns, tanks, and the like. But it is not children alone who play war games—and one must suppose that the fascination of the North American male with firearms of all kinds is, in the main, also a kind of playing with military toys. At a regular newsstand in a suburb of Toronto, I spotted the following magazines: *Guns and Ammo, Gung-Ho, Shooting Times, Eagle: for the American Fighting Man, Guns and Action, International Combat Weapons, Firepower, American Survival Guide, New Breed: The Magazine for the Bold Adventurer, Guns Magazine, Gun World, Official Gun Journal and Mercenary Guide, Combat Handguns,* and *Soldiers of Fortune.* All of these are glossy magazines about guns and/or combat. One must assume that there are not enough regular soldiers or mercenaries in a single Toronto suburb to support such a plethora of publications, and that therefore they are aimed at the general public—who are invited to imagine that they are soldiers or mercenaries interested, in a professional way, in the strengths and weaknesses of different weapons.

The hunting aspect is very much played down in these magazines. For example, most photos show people in battle dress of different kinds. And the advertisements emphasize the military aspect. To take just one example, in an advertisement in one of these magazines, a manufacturer claims that the sporting rifle that they make harnesses centuries of military experience, all the way back to the fourteenth century and including the Napoleonic Wars and the American Revolution. "Live the legend" they exhort their readers, in extolling the accuracy, reliability and stopping power of their product.[7]

"Live the legend" rather gives the game away. And it is very much the tone of most of these advertisements. One might easily gain from all this an image of the average male Toronto office worker getting home in the evening, donning his khaki fatigues, blacking his face, selecting a weapon (a rifle, a brace of grenades, a crossbow)—and perhaps also a gas mask—from his den, and popping out to ambush a neighbor, blow up the local McDonald's, or fight a desperate rearguard action against the local fire brigade. What these magazines seem to represent is a kind of pornography of aggression, an invitation to action without the means. Admittedly such pornography is of the soft kind. For the hard kind there is another, nastier and equally numerous, range of publications for the American male—although this time of the pulp rather than glossy variety, dealing with stories of violent crime.

A popular kind of outdoor sports, especially in the U.K. and in North America is "paintball." The most typical version of these commercially organized games is one played on a large tract of demarcated land, preferably wooded, between two teams of a dozen or more players, each team having a flag it has to guard. Teams set out from different positions, trying to capture the other's flag. There is usually a time limit (of say two hours), and the game is won when one or the other flag has been taken. Each player is issued an air-powered gun that shoots a paint pellet, and once a player has been struck and marked by such a pellet he must retire from the game.

In a publicity leaflet produced by a war game company a player describes how the game starts early in the morning with a strategy session with his team. They hear a horn being blown to signify that the exercise has started, and they set off cautiously through the woods. Suddenly he sees one of the "enemy," and freezes against a tree. He can feel his heart thudding in his chest, and his hands sweating. The opponent gets closer and closer.

In discussing this game we have really moved from the detachment frame to the safety-zone frame—since, while the individual playing the game may engage in make-believe and play-acting, the game in fact takes place in the *real* world and involves *actual* behavior. And the reality of the game is brought home particularly clearly by the fact that, although it takes place within a zone which is distant from real fighting, nevertheless accidents can happen and people can be genuinely hurt. The most usual injury occurs when the eye is hit by a pellet; this can be serious enough to result in permanent blindness. Aware of this, operators of the games provide players with goggles. But, as one injured player reported, he had taken his off because they had fogged up.

Again we see how excitement-seeking, even in a zone perceived to be safe, can lead to damage and injury. But this should not detract from the fact that such a game *is* only a game. The fear of a resident of a town near a war game site, that players who are not satisfied with the game "might come into town to pillage and rape,"[8] seems somewhat far-fetched. In fact, there is nothing new about such ritualized fighting, which goes back at least as far as jousting tournaments in Europe, and has a continuous history down to very recent times in that melodramatic, highly stylized (and often fairly safe) form of fighting known as dueling.

Interestingly, such war games seem to occur in primitive cultures as well. A good example is that of Dani tribes in New Guinea, who challenge each other to ritualized battles. To the untutored eye these may seem like real battles, and indeed there often are casualties, and even an occasional death. But the time and place of engagement are decided beforehand by mutual agreement (although if it rains there may be a postponement). The competing tribes, once battle lines are drawn up, take it in turns to advance, fire arrows, and retreat. But the arrows have no feathers on them, which means that they rarely fly true and injure anyone. In due course closer engagement occurs, the main weapon being the spear. A particular episode of such fighting is unlikely to go on for more than twenty minutes, and after a participant has thrown his spear he retreats to the sidelines. Eventually the whole thing subsides into a shouting match between the two sides, before they pack up and return home.

Paintball can be described as a kind of "war game." But the term is more usually used in reference to a kind of tactical board game in which miniature representations of soldiers and equipment are moved around on a map in accordance with a set of rules, rather like in chess. These kinds of games have been used for centuries, not just by military trainers but also by hobbyists. In the last twenty years, such "manual war games" have become increasingly replaced by computer war games that can provide complex and realistic simulations of particular historical battles or real-world events. People can play against each other in this way, or against the computer.

The idea is that one starts from the way that matters stood at a particular moment, e.g. on the morning of the battle, and then plays things out in ways that, in the event, may well not correspond to what actually happened. A company like Kuma Reality Games, which is one of the industry leaders, provides a variety of simulations, especially of recent military events. For example, it provides simulations of the Iran hostage rescue mission, the action in Korea for which John Kerry was awarded a Silver Star, and Operation Anacostia in Afghanistan. Most of its simulations, however, concern the Iraq conflict and include such "episodic games" as "Fallujah Police Station Raid," "Uday and Qusay's Last Stand," and "Battle in Sadr City." Amazingly, the company is able to produce simulations within weeks of the event occurring. This recency effect probably adds to the excitement of playing the games, and in any case demonstrates yet again how the entertainment industry is able to convert painful reality into playful pleasure by making use of the detachment and safety-zone frames. Just how effective these protective frames can be, is evidenced by the fact that even soldiers fighting in Iraq are known to play these Iraq war games.

THE JOY OF REAL COMBAT

If excitement can be obtained from observing, imagining, remembering, and playing at military combat, the excitement that can be obtained from combat itself must be infinitely greater—provided that such combat is viewed from within the context of a safety frame. In this case the safety frame would have to be of the type I have described as a confidence frame. This means that the danger is real but the individual confronted with it has sufficient confidence in himself and others, whether this is well-founded or not, that he does not feel genuinely threatened. It might seem amazing to those who have not experienced fighting that it can be experienced in this way, and that even intense joy can be obtained from it. And yet an examination of soldiers' accounts of their feelings during battle disclose precisely this to be the case. As Sir Francis Bacon put it many centuries ago, "Such a sweet felicity is that noble exercise, that he that hath tasted it thoroughly is distasteful for all other."[9]

A British D-Day soldier recalls:

> I was firing away at this Jerry machine gun and I didn't notice that our lot had pulled back a bit until I had wiped it out. Suddenly it was rather quiet and I was all alone. I was frightened, but at the same time there was this wonderful elation. It's like being in a pub punch-up—you may get a punch in the teeth or a black eye, but no young man can say he doesn't enjoy it.[10]

Another Second World War soldier wrote: "I know you will find this difficult to believe, and, yes, the war was terrible and I saw awful things, but I wouldn't have missed it for anything."[11] A British soldier who defended the Falklands against the Argentine invaders, when asked what he thought about the battle, replied "Exhilarating. Is that the right thing to say?"[12] And an American bomber pilot in the Gulf War described his thoughts during a daytime raid: "Here you are. You've never been to war. And they say you're going to Baghdad, and it's during the day, and everybody can see you. ... It was probably the most exciting day of my life."[13]

A more surprising testimony to the deep pleasure that war can provide comes from an essay written in 1917 on "Nostalgia for the Front" by the great French philosopher Teilhard de Chardin—surprising because of his deeply held religious-mystical convictions. In a letter about this essay he wrote:

> It goes without saying that at the front you no longer look on things in the same way as you do in the rear: if you did, the sights you see and the life you lead would be more than you could bear. This exaltation is accompanied by a certain pain. Nevertheless, it is indeed an exaltation. And that's why one likes the front in spite of everything, and misses it.[14]

Whether such exaltation is usual or unusual, the point is that it does seem to occur in at least *some* soldiers.

As S. L. A. Marshall says in his classic study of the soldier, *Men Against Fire*:

> The modern school of war correspondents seems to regard it as a duty to make the public cry over the hard lot of the soldier. The so-called realists of war fiction such as Erich Maria Remarque view through a glass darkly every last motion of the combat soldier. But what normal man would deny that some of the fullest and fairest days of his life have been spent at the front or that the sky ever seems more blue or the air more bracing than when there is just a hint of danger in the air?[15]

No doubt there are many reasons why experience of battle should on some occasions and for some people be a source of great satisfaction. These reasons include the chance it provides to prove one's ability to face up to risk and danger, the license it provides for the expression of violent aggression, the feeling of comradeship it can engender, and the sense of taking part in great and historic events. But the argument here is that one of the greatest sources of pleasure, at the time and in recollection later, is the feeling of excitement—even euphoria—that it can induce.

One of the by-products of the war in Vietnam has been to bring a new honesty and realism to writing about combat, and a major theme to emerge from such writing has indeed been the excitement of fighting. In the rest of this section I shall in particular be citing three books of reminiscences on the Vietnam War (by Herr, Caputo, and Baker). As you will see, it is interesting how similar these independent sets of writings are in relation to the ways in which this excitement—indeed euphoria—is described.

In perhaps the most highly acclaimed account of the Vietnam experience, *Dispatches* (by the war correspondent Michael Herr), the point is made in different ways time and again. Here he is describing the experience of "incoming," of being under bombardment:

> Amazing, unbelievable, guys who'd played a lot of hard sports said they'd never felt anything like it, the sudden drop and rocket rush of

the hit, the reserves of adrenaline you could make available to your-self, pumping it up and putting it out until you were lost floating in it, not afraid, almost open to clear orgasmic death-by-drowning in it, actually relaxed ...[16]

And again:

It came back the same way every time, dreaded and welcome, balls and bowels turning over together, your senses working like strobes, free-falling all the way down to the essences and then flying out again in a rush to focus, like the first strong twinge of tripping after an infusion of psilocybin, reaching in at the point of calm and springing all the joy and the dread ever known, *ever* known by *every-one* who *ever* lived, unutterable in its speeding brilliance.[17]

This same theme recurs in another notable Vietnam autobiogra-phy, *A Rumor of War*, by Philip Caputo. A Marine lieutenant in the early years of the war, Caputo later returned to Vietnam as a civilian war correspondent. He comments:

The rights or wrongs of the war aside, there was a magnetism about combat. You seemed to live more intensely under fire. Every sense was sharper, the mind worked clearer and faster. Perhaps it was the tension of opposites that made it so, an attraction balanced by revul-sion, hope that warred with dread. You found yourself on a *precari-ous emotional edge*, experiencing a headiness that no drink or drug could match.[18] (The italics are mine.)

He goes on:

The rare instances when the VC chose to fight a set-piece battle pro-vided the only excitement; not ordinary excitement, but the manic ecstasy of contact. Weeks of bottled-up tensions would be released in a few minutes of orgiastic violence, men screaming and shouting obscenities above the explosions of grenades and the rapid, rippling bursts of automatic rifles.[19]

Anyone who fought in Vietnam, if he is honest with himself, will have to admit he enjoyed the compelling attractiveness of combat. It was a peculiar enjoyment because it was mixed with a commensurate pain. Under fire, a man's powers of life heightened in proportion to the proximity of death, so that he felt an elation as extreme as his dread. His senses quickened, he attained an acuity of consciousness at once pleasurable and excruciating. It was something like the elevated state of awareness induced by drugs. And it could be just as addictive, for it made whatever else life offered in the way of delights or torments seem pedestrian.[20]

The third outstanding Vietnam book I shall refer to here is the collection of interviews with veterans carried out by Mark Baker and published under the title *Nam*. Again the theme of the excitement of fighting keeps breaking into the accounts. Here is an example: "When something went right in a fire fight—you call in a fire mission real good, you get your fields of fire right, deploy your men so that you outflank them and you stand up and walk right through them—it's thrilling. There's nothing like it. It's so real. Talk about getting high, this is beyond drugs—ultrareality."[21]

There has not been time yet for a literature to have built up about the way that the Iraq conflict has been experienced by soldiers. But an early and enthralling book in this genre is *One Bullet Away* by Nathaniel Fick. And like his Vietnam predecessors, Fick finds moments of high excitement to talk about:

> I saw in the platoon a glimmer of something I was starting to feel in myself. excitement. The adrenaline rush of combat and the heady thrill of being the law were addicting us. This was becoming a game. I was starting to look forward to missions and firefights in the way I might savor pickup football or playing baseball. There was excitement, teamwork, common purpose, and the chance to demonstrate skill. I didn't have the luxury of much time for reflection, but I was aware enough to be concerned that I was starting to enjoy it.[22]

Fick reports many bad moments too, really bad moments in the danger zone known as the "killing fields." But we seem to be faced here, in his testimony and that of the others I have cited, with a great and incontrovertible secret of masculine psychology. This is that confronting the dangers of war can be one of the surpassing joys of life. This does not mean of course that war is not also that hell which it is more frequently and conventionally depicted as being. But if there are depths there are also heights. If there is misery there is also adventure. It there is terror there is also ecstasy.

THE GREAT ILLUSION

None of this is to imply that countries go to war to satisfy a need for excitement in their citizenry and their soldiery. (Although who is to say that the craving for excitement on the part of kings and princes may not have played a part in the spawning of the Crusades and other campaigns of earlier ages?) But the fact that war can be presented as an enthralling game has been used since at least the beginnings of recorded history to overcome any doubts and fears, any reticence or resistance on the part of those who were actually required to put their lives at risk. As Churchill is reported to have said, "War is a game that is played with a smile."[23]

Not that this game-like aspect is necessarily used in a cynical and manipulative way by a country's leaders, but good politicians and generals seem intuitively to know the power of sporting rhetoric in creating a positive attitude towards war and good morale in the troops. General Norman Schwarzkopf, for instance, described his Desert Storm plan for the Gulf War in terms of the football play called a Hail Mary. In this use of sporting metaphor, military leaders appear to be aided and abetted by the troops themselves, from whose ranks such metaphors are often spontaneously created and developed. The cricket metaphor developed by British fighter pilots during the Battle of Britain is a case in point. The pilots would sit around in deck chairs between battles, as if watching a game of cricket, typically sporting cricket sweaters and keeping a tally of their "scores" on the sides of their aircraft—talking all the while of "sticky wickets" and "hitting the enemy for six."

A classic illustration of the way in which a sporting metaphor can be developed is the use of actual footballs in the First World War, these being kicked towards enemy lines while attacking. The best-known example is that of a certain Captain Nevill—who, as company commander, presented a football to each of his four platoons before an offensive on the Somme, offering a prize to the platoon that first kicked its ball up to the enemy's front line. Unfortunately, Nevill wasn't able to award the prize, he was killed during the subsequent attack.[24]

The point of all this of course is to give the illusion that the war action is taking place entirely in the safety zone, as in a game of cricket or football, thus producing a spurious confidence in the face of real danger. Technically, since the danger *is* real, we would *have* to categorize the psychological protective frame involved as a confidence frame—almost, one is tempted to say, as a "confidence trick" frame.

Certainly this seems to have worked in Vietnam. Here is what one of Baker's interviewees said:

> It was like the fantasy life of a kid. I'd played cops and robbers as a kid, so when I saw what was happening in Nam, I really wanted to cash in on it. Why not? It was like being invited to play with the big kids. They always called us men, Marines or troopers. Never boys. But during my first fire fight in Nam, I was giggling. ...You try to have fun with things. Ambush was fun. It's supposed to be professional, but it's not.[25]

This idea of fighting as a game is returned to frequently in Baker's interviews. One soldier said that when you killed someone you "scored a touchdown in front of the hometown fans."[26] Another reported, on being a door gunner in a helicopter: "I loved it, I loved flying. I liked shooting people as long as I wasn't too close. ... It was okay that they were shooting at me—that's part of the game."[27] The result of all this, at least for *some*, was that Vietnam was like a prolonged holiday camp: "It's hard to believe, but I didn't have a care in the world while I was in Nam. I'd get up in the morning all covered with mud, look up in the sky with the rain splashing in my face and just smile, 'I'm alive.' "[28]

In real fighting, then, we see a tendency to turn what is happening psychologically into a game—which is exactly the opposite of the tendency noted earlier in the chapter to make war games as realistic as possible. But the aim is the same in both cases: to maximize the feelings of *both* safety and danger. In one case the problem to be overcome is that of finding a way of feeling safe; in the other it is to find a way of experiencing danger. To return to an earlier metaphor, in one case the need is to find a cage for the tiger, in the other to find a tiger for the cage.

What seems to have happened in the cases cited of experiencing combat as a game is that the soldier has the illusion of being in the safety zone when he is in fact in the danger zone. An even greater illusion of safety can be provided if the soldier feels he is removed one degree farther from the danger zone by being detached from the situation, seeing himself as a spectator at a play. In this respect, he feels as if he is looking from the outside, seeing himself to be one of the actors. In other words, an even more effective illusion of being outside the danger zone is provided by the idea that a battle is not so much a game as a colorful piece of theater. Then the soldiers are actors with walk-on parts—who will walk off again when it is all over, having achieved their moment of glory. (Notice that "glory" is itself an essentially theatrical concept.) As Eric Hoffer has pointed out: "We speak of the theatre of war and of battle scenes. ... The great general knows how to conjure an audience out of the sands of the desert and the waves of the ocean."[29] In the same vein he writes:

> To our real, naked selves there is not a thing on earth or in heaven worth dying for. It is only when we see ourselves as actors in a staged (and therefore unreal) performance that death loses its frightfulness and finality and becomes an act of make-believe and a theatrical gesture. It is one of the main tasks of a real leader to mask the grim reality and killing by evoking in his followers the illusion that they are participating in a grandiose spectacle, a solemn or light-hearted

dramatic performance. Hitler dressed eighty million Germans in costumes and made them perform in a grandiose, heroic and bloody opera. ... The people of London acted heroically under a hail of bombs because Churchill cast them in the role of heroes.[30]

The theme of costumes is an interesting one in this context, since one of the points of donning a uniform—any kind of uniform—is to act out a role, to play a part; and there is always an element of fancy dress about a soldier's uniforms. This, of course, was even more the case before khaki and camouflage. As one writer has put it:

> If you examine early 19th Century uniforms, you will find that the message they carry is of the exotic, the far-fetched, the outlandish. This was done not so much to frighten the enemy as to attract recruits. But hussar uniform (from Hungary), lancer costume (from Poland), green light infantry uniform (from Germany and Austria), mamaluke swords, the roman helmets of heavy cavalry, the scimitars of light cavalry, bearskins from France worn by foot-guards—transformed the wearer into an enchanting stranger.[31]

Soldiers thus attired not only played a part, but a colorful and exotic one, emphasizing the distinctiveness of their world from that of ordinary everyday life. The other paraphernalia of the nineteenth-century army (and the modern army on the parade ground, at the march-past or in the tattoo)—the flags and emblems, the shining brass and leather, the drums and trumpets—also act to distance the soldier from reality, including the grim reality of pain and death.

As Paul Fussell points out, in a chapter devoted to the theater of war, in his marvelous book *The Great War and Modern Memory*:

> The wearing of 'costumes' not chosen by their wearers augments the sense of the theatrical. So does the availability of a number of generically rigid stage character-types, almost like those of Comedy of Humors: the hapless Private, the vainglorious Corporal, the

sadistic Sergeant, the adolescent, snobbish Lieutenant, the fire-eating Major, the dotty Colonel. If killing and avoiding being killed are the ultimate melodramatic actions then military training is very largely training in melodrama.[32]

Fussell also provides evidence that all this did indeed work for many soldiers, to produce the feeling of being on stage before and during battle. He quotes a major in the First World War who testified to "a queer new feeling these last few days, intensified last night. A sort of feeling of unreality, as if I were acting on a stage."[33] Another British soldier wrote that he: "had precisely the feeling that comes over one when the curtain goes up at amateur theatricals. Here were we, the performers, until so recently, idly sitting in the wings. There was the audience waiting to give us the reception we deserved."[34]

If we return to the Vietnam War we find the same feelings of acting, except that now the whole thing has been updated in imagination from the stage to the cinema, from the West End to Hollywood. Both Herr and Caputo, whose writings have just been referred to, mention the same effect. First, here is Herr:

I keep thinking about all the kids who got wiped out by seventeen years of war movies before coming to Vietnam to get wiped out for good. You don't know what a media freak is until you've seen the way a few of those grunts would run around during a fight when they knew that there was a television crew nearby; they were actually making war movies in their heads, doing little guts-and-glory Leatherneck tap dances under fire, getting their pimples shot off for the networks.[35]

And again:

It was the same familiar violence, only moved over to another medium; some kind of jungle play with giant helicopters and fantastic special effects, actors lying out there in canvas body bags waiting for the scene to end so they could get up again and walk off. But that was some scene (you found out), there was no cutting it.[36]

Caputo makes some similar statements. First this:

> As is frequently the case before an operation, we are filled with a 'happy warrior' spirit and tend to dramatize ourselves. With our helmets cocked to one side and cigarettes hanging out of our mouths, we pose as hard-bitten veterans for the headquarters Marines. We are starring in our very own war movie, and the howitzer battery nearby provides some noisy background music.[37]

Then this:

> I had enjoyed the killing of the Viet Cong who had run out of the tree line. Strangest of all had been that sensation of watching myself in a movie. One part of me was doing something while the other part watched from a distance, shocked by the things it saw, yet powerless to stop them from happening.[38]

IS MILITARY VIOLENCE EROTIC?

The adventure of war provides more than danger as a source of stimulation. In particular, it also offers the thrill of aggression, through the license it provides to maim, wound, torture, and kill. As one of Baker's interviewees says: "I enjoyed the shooting and the killing. I was literally turned on when I saw a gook get shot."[39]

Indeed, we see this playful enjoyment of aggression particularly clearly in the Vietnam War and the needless atrocities to which it gave rise. The concept of recreational violence can be applied to some of these incidents. There are some horrifying examples in Baker's book. Here is one. The soldier being interviewed by Baker described how he and some others had been in a tower guarding an air base, on a desperately hot day. They were all fed up and bored. One of them, spotting a peasant woman bent over working in a field some 500 yards away, bet the others that he could hit her at that distance. He took some pot shots, and eventually they all joined in, relieved to find some distraction. Finally, according to Baker's interviewee, he himself was the one to hit her, and she just keeled over dead.[40]

Another soldier describes how his unit stopped a Vietnamese man and his teenage daughter who are riding down the road on a motor scooter. He is carrying a tin of peas from the mess hall where he works. The peas are taken from him and eaten, and then the G.I.s, vaguely disgruntled, look for something else to do, and decide to rape the daughter "in punishment" for having the peas. So they all line up and rape her in turn. This still does not seem interesting enough, so they tear up the man's ID card, accuse him of being Vietcong, and shoot him. They go on and on shooting him until "the guy just bursts open. He didn't have a face anymore."[41] Then they turn on the girl, who is crying. They shoot her, too, laughing all the while, and then tear her body to pieces, each taking different parts as souvenirs and arguing all the while about who should have which piece.

In this account we see what looks like a close relationship between violence and sexuality. The relationship between eroticism and war has often been remarked. The very language of war—encounter, thrust, penetration, withdrawal—seems to attest to this, as do the traditional promises of rape as well as pillage, and the seemingly universal camp-following of prostitutes. The practice of some primitive tribesmen of wearing symbolic erect penises, and the use of depictions of the erect penis as warning signs among the ancient Egyptians and Greeks seems to point in the same direction.

Is combat therefore an aphrodisiac? Does it cause not just excitement, but specifically sexual excitement? And is warfare therefore a form of sexual perversion? If we turn to the three Vietnam books from which we have quoted, we seem at first to find support for this thesis of violence as sexual. Thus Caputo, talking of the conflict that the soldier feels between danger and the resolve to fight, puts it as follows: "This inner, emotional war produces a tension almost sexual in its intensity."[42] Michael Herr, describing his feelings after firefights, says:

And every time, you were so weary afterwards, so empty of everything but being alive that you couldn't recall any of it, except to know that it was like something else you had felt once before. It remained obscure for a long time, but after enough times the memory took shape and substance and finally revealed itself one afternoon during the breaking off of a firefight. It was the feeling you'd had when you were much, much younger and undressing a girl for the first time.[43]

And one of the soldiers interviewed by Baker says: "A gun is power. To some people carrying a gun constantly was like having a permanent hard on. It was a pure sexual trip every time you got to pull the trigger."[44]

However, we must not jump to conclusions too quickly. If we look at these statements carefully we see that they are metaphorical, not literal: intense arousal in war is *like* the intense arousal of sexuality. The excitement of combat is *like* undressing a girl. Carrying a gun is *like* "having a hard on." In fact danger, violence, and sex would appear to be among the most potent sources of intense emotionality known to man. If the aim of a description of the experience of any one of these is to emphasize its intensity, then this can be done in a way that draws out an analogy with either of the other two. Thus violent behavior can be described in sexual terms, and sexual behavior can be described in a way which emphasizes its violence; danger can be described as having sexual fascination, and sexual attraction can be described in a way which makes it seem dangerous.

What makes the sexual metaphor particularly apt in relation to those moments in war that are intensely enjoyed (either in relation to the expression of violence or because of the danger involved) is that sexual experience is the prototypical experience of pleasant high arousal. It is the form of very high arousal that is perhaps most typically experienced within a protective frame. So when a protective frame suddenly, and perhaps unexpectedly, falls into position during some other highly arousing activity (like fighting a battle), the sexual analogy is a natural one to make in describing the experience. But it is not the only one that can be made, and in the earlier quotations from Herr and Caputo we saw analogies being made to the experience of being high on drugs. This emphasizes that there is nothing intrinsically sexual about warfare; the similarity is simply in the enjoyment of exceptionally high arousal.

If one takes such metaphoric language too literally there is a danger of being seriously misled. If we see in the use of such military language as "thrust" and "penetration" evidence of sexual sublimation in warfare (or if, alternatively, we see in sexual activity an intrinsic expression of a need for violence and power), then we shall finish up with a theory, like Freud's or Adler's, that reduces all intense feelings to one type of need alone.

The view I have expressed here (and in the rest of this book) is of course different from such a reductionistic view, either in relation to warfare or to any other form of human activity. It is that there are many different sources of arousal, and that these can be added to each other to produce higher levels of arousal than would otherwise have been possible. No one source of arousal is more basic or primary than another. The situation is like that of a boat that moves forward under the power of sails or oars (or both) at the same time. We cannot reduce movement due to sails to movement due to oars, or vice-versa, and neither is more basic than the other. Although they both have the same effect in relation to forward movement, this does not mean that oars *are* sails or that sails *are* oars.

In these terms, "Make Love, Not War" makes good sense: these are alternative ways of achieving (among other things) intense experiences. But, in the excitement-seeking state, "Make Love *and* War" would make even more sense—were it not for the annoying physical impossibility of doing the two at the same time.

In summary, then, the theme of this chapter has been that war can be exciting, not only as a spectator sport (war fiction, television news, etc.), or in the form of games with war themes played by children and—increasingly—adults, but also in the form of the "real thing." Military combat is almost universally condemned as an immoral way of conducting affairs, and is typically depicted as unremittingly grim and traumatic. Yet an examination of interviews with soldiers, and the reading of autobiographical wartime writings, disclose a startling fact. This is that a combat situation can be, and on occasion is, a gloriously intense experience—not unlike sexual intercourse and orgasm.

This is not to condone combat, but rather to recognize something important about human (and especially masculine) psychology. Nor is it to suggest that wars are fought for the sake of this kind of pleasure-oriented experience. But the fact that war can be presented as a kind of game, or as a theatrical entertainment, makes it easier to encourage people to go and fight, to remain in the thick of things, and to think about it with nostalgia afterwards.

It may seem odd that in the first part of this chapter I discussed ways in which people who are not soldiers, at least at the time in question, do their best to pretend that they are. And, in the second part of the chapter, I discussed ways in which people who are soldiers do their best to pretend that they are *not*—or rather that they are really only acting at being soldiers, or playing games. To most psychological theories this would seem to be an inexplicable paradox. But in terms of the theory that I have been putting forward here, it all makes perfect sense: in the first case it is the tiger which is missing from the tiger-and-cage combination, and in the second it is the cage.

12

Risk, Rebellion, and Change

Up to now, my focus has been on how we can use the concept of excitement-seeking to understand a wide range of experiences and behaviours—both normal and abnormal. In this final chapter I am going to raise five basic questions about excitement-seeking. I am also going to tentatively suggest some answers. These questions have been left until the end of the book since they are about how we can explain excitement-seeking itself. Where does it comes from? How has it evolved? How does it relate to development—whether biological, cultural, organizational, or individual?

EXPLORATION AND BIOLOGICAL SURVIVAL

A few years ago, an experiment was carried out on monkeys who were placed in a compound with a set of vertical poles for them to climb. One of the poles was constructed in such a way that the top was electrified, so that when monkeys climbed the pole they suffered an electric shock. The interesting thing is that all the groups of monkeys observed showed an *increase* in climbing behavior for that particular pole. When the power was turned off, however, interest declined rapidly, demonstrating that there was nothing special about that particular pole other than its capacity to provide electric shocks. This capacity made it, presumably, a more exciting pole to explore than the others—an interpretation of the finding suggested by the experimenter himself.[1]

This reminds us that there is an evolutionary dimension to this whole matter of arousal-seeking. Man is not the only species to have an innate propensity for gratuitous risk-taking, a fascination for danger. Not all species seem to have it, but man appears to have it in a remarkably developed form. In evolutionary terms it must present some advantage, otherwise it would have disappeared long ago in the battle for survival.

Now, this presents something of a puzzle. Why should a tendency to take unnecessary risks and open oneself to avoidable danger be a biological advantage? Certainly it is not always a personal advantage, as we have seen in many of the examples of arousal-seeking in the previous four chapters. For instance, we saw how a young boy lost his life in doing the kind of thing the monkeys were doing in the experiment just cited: climbing a pole, the knowledge of the possibility of receiving an electric shock not withstanding.

The question here, however, is not about the welfare of the individual (which we shall look at later in this chapter), but the survival of the group—and ultimately the species. Putting it in this way helps us to begin to come to terms with the puzzle. After all, it is quite possible for an inherited characteristic to be disadvantageous for the individual who exhibits it, but advantageous to his family and social group. Thus, in some species the individual most in danger from a predator will sacrifice himself to enable others in the group to escape, and the majority to survive. For instance, some small birds, like robins and thrushes, warn of the approach of a hawk by means of special calls. Unfortunately for them, while drawing the attention of others to the danger from the predator, they also risk drawing attention to themselves.[2] Likewise, individual members of bee and wasp colonies may defend the colonies' nests with suicidal charges against intruders.[3] One cannot help here but see an analogy to terrorist suicide bombers who see themselves as guarding the community against invasion and occupation.

Presumably, some kind of advantage to the group might also be supposed to apply to arousal-seeking behavior. Sometimes, as we have seen, it leads to trauma (even death) for the individual concerned, but in the wider context of the group and the species it must nevertheless serve some purpose. So the first question in this chapter is: *what evolutionary advantages are provided by this propensity for seeking high arousal?*

It can be said straightaway that such advantages are in the main, and historically, to do with exploration in one form or another. It is advantageous for the group if certain individuals, at any given time, are willing to place themselves at risk through exploring various aspects of the environment—since others can learn from both their successes and their failures. Some gamble for everyone to be safe. Let me put this in more concrete terms: suppose a primitive tribal group is entering a new territory. It will be essential, for the group as a whole, for at least some of its members to test this environment to its limits in order to discover what is dangerous and what is not. Which water holes are safe to drink from, which sands are firm underfoot, which fruit can be eaten, which caves are empty of dangerous animals, which streams are shallow enough to ford? The group will look to its more adventurous members at a given time to make these discoveries and to test the limits of what is safe and what is dangerous—in other words, to establish where the dangerous edge runs. In doing so, some may go over the edge, but in the process show the rest where it is. It is better for one person to eat a poisonous fruit than for everybody, or for one person to drown trying to cross a river than for the whole tribe to do so.

Let us move from this to a more contemporary example of how an individual can benefit his group by testing the limits of some situation. Consider the modern test pilot. His task is to explore the limits of what is called the "flight envelope" of the aircraft he has been called on to put through its paces. This "envelope" describes the safety limits of the particular aircraft under different conditions (load, speed, etc.). When the envelope is known, a pilot can remain safe by staying within it. The test pilot, however, must discover where the margins of the envelope are, and can do so only by crossing them into the area of unpredictability, or at least coming close to doing so. "This remains true even in our present days of computers. In the end someone has to get into the airplane and find out if the designers and computers have got it right."[4] The same is true, of course, for astronauts, who also test the limits of their spacecraft, and sometimes go over the dangerous edge in doing so—as we have seen with the Challenger and Columbia tragedies. In other words, for others to benefit, someone has to take the risk of crossing over from the danger zone to the trauma zone.

What all this means is that it is adaptive for the group as a whole for some of its members at a given time to put themselves at risk, and this would seem to be the case whether we are talking about small groups or large societies. We must beware, of course, of dividing members of groups into adventurous arousal-seekers and cautious arousal-avoiders if by doing so we imply that these are fixed categories. Most people will experience life at different times in both of these ways, as has been emphasized in the whole body of this book. The point is that at any given time, or in relation to a given type of situation, *some* members of the group will be likely to be in an arousal-seeking state, and they will be the ones most likely to take the risks on behalf of the group at that time.

RISK-TAKING AND CULTURAL EVOLUTION

So far we have taken a biological perspective. But it is possible to ask a similar cultural question, namely: *what cultural advantages are provided by the propensity for seeking high arousal?* This is the second principal question of the chapter. In other words, if man has this biological characteristic, why might it be beneficial for a society to allow or even encourage its expression? What advantages might accrue? This is not unrelated to the previous question, since if arousal-seeking helps a culture to thrive and flourish it may also increase the chances of the biological survival of its members, as well as the survival of the culture as an entity in its own right. In fact, the mechanism would seem to be essentially the same at the cultural as at the biological level.

Let us return to our example of a primitive tribe. When the tribe becomes well established in its new territory, it is useful for some members of the group to continue to explore. Suppose a path has been established from a village to a fishing stream. Without the continuation by some of exploration, a more direct route, previously unsuspected, would not be discovered. So excitement-seeking through exploration by a few members of the tribe is a continuing motive force for change and improvement. It helps a society not only to survive, but to improve and progress and prosper. It helps to overcome the conservative, restrictive, and repetitive tendencies of society over time.

If this hypothetical tribe seems unconvincing, it is possible to make the same kind of point in relation to our own vastly more complex civilization. One could argue that the spectacular development of Western culture since the Renaissance has depended more than anything else on harnessing such voluntary risk-taking, be it of an intellectual, esthetic, or physical kind. Pioneers and innovators must take risks. Columbus set sail to the west, with the risk of sailing off the edge of the world. Galileo asked daring questions about the position of the Earth in the universe, putting at risk the whole comfortable medieval view of the cosmos. And so on.

This is not to say that Columbus, Galileo, and the thousands of scientists, artists, explorers, and others who succeeded them over the following centuries, were motivated by no more than the excitement that can arise from risk-taking. No doubt they were urged forward by such motives as conquest, honor, prestige, and money. The point is rather that these motives are likely in the normal way of things to have been tied up with arousal-seeking, and to have been sustained through adversity (at least in part) by the actual or prospective chance of excitement. According to the argument from earlier chapters, these motives at a given time would be tied up with either arousal-avoidance or arousal-seeking. But in the former case the tendency would be to avoid or minimize those risks that are in fact essential for real discoveries and advances to be made. The genuine innovator or hunter or entrepreneur needs to court danger, search out the unknown, and provoke the unpredictable. So whatever motives there are, we may expect arousal-seeking to be frequently part of the picture.

Sometimes risks pay off, sometimes they do not. Sometimes the edge turns out to be safe, sometimes dangerous and even deadly. Traveling faster than a horse was not, as some predicted when the steam engine was being developed, impossible for the human frame to withstand; nor, later, was traveling faster than sound. Attempting to fly by attaching wings to one's arms and jumping off a cliff edge, on the other hand, did turn out to be lethal. But whether the individuals who tested these ideas survived and prospered, or promptly killed themselves, society continued to progress through their trial-and-error behavior. In this sense the dangerous edge can also be part of the cutting edge of a developing society, providing the direction for discovery, change, and progress.

One of the inherent problems of communism, and perhaps one of the main reasons for its dismal failure over many years in the Soviet Union, and its eventual spectacular collapse in the summer of 1991, would appear to have been its inability to encourage people to take risks. Instead of a bubbling-up of diversity and invention there tended to be a sterile repetition of the old tried-and-trusted ways. The analysis of this book suggests that at least part of the reason for this lack of enterprise (and the same would probably be true for any totalitarian regime) may not be so much that people were not rewarded for taking risks. It may rather be that when people live in a climate of fear they have difficulty in establishing a protective frame for extended periods of time. And without the protective frame there can be no intrinsic joy in risk-taking and the excitement that can come from it.

THE PLACE OF NEGATIVISM IN CULTURAL CHANGE

So far, all the examples of the ways in which individuals displaying episodes of excitement-seeking can benefit themselves and their society have been about exploration of one type or another, including various kinds of risk. But many of the examples of the ways in which excitement-seeking can go wrong involved aggression and violence. Surely this latter type of arousal-seeking cannot aid the survival of the group—or the species—any more than it does the individual?

In addressing this question, we need to realize first of all the obvious fact that, at the biological level, aggression may be essential for the human species, as for many others. When it is used in the service of self-defence, or of hunting, it is clearly biologically functional. However, the issue here is the less obvious one of whether excitement-seeking aggression can ever be beneficial at the social/cultural level. Certainly, when physical aggression is used in a selfish and antisocial way as part of an excitement-seeking strategy, it may cause problems of the kind discussed earlier—vandalism, rape, and the like. And obviously these behaviors in themselves are not likely to benefit anyone other than the perpetrator. But if we look more closely we see that aggression is often an expression of what, in an earlier chapter, I called negativism (the desire to break away from rules and restrictions). The question now arises in the more interesting form of whether *negativism* in conjunction with arousal-seeking may have a beneficial role to play in society; and, if so, under what circumstances. This, then, becomes our third question in this chapter: *what cultural advantages are provided by the propensity for negativism, especially when it is combined with arousal-seeking?*

An answer to this may be constructed along the following lines: negativism of the non-violent kind, including negativism of a playful, stimulation-seeking type, can lead the individual to question and challenge, directly or implicitly, the assumptions on which a society is based—its values, ideals, and taboos. And it is useful, even essential, for these to be regularly re-examined if that society is to continue to adapt to changing conditions and circumstances, and to develop. As the historian A. J. P. Taylor so bluntly put it: "All change in history, all advance, comes from nonconformity. If there had been no trouble-makers, no dissenters, we should still be living in caves."[5]

An illustration of this would be the playful negativism of the avant-garde in all the arts during the past hundred years—of the ways in which proponents of each new movement have challenged the assumptions of previous ones about what art is and should be doing. Thus in the visual arts, *impressionism* challenged the assumption that art is about an objective reality which can be laid out in a way which does not take into account an observer; *expressionism* challenged the assumption that art is about what is seen rather than what is felt; *cubism* challenged the assumption that art is about what can be seen rather than what is known (e.g. what the other side of a three-dimensional object is like); *abstract art* challenged the idea that art has to be about anything. As Picasso said, "Every act of creation is first of all an act of destruction."[6] Similarly, Miró declared that he was going to "assassinate painting."[7] And Voltaire said "You must have the devil in you to succeed in any of the arts."[8] And not only the arts. One could argue that negativism enters into creativity and cultural development in every sphere, be it art, science, engineering, business, or politics.

In many cases artists have, in their work, attacked not only esthetic conventions but also the "ordinary" person's notions of freedom, sexual morality, beauty, justice, and the good life. The part that this sort of challenge has played in shaping contemporary culture has been considerable. For example, if we are all now freer in our sexual behavior, less governed by irrational taboos, this must be in part because of the negativism towards sexual conventions of such authors as D. H. Lawrence, Henry Miller, and Lawrence Durrell.

So the creative artist may play a part in overthrowing not only esthetic but social values and rule-systems. But artists of course are not alone in being able to do this: people in virtually all walks of life can play negativistically with accepted ways of doing things, in their own spheres of action. In this way, they are able to help society to change its contours—through altering people's habits, customs, beliefs, and lifestyles. We see this all the time in the world of business and organizations where the "difficult" employee is often the one whose criticisms lead to changes and improvements.

This is not to say that every crackpot idea will turn out to be socially beneficial. It is rather that the negativism of creative people produces a pool of ethical, political, commercial, and other ideas and attitudes that are different from the conventional ones. And some of these will start to make increasing sense to more and more people, as conditions change, while others will just disappear.[9] This situation is analogous to the way in which new species evolve: mutations in genetic material produce a variety of different versions of a given species. Some of these variations, in the struggle for survival, turn out to be fitter than others. At the level of ideas and attitudes, negativism plays the part of mutation. Which particular new ideas then survive and prosper depends on changing conditions.

Of course negativism does not occur in association with arousal-*seeking* alone. It can also occur in the service of arousal-*avoidance.* In the latter case, however, it often seems to take the form of a refusal to change, a denial of reality, an unwillingness to give up those tried-and-true ways of doing things that produce feelings of security. Negativism in this case thus seems to have a tendency to conservatism, to stubbornness in the face of change, to a reaction against new conventions and rule systems.

Negativistic arousal-seeking, then, tends to lead to change and exploration. The difference from the kind of exploration described earlier in this chapter (e.g. the playful exploration of a new island by some members of a tribe) is that negativistic exploration typically leads to attempts to explore beyond what is normally *permissible*, in society. This contrast with other kinds of arousal-seeking that rather tend to explore what is normally *accessible* (for example: geographically, intellectually) or physically possible. In other words, society makes dangerous edges of its own by creating limits and taboos, and by assuring trauma of some kind (loss of respectability, ostracism, fines, imprisonment) if the limits are transgressed. Here the precarious edge consists, as it were, of man-made barbed wire and searchlights, rather than the natural drop at the edge of the rock face. To enjoy playing on such a socially determined edge seems to require negativism as well as the quest for excitement.

If communism has failed as a way of organizing society, this may not only be—as I indicated above—because it discouraged arousal-seeking and risk-taking, but also because it discouraged negativism. Something similar could perhaps be said of Islam. Historians tells us that, throughout the medieval period, Islamic culture was more advanced that that of the Christian West. But in the modern period, Islam experienced no Renaissance, no Reformation, and no Enlightenment. The spirit of questioning, of independence of thought and of innovation that characterised the West over these centuries, in the main passed Islam by, the result being no full-blown scientific or industrial revolution in Islamic countries. The rebelliousness of mind and spirit that appear to be essential to such progress was largely missing from the Islamic world, with its emphasis on submission to the will of God and to the word of God. (The word "Islam" itself means, roughly, "submission".) In general there seems to be little puzzle about why there should be a relationships between fundamentalism (of any kind) and technological backwardness.

INDIVIDUAL DEVELOPMENT: OPEN ENDS AND DEAD ENDS

If it is important for society to include *some* people who are arousal-seekers at a given time, why must every individual have the capacity for both arousal-seeking and arousal-avoidance? Why did the species not develop in such a way that some individuals are arousal-seeking all the time and others are arousal-avoiding all the time—just as some people are naturally blonde and others brunette, or, to turn to a different species, some ants are workers and others are soldiers?

The answer must in some way be that both arousal-seeking and arousal-avoidance are essential to each individual's psychological make-up, and play a part in everyone's survival, development, and mental health. The utility of arousal-avoidance is obvious: the individual needs to overcome problems and difficulties that arise, and in doing so to reduce the arousal that is brought about by them. Thus, if bodily arousal comes from the need for fight or flight, then the individual needs to carry out one or the other to good effect in order to allow arousal to return to the level it was at before the emergency started. In the case of arousal-*seeking*, by contrast, the individual may be gratuitously looking for problems and difficulties—even creating emergencies—which will raise arousal. Whatever normal, healthy biological or psychological purpose could be served by this—especially since, as we have seen, it may on occasion be disastrous? So, our fourth question in this chapter can be stated as follows: *what individual psychological advantages are provided by the propensity for seeking high arousal?*[10]

We can discern the beginnings of an answer if we turn again, as we did in considering the biological and cultural foundations of arousal-seeking, to the idea that arousal-seeking often expresses itself through exploration of one kind or another. We can start by noting that it is essential for the growing child to explore his or her environment, and his or her own capabilities. Without this, he or she would tend to remain undeveloped, endlessly repeating only what could already be done and knowing only about a small part of the world. Parents, teachers, and other adults can push the child into new experiences. But they can only do a certain amount; the child must have an internal push in order to explore on the basis of the assistance offered. The argument here, then, is very much like that for society as a whole: it is necessary to discover what is actually safe and actually dangerous, see if there are better ways of doing things, and continually test the limits of action in order to change and progress. The difference from adult exploration is that trauma will normally mean no more than temporary failure, or perhaps momentary pain, and that adults are on hand to protect against anything more serious. This also means that the child can practice skills, within this safe context, which may aid survival when watchful adults, later in life, are no longer present.

When we come to consider adolescence and adulthood it becomes clear that, in relation to development, there are two broad categories of arousal-seeking strategy which subsume all the other categories cited in previous chapters (e.g. arousal from the sensory qualities of the environment, from cognitive synergies, from negativism, and so forth). On the one hand we have exploratory strategies, like those that are natural to the young child. These, in the normal ways of things, lead to enhanced skills and knowledge, and an enriched life. On the other hand we have strategies of arousal-seeking which lead nowhere beyond themselves and therefore make no contribution to development—and may even stunt it.

There are various ways we could label these two types of strategy: intelligent and unintelligent, open and closed, and so on. What it comes down to is this: in the one case the excitement is bound up in activities that become self-generating, each excitement leading naturally to the possibility of new excitement, usually because the excitements are part of learning more about some aspect of the world. In the other case each excitement, when achieved, leads no further than itself, and so one must start all over again to find some new source of arousal, or to reactivate yet again an old source. Some activities effectively lead to nowhere beyond themselves. Others lead towards an endless cornucopia of continuing fascination.

As an illustration of the latter point, let us consider mountain-climbing. This is a self-generating activity in the sense that the more one engages in it, the more one's skills develop—and, therefore, the more testing the climbs that one can undertake. And in turn the more testing the climbs that one engages in, the more one learns about mountaineering. So the excitement that comes from exploration continues to be generated by the intrinsic nature of the activity itself.

Suppose that you were to become fascinated with some historical period or person. The more you read and discovered, the more the new questions you would ask; and the more the questions you asked, the more again that you would read and learn. The more interested one is in something, the more interesting it becomes. Any hobby or passion, be it stamp-collecting or growing bonsai trees, can be a continuing source of new fascination and excitements which are bound up with the process of learning and therefore, in some respect at least, with self-development.

In such an upward spiral of challenges generating new responses, and responses generating new challenges, there would appear to be an optimal rate of change. At this rate the challenge never becomes too great for the individual's resources of knowledge and skill, but remains great enough to elicit continuing interest and response. At those times when the individual actually is in this optimal state of balance between challenge and skill, he or she may be said to be experiencing "flow." Mihalyi Csikszentmihalyi, who coined this term, describes flow as a state of mind in which one is so totally and deeply absorbed in what one is doing that one feels one is flowing along in it, typically losing all sense of time and selfhood. In many studies he has shown how this "flow state," which can be intensely gratifying, typifies people who are achievers and self-actualizers.[11] In the terms used in this book, we could say that the flow experience is likely to take place when the problems are not so great as to break through the protective frame, but *are* great enough to elicit high arousal. In other words, flow is a type of excitement experience. And it arises in this context of psychological growth and development.

Turning now to the opposite (unhelpful) kind of strategy: in this case the individual chooses some source of arousal which, once obtained, leads nowhere and so results in no new learning or skill, or any other kind of improvement. It is exemplified by boys hanging around on a street corner. Momentary excitement might come from seeing a pretty girl pass by and whistling at her, jeering at a man carrying parcels, throwing beer cans across the street, starting a fight. All of these are desultory, unimaginative, one-off activities that lead nowhere. (The same label applies to the great American institution of "cruising" a town's main street.) A more sinister example would be drug-taking for kicks. Not only does this lead nowhere, but the more one takes, the more one needs of it in order to produce the same effect. Simple acts of vandalism—breaking up telephone booths, heaving bricks through store windows, snapping off the antennas of parked cars— fall into the same general category of unhelpful strategies. In all these examples, there is precious little sign of flow. We might call these dead-end strategies, and contrast them with corridor strategies—since corridors lead to more corridors, and sometimes even to doors into new areas. In the dead-end case, the strategy only closes off new avenues.

Of course, many types of activities fail to fall clearly into either of these general categories. I have presented the categories as dichotomous only in order to make the point as clear as possible. In fact, we are talking about a dimension which runs the gamut from static to self-generating, and many activities fall somewhere in the middle: they generate some possibility for continuing interest, but not very much. Suppose one becomes interested in some TV soap opera. This interest develops from week to week, and one may even do such things as read about the actors, and even the plots, in magazines. But this interest does not lead to anything much beyond itself, so that when the stories finish, that is the end of the matter. In any case, the chances are that one's interest will have waned long before.

Now, it might appear that this distinction between arousal-seeking which aids and enhances development, and that which stunts it, is the same as the distinction between exploration and violence. Certainly many of the short sighted one-off strategies do seem to involve physical aggression. But violence can also enter into activities that help the individual to learn about the self and others, about courage and comradeship, about facing up to things. Soccer hooliganism may develop into an elaborate (and even subtle) game that allows the individual to explore both physical skills and social relationships.[12] Even certain kinds of crime may involve the development of skills and interests over a lifetime. Who is to say that the successful conman or blackmailer, while in a sense committing violence against society, is not "self-actualizing" in the process, however reprehensible his activities in other respects? The distinction between the open-minded and closed-off strategies is not about whether or not violence is part of the picture—it is about whether or not learning plays an intrinsic part in the activity. If the means to excitement, or other forms of pleasant high arousal, necessarily involve the learning of new ideas or skills, then the activity is part of a route to self-development, even if aggression is part of the package, and however immoral the activity might be.

CREATIVITY AND CRIME

As has been noted at several points in this book, some people seem to be more prone to boredom than others. When such people choose one or another kind of strategy, the open-ended or the dead-end type, therefore, they are liable to do so in ways that lead to extremes of one kind or another. Thus one gets the impression that creative people are often particularly prone to boredom. Furthermore, they also often seem to need particularly high levels of arousal in order to gain satisfaction. They then use their innate abilities to push ideas and materials along in novel, unexpected, and often defiantly negativistic ways. That is, they use particular kinds of psychologically enriching, open-ended strategies, especially those that involve the construction of convention-breaking structures of different kinds, to overcome their boredom.

A good example would be the case of Graham Greene, the novelist. In numerous writings and interviews he has described how, at the age of nineteen, he found his brother's revolver and bullets, and proceeded to play Russian roulette with it:

> I put the muzzle of the revolver into my right ear and pulled the trigger. There was a minute click, and looking down at the chamber I could see that the charge had moved into the firing position. I was out by one. I remember an extraordinary sense of jubilation, as if carnival lights had been switched on in a dark drab street. My heart knocked in its cage, and life contained an infinite number of possibilities. It was like a young man's first successful experience of sex.[13]

He repeated the experience a number of times on later occasions, although he reports that the effect of the "drug" began to wear off on repetition, and he had to find other stimulants and ways of giving chance a chance to overcome what he called his "boredom-sickness." Thirty years later he "diced with death" in a different way, by downing a pile of aspirin dropped into a tumbler of whisky. "But the effect of the whisky was offset by the medicine and I slept very well that night."[14]

Graham Greene appears to have been one of those creative people who feel naturally at home in the danger zone. He was fascinated by "moments of truth," and drawn to the "front line," the edge of political action, wherever it was—Haiti after Papa Doc seized power, Vietnam during the last days of French rule, and Kenya during the Mau Mau rebellion, for example. It is significant that he should call his second volume of autobiography *Ways of Escape*,[15] making it clear that the escape he was referring to in the title was a lifelong flight from boredom, his writing being a major strategy but not the sole one. His description of his experience of the blitz in London during the war is typical: "I loved the blitz. It was wonderful to wake up and know you were still alive and hear glass being swept up in the street. It was marvellous to walk down Oxford Street in the blackout and see the stars. I enjoyed the buzz bombs because you could hear them coming."[16]

Evelyn Waugh similarly described his escape from the "vicious spiral of boredom and lassitude" to write *Brideshead Revisited*.[17] Roland Barthes reported: "As a child, I was often and intensely bored. This evidently began very early, it has continued my whole life, in gusts ... and it has always been noticeable to others. A panic boredom, to the point of distress ...."[18] Any student of the lives of novelists and poets—indeed of painters and composers too— could point to endless similar examples of creative artists using their skills and originality in a constructive, open-ended way to escape from their special susceptibility to boredom.

Turning to the other side of things: those people who are particularly vulnerable to boredom, but who do *not* have the intellectual or other skills and capacities to amuse or occupy themselves creatively through open-ended strategies, are the ones who tend to become vending-machine vandals and street corner hooligans. Just like the creative person, they tend to use negativism. But they do so as part of dead-end strategies which (as we have to some extent seen) lead nowhere. So, in a sense, the vandal is the failed creative artist, and the artist the successful vandal. Both want extra large portions of excitement from life, and attempt to get it especially from being negativistic. But they use different tactics in this life game, and have very different amounts of success. The result is that the one tends to become increasingly desperate, the other increasingly fulfilled; the one increasingly condemned by, the other increasingly feted by, society.

In the case of the person who is truly creative, negativism launches him or her off on new and exciting voyages of discovery, and remains a continuing part of the motive force. In the case of the vandal, the dropout, the angry unwashed, the negativism is like a starter motor which fails to ignite the engine. There is much noise and commotion, but little or no forward movement, or at most only as much as can be gained from jolting forward by using the starter motor with the gears engaged.

We should note, though, that the successful criminal is very different from the vandal. As was suggested in the previous section of this chapter, the successful criminal may well be a self-actualizing person, and if successful may indeed be psychologically similar to the creative artist.[19] As W. Somerset Maugham put it, "It is only the artist, and maybe the criminal, who can make his own [rules]."[20] It is interesting that Degas said, "A picture must be painted with the same feeling as that with which a criminal commits a crime."[21] And to return to Graham Greene again, he is quoted in an interview as reporting: "I feel that several times in my life I was saved by fate from becoming a criminal. I was drawn towards crime by boredom, which caused me unbearable suffering."[22] Fortunately for the rest of us, he used his writing to rescue him from boredom.

Naturally, this is not to imply that crime is as valuable to the community as is creative writing. The point is that, to the individual (speaking psychologically and not ethically), it *may* be. It may rescue that person from boredom, and allow him or her to develop skills and make use of originality in highly satisfying ways.

EXCITEMENT IN THE AGE OF BOREDOM

For people to develop in a healthy way, then, it would seem that they have to experience arousal-seeking on a regular basis, and, when they are in that state, use open-ended types of strategy which involve learning.[23] Ideally, these learning strategies, even if negativistic, will not be antisocial or violent. For the various reasons we have considered, society in general should also benefit if this combination of qualities characterizes most of its members.

Having reached this point in the argument, however, we need to confront one final question: *what is the place in contemporary society of the propensity for seeking high arousal?* The emphasis in this question is on "contemporary" because, as we shall see, modern society has evolved in such a way as to make arousal-seeking more problematic for its members than it may have been in the past.

First of all, modern Western society has developed in a manner which radically changes the situation by helping its members to become increasingly secure, and feel themselves to be increasingly safe. On the one hand, social welfare in most Western countries, such as the countries making up the European Union, has removed some of the worst dangers of poverty, unemployment, and illness. On the other hand, technology has removed many of the sources of danger, and especially those that derive from ill health.[24] Now, if people feel themselves to be safe, then for reasons we have explored throughout this book they are more likely to be in the arousal-seeking state, and therefore to be looking for danger and risk. So there is a paradox here: the safer we make life, the more people seem to want to take risks and court danger.

In this respect, at least, all the efforts of social reformers have been counterproductive. We can see a specific instance of this in relation to travel. The law insists that cars meet various safety requirements. Some countries require regular retesting for roadworthiness, and demand the wearing of safety belts. The result is that we are more likely to be in the excitement-seeking state of mind than we otherwise would be when driving, because of the seemingly safe context in which we find ourselves. We are therefore more likely to take risks for the sake of excitement. Similarly, the motorbike rider feels safer in a leather protective suit and crash helmet, and is likely therefore to ride even faster than otherwise. So, by making things safer, the so-called "Nanny society" often unwittingly contrives to encourage people to take greater risks—thereby endangering not only themselves, but others. It might produce safer driving if the driver were required to tie a garrotte around the throat, to tighten on impact, rather than to buckle up a safety belt (or rely on an airbag) and if the motorcyclist were forced to ride naked.

At the same time, the areas in which people (particularly youngsters) can take risks have been narrowed down. For example, the age-old solution to the problem of the young man looking for excitement—to go off to war—has become much restricted, even though wars continue to occur, as in Iraq. The reason is that, as weapons become smarter, so fewer, but more expert, soldiers are needed.

Nor are there more empires to be built. Even geographical exploration is difficult. There may still be mountains, deserts, jungles, and wildernesses—but none that have not been mapped, written about in guidebooks, photographed for glossy coffee-table books, presented on endless series of television programs, and (for all one knows) included in the expansion plans of MacDonald's and Starbucks. Furthermore, pioneering now requires technical expertise. At one time in America the frontier was the West, and anyone could go off and chance his or her luck in pushing the frontier forward. The only analogous new frontier is space—for the discovery and settlement of which one must be a qualified physicist, engineer, computer specialist, or test pilot.

As society becomes more sophisticated, specialized, technological, and advanced, the risks that are likely to benefit it are increasingly those that can be taken only by technicians, professionals, and others who are trained to work at the frontiers of research. Even businessmen and entrepreneurs increasingly need to become experts in their sectors. Although, in evolutionary terms, the willingness of the individual to take certain kinds of uneducated risks—eating unidentified fruits, setting sail in a new direction—has been invaluable, and indeed essential to the survival of man, the important risks are now likely to be taken only by the experts: the surgeon willing to risk a career in some chancy and untested operating technique, the physicist staking a reputation on a radical new theory, the entrepreneur coming up with venture capital for promising developments in computer technology. So the earlier part of this chapter was really about cultural development up to the

present. And the present may have become fundamentally different. It may be that, from the point of view of society, risk-taking is
now only needed from a small class of people.

If we put together the two general developments that have been
touched on here—a growing need for excitement, and a decreasing
possibility for meaningful risk-taking—then we have a perfect
recipe for a major social problem. Our time has been called the age
of anxiety, but it could equally well be called the age of boredom. It is
hardly surprising that, especially in the most prosperous countries,
we see the phenomenon of the teenage terrorist and the suburban
saboteur. Somehow society has to find a means, especially for its
relatively uneducated youngsters, to excitement-seek in ways which
are not damaging to others. It has to do so both for the mental health
of these individuals themselves, and for the health of society as a
whole—which can be put at risk by such disaffected members.

The main solution, and the one implied by all the discussion in the
last section of this chapter, is that of education. Specifically, what is
needed is for youngsters not just to be taught, but to be taught how
to teach themselves. What should be imparted is the open-ended
skill of learning new skills, together with a fascination for the world
around in all its aspects, an enthusiasm for new challenges, and a
belief in the possibility of self-improvement. Even if this has been
said many times before in one form or another by educationalists
and other reformers, it is no less true now than it has ever been.

Meanwhile, it is no good just clamping down on such outlets for
excitement-seeking as there are, like soccer hooliganism or graffiti
spraying. Instead, we perhaps need to encourage people to do *really*
dangerous things, like going over Niagara Falls in any kind of vessel.
In this specific case, it is clear that the relevant authorities will do
everything they can to prevent people from taking personal risks.
Thus, when someone was about to go over the Falls in a silver-and-
red barrel, the Ontario Hydro (which generates hydroelectric
power from the river), lowered the water in the retaining pool
where the barrel was floating. Within several minutes it had become
jammed on a set of retaining logs. The occupant was not at all
pleased when they knocked on the hatch to get him out.[25]

Even when someone makes it over the Falls safely, they are dealt with in what one might call an unappreciative manner. For example, someone who went over safely in a rubber ball of his own design in 1961 was fined, and his invention was confiscated by Canadian Customs as a "foreign vessel in their waters."[26] Another man who went over in 2003, surviving even though he used no safety devices, was charged with "mischief and performing a stunt" and fined $3,000 plus certain expenses.[27]

The argument here is that society might want to help, not hinder, people who have a desire to take personal risks—provided the ways they choose are neither harmful to others nor threatening to the fabric of society itself. Indeed, if risk-taking is not channeled into forms which are harmless to others, it may take even more disruptive forms. Many people need not "breathing space" but "risky space." I am suggesting that we should allow people to play with fire, generate new games of violence, duel, crash cars in specially prepared runways, climb the outside of skyscrapers, swim where there are powerful currents, and undertake other even more imaginative and dangerous activities. We should perhaps permit aggression between consenting adults. We should allow danger where only the individual who chooses the danger is at risk. The running of the bulls in Pamplona is an object lesson here, a model of socially sanctioned—indeed, socially *encouraged*—risk-taking.

This is not to claim that frustrated arousal-seeking is the only cause of social unrest. Far from it. But it *is* to point to one major factor that is often overlooked, especially by politicians and economists: boredom has always been a social problem. In previous centuries it went by other names, such as "accidie" and "spleen." But now, with increased leisure time, growing unemployment, better health services, people living longer into retirement, and the reduced chance of taking interesting risks, it has become a social crisis—a virtual boredom epidemic. In the years ahead we are going to have to learn how to cope with it.

Whether or not encouraging youngsters in their quest for risk is really viable, we should certainly be willing to spend much more money on providing safety zones like public sports areas and facilities for artistic activity, where teenagers (in the main) can go to satisfy their needs for fulfilling action and excitement. This is particularly true in poor communities. If crime, vandalism, and other social evils are more prevalent in such communities, this may not be only for the obvious reason that people in those communities need the money that comes from crime, or even that they need to express their frustration and anger. It may also be because they do not have available a range of alternative ways of achieving excitement. If crime is the only "game in town", the individual may have little option but to choose it. What is needed from public authorities is not just a clamping down on unacceptable behavior, but a commitment to provide many alternative "games in town."

EXCITEMENT-SEEKING AND RISK-TAKING

It should be clear that excitement-seeking and risk-taking cannot be equated. This is because the pleasant arousal of excitement may be sought out and obtained in many different ways, and taking risks is only one of these. Other forms of excitement-seeking that we have looked at earlier in this book include the use of sensory stimulation, the competition of sport, the confrontations of negativism, and the experience of the kinds of intriguing incompatibilities that I have referred to as "cognitive synergies."

Conversely, risk-taking may be undertaken primarily for reasons other than that of obtaining excitement. Since the taking of risks, as we have just seen in this chapter, is in itself an important ingredient of cultural and personal change, especially through exploration and learning, we should be aware of some of these other motivations even if they do not in themselves form the central subject-matter of the present book.[28]

For example, we may take a risk because we wish to fulfill our professional obligations. The sort of risks taken by soldiers, firemen, and members of other risky professions may often come into this category. We may take a risk in order to feel courageous, or to demonstrate to ourselves, and others, just how clever we are. Many kinds of risky sports may come under this heading. We may take a risk in developing an intimate relationship, when we undertake an action that could lead to rebuff and embarrassment (for example, the first kiss). The point, however, is that each of these kinds of risk and uncertainty must be undertaken in combination with either the arousal-seeking or the arousal-avoiding state of mind. In the former case, the heightened awareness and engagement will be experienced as "being alive" and welcomed, while in the latter it will tend to be tolerated at best and experienced as highly stressful at worst. The moral is obvious: people are more likely to take risks, and benefit from the advantages that can accrue from this, if they are in the arousal-seeking than if they are in the arousal-avoiding motivational state.

This has implications, among other things, for businesses. Business enterprises generally depend for their success on the innovations and inventions that can only come through risk-taking. It is better therefore for those involved to be able to experience what they are doing, at least on occasion, as a form of excitement-seeking. This does not mean that people at work, including managers, should take stupid risks, or ill-advised risks, or badly-thought-out risks—but simply that they should be willing to take risks. In this way they can help to keep the company moving forwards in terms of its product, the techniques it uses to produce the product, and its understanding of what its customers need. And yet many businesses develop a culture in which risk-taking is frowned on, and "playing it by the book" and "being sensible" are encouraged at all times.[29]

TOWARDS A WIDER PERSPECTIVE

In this book we have been exploring a topic which, for all its obvious importance in everyday life, has received rather little attention from psychologists. Certainly there has been little research on excitement in comparison with its ugly twin sister, anxiety.

All the questions I raised in the first chapter have been given answers within a coherent general framework of ideas. It should by now be evident to the reader why people enjoy the simulated dangers of the amusement park, the vicarious thrills of the horror film, and even the real dangers of such sports as bungee-jumping. It ought to be clearer why people are attracted to potentially calamitous events like expected earthquakes—and also to certain other predictably unpleasant ones, like those involved in the Catalan fire festivals. Antisocial activities like wilding can now be understood in a new light. And the reason why my panic switched to euphoria when I was buzzed by a light plane (recall the opening paragraph of the book) should now make more sense. My hope is that all this will give you some insight into some of your own more curious behaviors, through an appreciation that the seeming paradoxes of human nature make sense if we understand that emotions are "turned upside down" when experienced within a protective frame.

If much of this now seems obvious to you, you may be surprised to learn that the ideas expressed here are not widely accepted in the psychology of motivation and emotion. In fact they fly in the face of assumptions commonly made by psychologists. These include the assumption that people like only middling levels of arousal, that within this middling level each individual has pretty much a fixed amount of arousal which he or she prefers to all others at all times, and that each emotion can be experienced in only one fixed way.

I should also add this: the theory that has informed the analysis presented here is a general one that goes way beyond the topic of this book. For reasons which at this stage should be obvious, it is called *reversal theory*.[30] The pair of mental states that have been at the focus of attention in this book—the arousal-seeking and arousal-avoidance pair—is, in the more general theory, only one of a whole *set* of pairs of states. These pairs, taken together, underlie the whole of emotional experience, including such emotions as guilt, triumph, gratitude, and resentment. But that is another story.

My hope is that you have been able to hang on during our bumpy journey, with all its ups and downs, twists and turns—and that you have managed to maintain a detachment frame, and enjoy the excitement. There is no doubt that the world we have been visiting seems to resemble the world of "Alice Through the Looking Glass."

It is one in which danger leads to a need for safety, and safety to a need for danger; in which pleasant emotions can become unpleasant, and vice-versa, while still remaining the same emotion; in which work can become play, and play can become work, in the course of the very same activity; in which everyday behaviors come to seem strange and paradoxical, and perverse behaviors can be seen as extensions of perfectly normal desires; in which "good" behavior can lead nowhere, and destructive behavior can lead to creativity and construction; in which stability can be unhealthy, and instability healthy.

We have, in other words, been visiting a complex world of real, living people rather than the simple world of rather static wooden figures that is so often presented to us by academic psychology. This is another way of saying that here is a book about you and your own world of experience—the one you will step back into when you close these covers, put the book down, and look around you.

Notes

1 PLAYING WITH FIRE

1. Crace, J. "Scream tests", *Radio Times* (UK), 15–21 March 1988, pp. 12–13. An enthralling book celebrating the creativity of the designers of what he calls "scream machines" is Coker R., *Roller Coasters: A Thrill Seekers Guide to the Ultimate Scream Machines*, New York: Main Street, 2002.

2. The history of the X Games is well documented in Soden, G. *Falling: How Our Greatest Fear Became Our Greatest Thrill*, New York: Norton, 2003. For more about the experience of participating in extreme sports, see Gutman, B. and Frederick, S. *Being Extreme: Thrills and Dangers in the World of High-Risk Sports*, London: Citadel Press, 2002.

3. Robbins, W. "Waiting for a quake to happen," *New York Times*, National Edn., 4 December 1990, p. 1, section B.

4. To take a single example, eight schoolboys in Scotland went on a rampage in which they beat up three passengers on a bus. This was described by the newspaper *The Scotsman* (18 August 2005) as a wilding attack.

5. Reversal theory, a general psychological theory that I have developed with colleagues, identifies eight basic emotional needs that people can experience, the need for excitement being just one of these. Risk-taking may arise in the pursuit of any of these basic needs, not just the pursuit of excitement. Some references on reversal theory will be provided in the final chapter.

6. For example, a search of *Psychological Abstracts* for 2005 showed that 8,629 papers were published during the year with the word "anxiety" in their title or abstract, but that only 176 papers were published with the word "excitement" in their title or abstract.

2 THE PROTECTIVE FRAME

1. Cannon, W. B. *Bodily Changes in Pain, Hunger, Fear and Rage: An Account of Researches into the Function of Emotional Excitement*, New York: Appleton-Century, 1929.

2. Schachter, S. and Singer, J. "Cognitive, social and physiological determinants of emotional state," *Psychological Review*, **69**, 1962, pp. 378–399.

3. This derives from a theory known as "Optimal Arousal Theory," which was originally put forward by Canadian psychologist D. O. Hebb in the mid-1950s. A landmark paper by Hebb was "Drives and the CNS (Conceptual Nervous System)," *Psychological Review*, **62**, 1955, pp. 243–254.

4. Olivier, L. *On Acting*, London: Weidenfeld and Nicolson, 1986. Consistent with this, Olivier is reported, memorably, as having said that acting is "like coming for a living." Review by S. Spencer of *"Olivier"* by T. Coleman, London: Bloomsbury, in *The Sunday Telegraph*, 4 September 2005, p. 15.

5. Dawson, L. *A Clown Too Many*, London: Fontana/Collins, 1986, pp. 192–193.

6. Apter, M. J. and Batler, R. 'Gratuitous risk: A study of parachuting', in, S. Svebak, and M. J. Apter, (Eds.), *Stress and Health: A Reversal Theory Perspective*, Washington, D.C.: Taylor and Francis, 1997, pp. 119–129.

7. Legrand, F. D. and Apter, M. J. "Why do people perform thrilling activities? A study based on reversal theory", *Psychological Reports*, **94**, 2004, pp. 307–313.

8. Kerr, J. H., Kawaguchi, C., Oiwa, M., Terayama, Y., and Zukawa, A. "Stress, anxiety and other emotions in Japanese modern dance performance," *Pacific Journal of Psychology*, **11**, 1, 2000, pp. 16–33.

9. Television documentary, "The Most Swirling, Swinging, Sliding, Spinning, Up-and-Down Ride of Your Life," broadcast in the UK on BBC2, 26 December 1986.

3 DANGER'S DELIGHT

1. This theme of the need to be in control comes out clearly in interviews with six of the world's highest-ranking stuntmen: Piet, S. "What motivates stunt men?", *Motivation and Emotion*, 11 (2), 1987, pp. 195–213.

2. Lundy, D. *Godforsaken Sea: Racing the World's Most Dangerous Waters*, Chapel Hill: Algonquin Books, 1999, p. 187. This book is specifically about the Vendée Globe race that took place in 1996–7. It can be seen from this quotation that Lundy explicitly uses the protective frame concept as developed by the present author.

3. Chris Bonington, interviewed in de Bono, E. *Tactics: The Art and Science of Success*, London: Fontana/Collins, 1986, p. 200. Bonington's expeditions have been the first to climb many of the world's most difficult mountains, and he was the first to complete an ascent of the South West face of Mount Everest.

4. Smoke Blanchard, interviewed in the *San Francisco Chronicle*, 25 February 1985. Blanchard is one of the pioneers of modern rock climbing and bouldering.

5. Bonington, C. *Annapurna South Face*, London: Cassell, 1971, p. 41.

6. Herzog, M. *Annapurna*, New York: Dutton, 1952, p. 167.

7. Pat Ament, interviewed in *Newsweek*, 15 October 1984.

8. Jeff Achey, interviewed in *Newsweek*, 15 October 1984.

9. Ibid.

10. *Toronto Star*, 27 June 1985.

11. Ibid.

12. All the quotations in this paragraph are from Turner, G. "The hectic life of our top surgeons," *Sunday Telegraph* (UK), 29 January 1984, p. 8.

13. Robin Skynner, interviewed in Cleave, M. "Squaring the family circle," *Observer Magazine* (UK), 14 February 1988, pp. 60–62.

14. Chris Thorsen, quoted in Fine, S. *Toronto Globe and Mail*, 29 July 1985, p. 14.

15. Cus D'Amato, cited in Calvin, M. "The big fight terror that excites Spinks," *The Daily Telegraph* (UK), June 1988.

16. Truman, J. "Mike Tyson—baptism for a heavyweight," *Arena*, December/January 1986/1987, pp. 90, 94.

17. Ball, C., Chester, L., and Perrott, R. *Cops and Robbers*, London: Andre Deutsch, 1978.

18. Boerlage, M. "Ascent of Brammah 11, Kashmir, 1985," *Berggids* (Journal of the Royal Dutch Alpine Club), December 1985, p. 15.

19. Chay Blyth, interviewed in McIlvanney, H. *Observer* (UK), 31 October 1982. His exploits led, among other things, to the establishment of the BT Global Challenge, a race in which yachts sail around the world in the 'wrong direction,' i.e. against the prevailing winds and currents. The most recent race started from Portsmouth in October 2004 and finished in July 2005.

20. Ibid.

21. Stirling Moss, cited in Kerr, J. H. "Speed sports: The search for high arousal experiences," *Sportwissenschaft*, **18** (2), 1988, p. 186.

22. Henderson, K. "Racing against Myself," *Washington Post Magazine*, 14 August 2005.

23. Hemingway, E. *Death in the Afternoon*, Harmondsworth: Penguin, 1976, p. 210.

24. Ibid. (photograph caption).

25. Tynan, K. *Bull Fever*, London: Longmans, 1966, p. 55.

26. Conrad, B. *Gates of Fear*, New York: Bonanza, 1957, p. 28.

27. Ibid., p. 147.

28. Ibid., p. 192.

29. *The Sunday Telegraph* (UK), 22 January 1984, p. 28.

30. *Lookout*, June 1989, p. 72.

31. Ibid.

32. Michener, J. A. *Iberia: Spanish Travels and Reflections*, Greenwich, Connecticut: Fawcett Crest, 1968, p. 595.

4 INTO THE SAFETY ZONE

1. What makes a home a home has become of interest to anthropologists. See McCracken, G. *Culture and Consumption*, Indiana University Press, 1990. Also of relevance to the psychology of homes is Csikszentmihalyi M. and Rochberg-Halton, E. *The Meaning of Things*, Cambridge University Press, 1981.

2. Dobereiner, P. "Sport's own world of make-believe," *The Observer* (UK), 22 January 1984.

3. Dobereiner, P. "Fear is the spur for game heroes," *The Observer* (UK), 30 October 1983.

4. According to soccer mythology, it was said originally by Bill Shankly during his time as manager of Liverpool. In any case, it has been repeated by many other managers and coaches.

5. Real life examples of the way that athletes reverse backwards and forwards between these two states will be found in Kerr, J. H. *Counselling Athletes: Applying Reversal Theory*, London and New York: Routledge, 2001.

6. A clinical measurement aimed at establishing, in particular cases, which of these and other reasons for losing the protective frame in sexual situations actually occurs, will be found in Bonierbale, M., Clement, A., Loundou, A., Simeoni, M. C., Barrau, K., Hamidi, K., Apter, M. J., Lancon, C., and Auquier, P., "A new evaluation concept and its measurement: Male sexual anticipating cognitions," *Journal of Sexual Medicine*, **3** (1), 2006, pp. 96–103.

7. In reversal theory, this serious frame of mind, of which anxiety-avoidance is an aspect, is called the *telic* state; the playful frame of mind, of which excitement-seeking is an aspect, is known as the *paratelic* state.

8. "Playboy Interview: Donald Trump," *Playboy*, March 1990, p. 63.

9. Ibid., p. 72.

10. This is one of the main themes of Anthony Fry's book *Safe Space: How to Survive in a Threatening World*, London: Dent and Sons, 1987.

5 ON THE SIDELINES

1. See Chua-Eoan, H. "The new rules of fight club", *Time*, 26 September 2005.

2. Levin, B. *Enthusiasms*, London: Coronet Books (Hodder and Stoughton), 1985, pp. 144–145.

3. Bettelheim, B. *Freud's Vienna and Other Essays*, New York: Vintage Books (Random House), 1991, p. 114.

4. Nabokov, V. *Lectures on Literature*, New York: Harcourt Brace Jovanovich, 1980, p. 6.

5. Weldon, F. *Letters to Alice: On First Reading Jane Austen*, London: Coronet Books (Hodder and Stoughton), 1985, pp. 77–78.

6. See, for example, Hariton, E. B. and Singer, J. L. "Women's fantasies during sexual intercourse: Normative and theoretical implications," *Journal of Consulting and Clinical Psychology*, **42**, (3), 1974, pp. 313–322; and Sue, D. "Erotic fantasies of college students during coitus," *Journal of Sex Research*, **15**, 1979, pp. 299–305.

7. *Preface to Lyrical Ballads*, 2nd edn. 1801.

8. King, S. *Danse Macabre*, London: Macdonald, 1982, p. 10.

9. Apter, M. J. *The Experience of Motivation: The Theory of Psychological Reversals*, London: Academic Press, 1982.

10. Edmund Burke, the British politician and philosopher, defined "the sublime" in his book *A Philosophical Inquiry into the Origin of our Ideas of the Sublime and Beautiful* (1756) as that which excites "passions" which "are delightful when we have an idea of pain and danger, without being actually in such circumstances ..." (p. 125, 1857 edn.).

11. This idea is developed in Coulson, A. "Cognitive Synergy in Televised Entertainment," in M. J. Apter and J. H. Kerr (Eds.) *Adult Play*, Amsterdam: Swets and Zeitlinger, 1991, pp. 71–85.

12. This phrase was coined by John Lennon and Malcolm Foley. See *Dark Tourism: The Attraction of Death and Disaster*, London and New York: Continuum, 2000. A related neologism is "catastrophilia" coined by Mark Svengold in his book *Big Weather: Chasing Tornadoes in the Heart of America*, New York: Holt, 2005.

6 HOW PEOPLE DIFFER

1. Walters, J., Apter, M. J., and Svebak, S. "Color preference, arousal, and the theory of psychological reversals," *Motivation and Emotion*, **6** (3), 1982, pp. 193–215.

2. For example, the Telic Dominance Scale. This is given in full in Apter, M. J. *The Experience of Motivation*, London: Academic Press, 1982. It is also provided in Appendix D of Kerr, J. H. *Motivation and*

Emotion in Sport: Reversal Theory, Hove, Sussex: Psychology Press (Taylor & Francis), 1997. An alternative known as the Paratelic Dominance Scale has been constructed by Cook, M. and Gerkovich, M. M. See: "The development of a Paratelic Dominance Scale," in Kerr, J. H., Murgatroyd, S. and Apter, M. J. (Eds.) *Advances in Reversal Theory*, Amsterdam: Swets & Zeitlinger, 1993, pp. 177–188. The items for the scale are given in table 7 of this paper.

3. Lafreniere, K., Cowles, M., and Apter, M. J. "The reversal phenomenon: Reflections on a laboratory study," in M. J. Apter, J. H. Kerr, and M. Cowles (Eds.) *Progress in Reversal Theory*, Amsterdam: North Holland, 1988; and Frey, K. "Correlates and distributions of arousal preferences over time," paper presented at the Fifth International Conference on Reversal Theory, Midwest Research Institute, Kansas City, Missouri, June 1991.

4. Eddy, M., Frey, K., and Apter, M. J. "Parental upbringing style and the development of telic dominance," paper presented at the Fifth International Conference on Reversal Theory, Midwest Research Institute, Kansas City, June 1991.

5. This is reviewed in Apter, M. J. *Reversal Theory: The Dynamics of Motivation, Emotion and Personality*, Oxford: Oneworld Publications, 2006, chapter 5.

6. Svebak, S. "Personality and sports participation," in G. P. H. Hermans (Ed.) *Sports, Medicine and Health*, Amsterdam: Elsevier, 1990, pp. 87–96.

7. Marvin Zuckerman and his colleagues have also argued that there are physiological, especially biochemical, differences between what they call high and low "sensation seekers." They measure the latter with a psychometric scale called the "Sensation Seeking Scale." This represents a solid body of research over many years. Unfortunately, from the perspective of the present book, it is tied to a theoretical structure that makes no reference to different states of mind. Rather, it assumes that people differ from each other only in terms of a single preferred level of arousal which is essentially unchanging for each individual, although different between individuals. It is therefore difficult to assimilate Zuckerman's data to the present argument. But see Zuckerman, M. *Sensation Seeking: Beyond the Optimal Level of Arousal*, Hillsdale, NJ: Lawrence Erlbaum, 1979; Zuckerman, M.

Psychobiology of Personality, Cambridge, UK: Cambridge University Press, 1991; and Zuckerman, M. *Behavioral Expression and Biosocial Bases of Sensation Seeking*, Cambridge UK: Cambridge University Press,1994. The same applies to the work of Frank Farley on what he calls the "Big T" (i.e., thrill-seeking) personality type. See his article "The Big T in Personality," *Psychology Today*, May 1986, pp. 44–50. See also: Farley, F. "The Type T personality" in L.P. Lipsett and L. L Mitnick (Eds.) *Self-regulatory Behavior and Risk Taking: Causes and Consequences*, Norwood, NJ: Ablex Publishers, 1991.

8. I am indebted to the Romanian psychologist Catalin Mamali for drawing my attention to the concept of crucial experiences, and to his own work on this topic, which is largely unpublished in English.

9. Girodo, M. "Telic and paratelic modes in operational undercover and field narcotics agents," paper presented at the Second International Conference on Reversal Theory, York University, Toronto, May 1985

10. Tacon, P. and Abner, B. "Normative and other data for the Telic Dominance and Negativism Dominance Scales," in J. H. Kerr, S. Murgatroyd, and M. J. Apter (Eds.) *Advances in Reversal Theory*, Amsterdam: Swets & Zeitlinger, 1993, pp. 165–175. This study tested 1,414 Canadian adults aged 20 to over 60. The same trend was found earlier by Murgatroyd, S. using the same scale with 945 respondents in the UK aged 21 to 70. See Murgatroyd, S. "The nature of telic dominance", in M. J. Apter, D. Fontana, and S. Murgatroyd (Eds.) *Reversal Theory: Applications and Developments*, Wales: University College Cardiff Press/Hillsdale, NJ: Lawrence Erlbaum, 1985, pp. 20–41.

11. Tacon and Abner, op.cit. found no significant difference on the arousal-avoidance subscale of the Telic Dominance Scale between males and females. Murgatroyd, op.cit. also failed to find a significant difference on this subscale.

7 GETTING TURNED ON

1. This threefold classification is based on Berlyne, D. E. *Aesthetics and Psychobiology*, New York: Appleton-Century-Crofts, 1971. He used

the terms "psychological properties," "ecological properties," and "collative properties."

2. Levin, B. *Enthusiasms*, London: Coronet Books (Hodder and Stoughton), 1985, p. 36.

3. Ibid., p. 179.

4. This term was coined in Apter, M. J. *The Experience of Motivation: The Theory of Psychological Reversals*, London: Academic Press, 1982, chapters 6–8.

5. Vinograd, C. "Aping the apes: Humans go wild at London Zoo," *Washington Post*, 28 August 2005.

6. Ibid., chapter 8. See also Apter, M. J. *Reversal Theory: The Dynamics of Motivation, Emotion and Personality*, Oxford: Oneworld Publications, 2006, chapter 8.

7. Wilson, E. O. "The drive to discovery," *Dialogue*, **70**, 1985, pp. 64–70.

8. An entertaining book on all the different ways in which we play with falling and gravity is Soden, G. *Falling: How Our Greatest Fear Became Our Greatest Thrill*, New York and London: W.W. Norton, 2003.

9. Defined in Apter, M. J. (reference 4 above, 1982), chapter 9. See also McDermott, M. "Negativism as play: Proactive rebellion in young adult life," in J. H. Kerr and M. J. Apter (Eds.) *Adult Play*, Amsterdam: Swets and Zeitlinger, 1991, pp. 87–99; Apter, M. J. *Reversal Theory: The Dynamics of Motivation, Emotion and Personality*, Oxford: Oneworld Publications, 2006, chapter 6.

10. Schememann, S. "Across East Europe to Moscow, the trail of freedom reaches tyranny's epicenter," *The New York Times*, Sunday, 25 August 1991, Section 4 ("The Week in Review"), p. 1.

11. Stassinopoulos, A. *Maria Callas*, London: Hamlyn, 1981, p. 285.

12. *Bookcase: The W. H. Smith Book Review*, No. 12, 1986, p. 11.

13. Adler, N. *The Underground Stream: New Life Styles and the Antinomian Personality*, New York: Harper Torchbooks, 1972, p. 3.

14. Becker, H. S. "Becoming a marihuana user," in Open University, *School and Society: A Sociological Reader*, London: Routledge and Kegan Paul, 1971, p. 145.

15. Ibid., p. 145.

8 FUELING THE FLAMES

1. Zillmann, D. *Connections Between Sex and Aggression*, Hillsdale, NJ: Lawrence Erlbaum, Second edition, 1998. Among other things, this book contains a good review of all the research on excitation transfer, pp. 147–210.

2. Dutton, D. G. and Aron, A. P. "Some evidence for heightened sexual attraction under conditions of high anxiety," *Journal of Personality and Social Psychology*, **30**, 1974, 510–517.

3. E.g. Rosselló, J. "Las Corridas de Toros (1)," an article which appeared in the Spanish magazine *Integral*, **8** (75), February, 1986, pp. 4–8.

4. A more extended account of the pleasures of antique collecting, as interpreted from the reversal theory point of view, will be found in Smith, K. C. P. and Apter, M. J. "Collecting antiques: A psychological interpretation," *Antique Collector*, **7**, 1977, pp. 64–66.

5. Barbach, L. and Levine, L. *Shared Intimacies: Women's Sexual Experiences*, London: Corgi, 1981, p. 238.

6. In this respect, the books by Nancy Friday have become classic: *My Secret Garden: Women's Sexual Fantasies* (1973), *Forbidden Flowers: More Women's Sexual Fantasies* (1975), and *Women on Top* (1991), all published by Simon and Schuster, New York. Michael Bader argues that the function of sexual fantasies during sexual encounters is to help the individual to feel safe rather than to add to the arousal. In the language of the present book, the aim is to establish and maintain the protective frame during intercourse. Bader, M. *Arousal: The Secret Logic of Sexual Fantasies*, London: Virgin, 2003.

7. Letter published in Ann Landers' advice column, *Chicago Tribune*, 26 April 1991.

8. Apter, M. J. *The Experience of Motivation: The Theory of Psychological Reversals*, London: Academic Press, 1982, p. 219.

9. One of the many surprises that emerged from Kinsey's research was that nearly 60% of all males had practised oral sex: Kinsey, A., Pomeroy, W. P., and Martin, C. E. *Sexual Behavior in the Human Male*, Philadelphia: Saunders, 1948, p. 371. The most recent estimate comes from the most comprehensive national survey ever released by the federal government: Mosher, W. D. "Sexual behavior and selected

health measures: Men and women," *Vital & Health Statistics*, 2005. This survey found that 90% of men and 88% of adult women have had oral sex with an opposite sex partner. It was also found that 50% of teens had engaged in oral sex.

10. Samenow, S. E. *Inside the Criminal Mind*, New York: Times Books, 1984, p. 177. Revised edition: New York: Crown, 2004.

11. Noguchi, T. T. *Coroner*, New York: Simon and Schuster, 1983.

12. Boss, M. *Meaning and Content of Sexual Perversions: A Dasein-analytic Approach to the Psychopathology of the Phenomenon of Love* (translated by L. L. Abell), New York: Grune and Stratton, 1949, pp. 88–89.

13. Bosworth, P. "Let's call it suicide," *Vanity Fair*, March 1985, p. 52.

14. Op.Cit.

15. Litman, R. E. and Swearingen, C. "Bondage and Suicide," *Archives of General Psychiatry*, **27**, 1972, pp. 80–85.

16. Ibid.

9 THE FALLACIOUS FRAME

1. Edgerton, C. *Solo: My Adventures in the Air*, Chapel Hill: Algonquin, 2005.

2. Monaghan, E. "Soldiers survive war, then die on the roads," *The Times* (UK), 5 May 2005, p. 47.

3. Mason, P. *Niagara and the Daredevils*, Niagara Daredevil Gallery, 1969; Gromosiak, P. *Daring Niagara: 50 Death-Defying Stunts at the Falls*, New York: Buffalo Books, 1999.

4. According to one list, 90 BASE jumping deaths have been recorded since 1981. Tanner, A. "Base jumpers falling madly for Idaho bridge," *Washington Post*, September 18, 2005, section A p. 10.

5. "Parachutist is killed in Eiffel Tower base jump," *The Times* (UK), 18 May 2005, p. 39.

6. *South Wales Echo*, 19 October 1983 (front page).

7. Gowen, A. and Berselli, B. "Teenagers' game had deadly end," *Washington Post*, 29 January 1999, section B p. 1.

8. "Man sneaks lap at Indy, dies in crash," *Chicago Tribune*, 30 May 1991, p. 27.

9. Lidz, F. "Retired daredevil Evel Knievel has watched his son's career take off," *Sports Illustrated*, **64**, 17 March 1986, pp. 8–12.

10. Playfair, G. and Sington, D. *The Offenders*, London: Secker and Warburg, 1957, p. 160.

11. Spanier, D. "Aces of Vegas," *Daily Telegraph* (UK) "Weekend" section, 16 May 1987, p. 1.

12. Marsh, P. "Life and careers on the soccer terraces," in R. Ingham, S. Hall, J. Clarke, P. Marsh, and J. O'Donovan, *Football Hooliganism: The Wider Context*, London: Inter-Action Inprint, 1978.

13. Marsh, P., Rosser, E., and Harré, R. *The Rules of Disorder*, London: Routledge and Kegan Paul, 1978, p. 95.

14. Kerr, J. H. *Understanding Soccer Hooliganism*, Buckingham, UK and Philadelphia: Open University Press, 1994.

15. Baldwin, J. I., Whiteley, S., and Baldwin, J. D. "Changing *AIDS* and fertility-related behavior: The effectiveness of sexual education," *Journal of Sex Research*, **27** (2), 1990, pp. 245–262.

16. Evidence in support of this is reviewed in Gerkovich, M. M. "Risk-taking," in M. J. Apter (Ed.) *Motivational Styles in Everyday Life: A Guide to Reversal Theory*, Washington, D.C.: American Psychological Association, 2001, pp. 215–228.

17. I am indebted to Dr. Mary Cook at the Midwest Research Institute, Kansas City, Missouri, for this ingenious suggestion.

18. See, for example, O'Connell, K. A., Cook, M. R., Gerkovich, M. M., Potocky, M., and Swan, G. E. "Reversal theory and smoking: A state-based approach to ex-smokers' highly tempting situations," *Journal of Consulting and Clinical Psychology*, **58**, 1990, pp. 489–494. The whole series of studies is reviewed in: O'Connell, K. A. and Cook, M. R. "Smoking and smoking cessation," in M. J. Apter (Ed.) *Motivational Styles in Everyday Life: A Guide to Reversal Theory*, Washington, D.C.: American Psychological Association, 2001, pp.139–153.

19. Wolfenstein, M. *Disaster: A Psychological Essay*, London: Routledge and Kegan Paul, 1957, p. 45.

20. *The Times* (UK), 1, 2, and 3 July 1954.

21. Colbert, E. and Chamberlin, E. *Chicago and the Great Conflagration*, New York: Vent, 1871; cited by Wolfenstein (reference 19 above, 1957).

22. James, W. "On some mental effects of the earthquake," in *Memories and Studies*, New York: Longmans Green, 1911; cited by Wolfentein (reference 15 above, 1957).

23. Sullivan, C. L. *Hurricanes of the Mississippi Gulf Coast: 1717 to Present*, The Gulf Publishing Company/The Sun Herald, 1986, p. 97. My thanks to Randall Braman, Kirsey Stewart, John McFarland, and Marilyn Pustay for helping to find this quotation.

24. Ibid., p. 102.

25. Gibbs, W. *San Francisco Examiner*, 27 January 1985.

26. Dear, W. *The Dungeon Master: The Disappearance of James Dallas Egbert III*, Boston: Houghton Mifflin, 1984.

27. Zarzour, K. *Toronto Star*, 3 and 5 June 1985.

28. *San Francisco Examiner*, 6 January 1985.

29. Tendler, S. *The Times* (UK), 8 December 1982, p. 5.

30. Hughes, R. *The Shock of the New: Art and the Century of Change*, London: British Broadcasting Corporation, 1980, p. 281.

31. Murgatroyd, S. and Apter, M. J. "A structural-phenomenological approach to eclectic psychotherapy," in J. Norcross (Ed.) *Handbook of Eclectic Psychotherapy*, New York: Brunner/Mazel, 1986, pp. 260–280.

32. Ochberg, F. M. "Post-traumatic therapy and victims of violence," in F. M. Ochberg (Ed.) *Post-Traumatic Therapy and Victims of Violence*, New York: Brunner/Mazel, 1988, p. 12.

33. The importance of such illusion to normal mental health is well documented in Taylor, S. E. *Positive Illusions: Creative Self-Deception and the Healthy Mind*, New York: Basic Books, 1991. This idea goes back at least to the writings of the psychiatrist Alfred Adler in the early years of the last century, and to his concept of fictional goals. In turn, Adler was influenced by the philosopher Vaihinger and his notion of "As If."

10 CRIME AND ITS PLEASURES

1. *South Wales Echo*, 10 December 1983, p. 7.

2. *Daily Mail* (UK), 10 June 1982, p. 258.

3. Bowd, G. *Daily Express* (UK), 30 September 1985, p. 3.

4. This phrase was used in Amiel, B. "Leisure riots mark the price of

peace," *Sunday Times* (UK), 15 September 1991, which dealt with the riots which had occurred just before in a number of cities in Britain, especially Newcastle.

5. Gerard Gaudron, Mayor of Aulnay sous Bois, as reported in Henly, J. *The Guardian*, 5 November 2005. This idea that riots are about fun received its classic expression in the book *The Unheavenly City* by Edward Banfield (New York: Little Brown, 1968), especially in the chapter on "Rioting for fun and pleasure."

6. Especially in the classic study of a thousand delinquent boys in Glueck, S. and Glueck, E. *Delinquents in the Making: Paths to Prevention*, New York: Harper, 1952.

7. Jones, R. and Walter, T. "Delinquency is fun," *Community Care*, 9 August 1978, p. 20.

8. Ibid.

9. Ryder was convicted on 6 November 2002 and sentenced to perform community service and reimburse the value of the goods. It seems that nobody believed her excuse that her director (unnamed) instructed her to do it, to prepare for a role in a movie (unnamed).

10. *Daily Express* (UK), 24 October 1980, p. 32.

11. Frischer, D. "Les delices de la 'fauch'," *Le Monde Dimanche*, 13 July 1980, p. 4 (Author's translation).

12. Ibid.

13. Walsh, D. P. *Shoplifting: Controlling a Major Crime*, London: Macmillan, 1978.

14. Katz, J. *Seductions of Crime: Moral and Sensual Attractions in Doing Evil*, New York: Basic Books, 1988.

15. MacDonald, J. M. *Rape: Offenders and their Victims*, Springfield, Illinois: Charles C. Thomas, pp. 150–151.

16. Interview with the ex-wife of the "Monster of the M5," *The Sun* (UK), 10 March 1981, p. 4.

17. Dr. K. C. P. Smith, working at Horfield Prison in Bristol, England (personal communication).

18. This sequence is based on a passage in Apter, M. J. and Smith, K. C. P. "Reversal Theory," in B. McGurk, D. Thornton, and M. Williams (Eds.) *Applying Psychology to Imprisonment: Theory and Practice* London: H.M.S.O., 1987, pp. 78–95.

19. Benson, R. *Daily Express* (UK), 23 October 1979.

20. The account that follows is based on Critchley M. (Ed.) *The Trial of Neville George Clevely Heath*, London: Hodge, 1951; Playfair, G. and Sington, D. *The Offenders*, London: Secker and Warburg, 1957; and Gaute, J. H. H. and Odell, R. *The Ladykillers, 2*, London: Granada, 1981.

21. Dr. K. C. P. Smith, personal communication.

22. Deer, B. "Maniacs who kill for pleasure," *Sunday Times* (UK), 27 July 1986.

23. Steve Cattell, a serial burglar, as reported in Franks, A. "My name's Steve and I'm a thief," *The Times Magazine* (UK), 5 November 2005, p. 50.

24. Katz, J. (reference 14 above).

25. Samenow, S. E. *Inside the Criminal Mind*, New York: Crown, 2004 (originally published 1984, New York: Times Books).

26. Ibid 1984 edn., p. 123.

27. Honigsbaum, M. "Concern of 'happy slapping' craze," *The Guardian*, 26 April 2005.

28. "Fire Brigades Union backs private members bill aimed at tackling violence against emergency workers," *Management Issues*, 21 June 2005.

29. Scobie, W. "Terror of kids who kill for fun," *Sunday Times* (UK), 6 November 1983.

30. Will, G. F. "America's slide into the sewer," *Newsweek*, 30 July 1990, p. 64.

31. Boys "boasted of killing man for enjoyment," *The Times* (UK), 26 October 1999.

32. Kerr, J. H. *Rethinking Aggression and Violence in Sport*, London and New York: Routledge, 2005.

33. Katz, J. (reference 14 above).

34. Collins, J. *Chances*, London: Pan Books/William Collins, 1982.

11 THE GLAMOR OF WAR

1. Libretto, by F. M. Piave, translated by Andrew Porter for Welsh National Opera performance of *La Forza del Destino*, 1981.

2. Brittain, V. *Chronicle of Youth: War Diary 1913–1917*, London: Fontana, 1982, pp. 100–101.

3. Ibid., p. 102.

4. Royko, M. "War televised much like American football game," syndicated column in the *Purdue Exponent*, 8 February 1991.

5. Rivers, C. "Front Lines: It's tough to tell a hawk from a lonesome dove," *New York Times*, 10 February 1991.

6. Pritchett, V. S. *The Spanish Temper*, London: The Hogarth Press, 1984, p. 184 (originally published in 1954).

7. Advertisement in *Soldier of Fortune*, July 1985.

8. Taylor, S. *Toronto Star*, 4 June 1985.

9. Hart, L. (Ed.) *The Sword and the Pen*, London: Book Club Associates, 1978, p. 3.

10. Vincent Osbourne, interviewed in the *Daily Mirror* (UK), 7 June 1984.

11. Liddle, P. "One man and his war," *Times Higher Educational Supplement* (UK), 5 October 1984.

12. Mike Norman, interviewed in Plaice, E. *Daily Mirror* (UK), 6 April 1982.

13. Capt. James Johnson, interviewed in Atlas, T. and Evans, D. "Aerial war on a moonless night," *Chicago Tribune*, 18 January 1991.

14. Teilhard de Chardin, P. *The Heart of the Matter*, London: Collins, 1978, p. 168.

15. Marshall, S. L. A. *Men Against Fire*, New York: William Morrow and Co., 1964, p. 185.

16. Herr, M. *Dispatches*, London: Picador (Pan Books), 1978, p. 57.

17. Ibid., p. 111.

18. Caputo, P. *A Rumor of War*, London: Arrow Books, 1978, p. 230.

19. Ibid., xiii.

20. Ibid., xv.

21. Baker, M. *Nam*, UK edition, London: Abacus, 1982, p. 66.

22. Fick, N. *One Bullet Away: The Making of a Marine Officer*, Boston and New York: Houghton Mifflin, 2005, p. 261.

23. Sheppard, R. Z. Review in *Time*, 9 May 1983, of W. Manchester, *The Last Lion, Winston Spencer Churchill: Visions of Glory, 1874–1932*, (New York: Little, Brown).

24. See Fussell, P. *The Great War and Modern Memory*, New York: Oxford University Press, 1977, p. 27. Fussell gives an extended discussion of the sporting metaphor in war.

25. Baker, M. (reference 21 above), p. 56.
26. Ibid., p. 66.
27. Ibid., p. 160.
28. Ibid., p. 58.
29. Hoffer, E. *The True Believer*, New York; Harper and Row (Perennial Library), 1966, p. 65.
30. Ibid., p. 64.
31. Giddings, R. "Something about a soldier," *New Society*, 27 September 1979.
32. Fussell, P. (reference 24 above), pp. 191–192.
33. Ibid., p. 192.
34. Ibid., p. 201.
35. Herr, M. (reference 16 above), p. 169.
36. Ibid., p. 169.
37. Caputo, P. (reference 18 above), p. 106.
38. Ibid., pp. 305–306.
39. Baker, M. (reference 21 above), p. 51.
40. Ibid., p. 85.
41. Ibid., p. 149.
42. Caputo, P. (reference 18 above), p. 294.
43. Herr, M. (reference 16 above), pp. 111–112.
44. Baker, M. (reference 21 above), p. 146.

12 RISK, REBELLION, AND CHANGE

1. Bernstein, I. S. "Taboo or toy?" in J. S. Bruner, A. Jolly, and K. Sylva, (Eds.) *Play*, Harmondsworth, England: Penguin, pp. 194–198.
2. For other examples, see Wilson, E. O. *On Human Nature*, Harvard University Press, 1978.
3. Ibid., p. 150f.
4. Phillips, P. "Where science and courage meet," *Telegraph Sunday Magazine* (UK), 16 March 1986.
5. Wansell, G. "Man of the week: A. J. P. Taylor," *Telegraph Sunday Magazine* (UK), 16 March 1986.

6. May, R. *The Courage to Create*, London: Collins, 1976, p. 60.

7. *The Great Artists, Volume 87*, London: Marshall Cavendish, 1986, p. 2757.

8. Durant, W. *The Story of Philosophy*, New York: Pocket Books (Simon and Schuster), 1961, p. 199.

9. This is an example of a principle known in cybernetics (the study of control and communication systems) as the Law of Requisite Variety. This states, roughly speaking, that a system needs as much internal variety as its environment has, in order to be able to adapt when the environment changes. See Ashby, W. R. *An Introduction to Cybernetics*, London: Chapman and Hall, 1956.

10. I am here dealing with psychological rather than physiological advantages of overcoming boredom and achieving excitement. At the physiological level, Augustin De La Pena, intriguingly, has argued that some types of cancer are related to the experience of boredom and suggests that there are other forms of bodily disorder that are also due to under-stimulation. For more about this, see his book *The Psychobiology of Cancer: Automatization and Boredom in Health and Disease*, New York: Praeger, 1983.

11. Probably the best way into Mihalyi Csikszentmihalyi's work is his book entitled *Flow: The Psychology of Optimal Experience*, New York: Harper and Row, 1990. See also by the same author *Beyond Boredom and Anxiety: Experiencing Flow in Work and Play*, 25th anniversary edition, New York: Jossey-Bass, 2000.

12. Kerr, J. H. *Understanding Soccer Hooliganism*, Buckingham, UK: Open University Press, 1994; Kerr, J. H. *Rethinking Aggression and Violence in Sport*, London: Routledge, 2004.

13. Greene, G. *A Sort of Life*, Harmondsworth, UK: Penguin, 1974, p. 94 (originally published 1971).

14. Allain, M. F. *The Other Man: Conversations with Graham Greene*, London: The Bodley Head, 1983, p. 50.

15. Greene, G. *Ways of Escape*, London: The Bodley Head, 1980.

16. Interview with Graham Greene in Mortimer, J. *In Character*, Harmondsworth, UK: Penguin, 1984, p. 74.

17. Granger, D. "The Writing of 'Brideshead Revisited'," *The Listener*, 8 October 1981, p. 394.

18. Barthes, R. *Roland Barthes*, translated by Richard Howard, New York: Farrar, Strauss and Giroux, Inc., 1977.

19. The psychologist Frank Farley has similarly noted the relationship between criminality and creativity in "The Big T in Personality," *Psychology Today*, May 1986, pp. 44–50.

20. Maugham, W. S. *The Summing Up*, London: Pan Books, 1976, p. 36.

21. May, R. *The Meaning of Anxiety*, New York: Norton, 1977, p. 44.

22. "World war not inevitable says Graham Greene," *The Times* (UK), 17 August 1981.

23. Related arguments can be found in van der Molen, P. "Learning, Self-Actualization and Psychotherapy," in M. J. Apter, D. Fontana, and S. Murgatroyd (Eds.) *Reversal Theory: Applications and Developments*, Wales: University College Cardiff/Hillsdale, NJ: Lawrence Erlbaum, 1985, pp. 103–116.

24. The sociologist Ulrich Beck has argued in his much cited book *Risk Society* that modern technology, while reducing minor risks in our lives, increases the chances of catastrophe through global warming, nuclear accident, and the like. Unfortunately, as he points out, these major risks tend to escape perception—unlike earlier environmental hazards that assaulted the senses. Using the concept of the protective frame, we could say that this invisibility makes it easier to maintain such a frame even if it turns out to be, in the terms of an earlier chapter, a fallacious frame. See Beck, U. *Risk Society: Towards a New Modernity*, London: Sage, 1992. On the subject of the potentiality for major catastrophe, see Rees, M. *Our Final Century*, London: Arrow Books, 2003.

25. *Globe and Mail* (Toronto), 29 July 1985.

26. *The Times* (UK), 17 July 1961.

27. CNN.com/world, posted 21 October 2003.

28. The reader wishing to learn about the sociology of risk-taking (rather than the psychology of excitement-seeking) might usefully consult publications on what sociologists call "edgework." While the excitement that can come from risk-taking is recognized in this field, as is the pleasure of overcoming the restraints of society, the emphasis tends to be more on the satisfactions that can arise from exerting control. See Lyng, S. (Ed.) *Edgework: The Sociology of Risk Taking*, London

and New York: Routledge, 2005. See also Lyng, S. "Crime, edgework and corporeal transaction," *Theoretical Criminology*, **8**, 2004, pp. 359–357; Tulloch, J. and Lupton, D. *Risk and Everyday Life*, London: Sage, 2003.

29. Carter and Kourdi show how all the eight basic motivations identified in reversal theory need to be linked in to excitement-seeking if individuals and organizations are to flourish: Carter, S. and Kourdi, J. *The Road to Audacity: Being Adventurous in Life and Work*, London: Palgrave Macmillan, 2004. The eight kinds of risk-taking are usefully summarized on page 47 of their book. It may be helpful to repeat that the present book focuses on just one of these eight needs, namely the need for excitement. But this need engages joyously with risk, while the other needs typically do no more than tolerate risk—unless they occur in conjunction with the quest for excitement. See also Apter (2005), op.cit. in note 30 below, pages 17–18. This is one of the main themes in the work of Apter International; this management consultancy company applies reversal theory to the needs of businesses and other organizations worldwide.

30. The reader interested in learning more about this theory might want to consult one or more of the following:

Apter, M. J. (Ed.) *Motivational Styles in Everyday Life: A Guide to Reversal Theory*, Washington, D.C.: American Psychological Association, 2001.

Apter, M. J. *Personality Dynamics: Key Concepts in Reversal Theory*, Loughborough: Apter International, 2005.

Apter, M. J. *Reversal Theory: The Dynamics of Motivation, Emotion and Personality*, Oxford: Oneworld Publications, 2006.

Index

A

Abelam people 99
abstract art 193
actors, soldiers as 178–9, 180–1
adrenaline 15
agoraphobia 63, 142
alcohol 136–7
antique collecting 116–19
anxiety
    anxiety disorders 63
    chronic/acute 142
    enjoyment of 73
    and excitement 6–7, 9–10,
        13, 15, 16–19, 33–4, 42–4,
        58
    protective frames 142–3
    sexual behavior 61
    treatments for 143
anxiety-avoidance state
    and excitement-seeking state
        22–4
    'frame' metaphors 32–3
    pleasure/displeasure
        possibilities 31–2

protective frames,
    presence/absence of 29–31
Apprentice, The 62
arousal
    acting on world 101–7
    cognitive synergy 98–101
    drug-taking 108–9
    examples 115–19
    excitation transfer 112–13
    exploration 101–2, 106
    frustration, confronting
        102–3, 106
    impending pleasure/pain 96
    individual development
        195–6
    individual differences 80–92,
        114–15
    low/high, as mirror images
        20–2, 23–4
    motivation 109, 114
    negativism 104–6
    physical limitations,
        overcoming 103–4, 106
    physiology of 13–15

arousal (*cont.*):
    pleasant/unpleasant 13–22, 108–9
    and protective frames 93
    range of sources of 93–5
    responding to world 95–8
    risk-taking 107–8
    sensory excitement 95
    sexual 119–24
    situations, structural aspects of 97–8
    unitary character of 113–14
arousal-preference states (seeking/avoidance)
    age factor 87
    control 88–91
    'crucial experiences' 86–7
    fallacious frame 141–2
    gender factor 87–8
    learning 83–4
    needs, changing 81–2
    protective frames 89–92
    situations, avoiding 88–9
    state dominance 82–6
    state-switching 90–1
arts, and nonconformity 192–4
artworks 100
Assassin game 139–40
Auschwitz 75
autoerotic asphyxiation (scarfing) 122–3
autonomic nervous system 14–15

B
Bacon, Sir Francis 171–2
Baker, Mark 175, 181, 183
Barnett, Lady Isabel 150
Barthes, Roland 201
BASE jumping 127–8
Bettelheim, Bruno 68
biological survival, and excitement-seeking 186–9

Bishop, Jessie 155
Blanchard, Smoke 39
Blyth, Sir Chay 44
Bonington, Sir Chris 38–9
boredom
    age of 205
    arousal dimension 20–4
    creative people 199–201
    crime 145–9, 160
    dead-end strategies 201
    excitement 25–6
    risk-taking 145–6, 203–7
boxing matches 65
brain, arousal of 15
Brideshead Revisited (Waugh) 201
Brittain, Vera 165
Browing, Iben 4
Bulger, James 161
Bull Fever (Tynan) 46
bulls, running with *(encierro)*
    danger, and excitement 47, 50–1
    'going up to the edge', as fine art 45
    gratuitous risks 46
    protective frames 51–2, 78–9
    public, risks taken by 46–52
    spurious safety 52
    supreme moment of risk 46
Bundy, Ted 158
Bunuel, Luis 72
business
    creative people in 193–4
    risk-taking 107, 208
    safety-zone frame 62–3

C
cage fighting 65
Camille, hurricane 138
Cannon, Walter 13
canyoneering 3
Capilano Suspension Bridge experiment 112–13

Capriati, Jennifer 150
Caputo, Philip 174–5, 180–1, 182
car racing 128–9
Challenger spacecraft disaster 74
Chernobyl disaster 75
Chicago, great fire of 138
Churchill, Winston 176
claustrophobia 142
CN Tower, Toronto 40
coasteering 3
cognitive synergy 207
   arousal-preference states 100
   defined 98
   examples 98–100
   humor 100–1
   multiple arousal 116, 117,
     118–19
   science 100
   works of art 100
college football games 116–17
Columbia spacecraft tragedy 189
Columbus, Christopher 190
communism 191, 194
confidence frame 53–4, 64, 77–9
   definition 53–4, 77
   fallacious 126–30
   see also danger; dangerous edge
Conrad, Barnaby 47
creativity, and crime 199–202
crime
   boredom 145–9, 160
   creativity 199–202
   economic motives 159
   excitement-seeking 149, 158–60
   negativism 105
   psychological needs 159
   psychopaths 154–8, 162
   rape 151 4
   shoplifting 150–1
   violence as sport 161–3
'crucial experiences' 86–7
Csikszentmihalyi, Mihalyi 198

cubism 193
cultural evolution, and risk-taking
   189–91

D
Dahmer, Jeffrey 158
D'Amato, Cus 43
danger
   attraction to 4–5
   bulls, running with 45–52
   definition 26
   excitement-seeking 36–7
   meaning of 26
   protective frames 29–31, 37–8
   stimulation, search for 36 8
   unrealistic assessments of 126
   see also confidence frame
dangerous edge
   definition 7
   excitement/anxiety, switching
     between 42–5
   metaphor 10
   mountaineering 38–40
   others, putting at risk 145–6
   professions, risky 40–1
   safety/danger/trauma zones
     27–9, 31, 42
   trauma, meaning of 26, 28
Dani tribes 170
'dark tourism' 75–6
Dawson, Les 18–19
de Chardin, Teilhard 172
Death in the Afternoon (Hemingway)
   45–6
defense mechanisms 70–1
detachment frame
   anxiety-avoidance 72
   defense mechanisms 70–1
   definition 54, 67, 77
   detachment zone 54, 77–9
   make-believe process 69, 70,
     71, 72, 139–41

detachment frame (*cont.*):
   observing 64
   parapathic emotions 72–7
   psychopaths 157–8
   retrospection process 69–71,
     72, 139
   safety/danger/trauma zones
     65–6
   self-substitution process 66–8,
     71, 72, 78, 137–9
   spectator sports 64–5, 165
dictators 137
Dispatches (Herr) 173–4
distance, overcoming 104
down hill sports 3
drug-taking 108–9, 136–7
dueling 170
Dungeons and Dragons game 140–1
Durrell, Lawrence 193

E
earthquake 4
'emotion recollected in tranquility'
   69–70
emotions, enjoyment of 72–4,
   76–7
   see also parapathic emotions
encierro see bulls, running with
Enthusiasms (Levine) 68
espionage, for fun 141
excitement
   and anxiety 6, 9–10, 13, 15,
     16–19, 33–4, 42–4, 58
   panic, and exhilaration 1–2
   risk-taking 2–3, 8–9
   violence 5–6
   what is it? x
excitement-seeking state
   biological survival 186–9
   boredom, age of 202–7
   creativity, and crime 199–202
   cultural change 189–95

   extreme, conditions for 36–7
   human nature 7–8
   individual development 12,
     195–9
   risk-taking 207–8
   see also anxiety-avoidance state;
     crime; danger
exhibitionism 121
expressionism 193
extreme sports 3–4

F
fairgrounds 1–2
fallacious frames
   confidence frame 125–30
   detachment frame 137–41
   frame, unavailable or damaged
     141–4
   safety-zone frame 130–7
falling activities 103
fantasy 69, 220n6
   and reality 140–1
   sexual behavior 120
   see also make-believe process
fear, and exhilaration 44–5
Fick, Nathaniel 175
fiction
   excitement-seeking state 66–7
   and fact 140–1
   parapathic emotions 72–3
'fight or flight' reactions 14–15
fire festivals 4–5
firemen, attacks on 161
'flow' 198
Freud, Sigmund 8, 70–1, 114
fugu (poisonous fish), eating 111
fundamentalism 194–5
Fussell, Paul 179–80

G
Gacy, John 158
Galileo 190

gambling 131
game-playing
  psychopaths 156–7
  see also sports; war games
Gerlach, Mary Ann 138
Great War and Modern Memory, The
  (Fussell) 179–80
Greene, Graham 141, 200, 202
'grief tourism' 75–6
Ground Zero 76

H
Hall, Stuart 150
Hambleton, Hugh 141
Hamlet (Shakespeare) 98
'happy slapping' 161
Heath, Neville 155–8
heli-skiing 3
Hemingway, Ernest 45–6
Herr, Michael 173–4, 180, 182
Herzog, Maurice 39
Heysel Stadium deaths 134
Hill, William 'Red' 127
Hiroshima 75, 76
HIV
  condom use 135–6
  high-risk groups 122
hoaxes 146
Hoffer, Eric 178
holidays 60
home 56
horror films 73
humor 100–1
hurricanes 76, 130–1, 138

I
Iberia (Michener) 51
impressionism 193
individual development
  arousal-seeking propensity
    195–6
  exploration, childhood 196

strategies, open and closed
  196–9
Inside the Criminal Mind (Samenow)
  160
intellectual exploration 101–2
invincibility, feelings of 126–7
Iraq War 166–7, 175–6
Islam 194–5, 195

J
James, William 138
jousting 170
juvenile delinquency 148–9, 160

K
Kafka, Franz 35
Katrina, hurricane 76, 130–1
Katz, Jack 159, 162
Kennedy, John F. 74, 75
King, Stephen 73
Knievel, Evel 129
Kuma Reality Games 171

L
La Forza del Destino (Verdi) 164
Lamarr, Hedy 150
Law of Requisite Variety 227–28 n9
Lawrence, D.H. 193
Le Carré, John 141
'leisure riots' 148
Lessing, Doris 107
Letters to Alice (Weldon) 68
Levin, Bernard 68
Lundy, Derek 38

M
make-believe process 69, 70, 71,
  72
  and real dangers 139–41
Marsh, Peter 132, 134
Marshall, S.L.A. 172–3
Maugham, W. Somerset 202

Men Against Fire (Marshall) 172–3
Michener, James 51
Miller, Henry 193
Moss, Stirling 44
mountaineering
    calculated risk 39
    free soloing 39–40
    self-generating activities 197
Munch, Edvard 142
murder
    by juveniles ('thrill kill') 161
    see also psychopaths

N
9/11 disaster 74–6
Nabokov, Vladimir 68
Nam (Baker) 175
negativism
    arousal 104–6
    crime 105, 201–2
    cultural change 191–5
    sexual behavior 120–1
nervous system 14–15
Nevill, Captain 176–7
nonconformity 192–4
nudism 60

O
obsessional-compulsive disorder
    63
offense mechanisms 71
Olivier, Sir Laurence 18
On Acting (Olivier) 18
One Bullet Away (Fick) 175
Optimal Arousal Theory (Hebb)
    212n3

P
paintball 169–70
parachuting 23–4, 29–30, 43
parapathic emotions
    definition 73

emotions, enjoyment of 72–4,
    76–7
'grief tourism' 75–6
TV news, as entertainment
    74–5, 162–3, 166–7
unreal contexts 73–4
parasympathetic nervous system 14
Paratelic Dominance Scale 217n2
Patch, Sam 127
pornography 72
post-traumatic stress disorder
    143–4
projective tests 113
protective frames
    anxiety 142–3
    chance 51–2
    changeability 80–92
    concept of 10
    contrasting 77–9
    danger 10, 36–8
    definition 10, 29
    encierro example 78–9
    excitement-seeking state
        29–31, 36–7
    misperception of 125–30
    parapathic emotions 74
    removing and setting up 89–90
    reversals over time 33–5
    safety, spurious 52
    security, subjective 37–8
    switching between 71–2
    thrill-seekers 91–2
    see also confidence frame;
        detachment frame; safety-
        zone frame
Psycho (Hitchcock) 73
psychology, and emotions 7, 9
psychopaths
    arousal-avoidance state 154
    arousal-seeking state 154
    extreme type 155
    game-playing 156–7

immediate thrill 154–5
Neville Heath example 155–8
and ordinary people 162
personal protective frames 154
risk-taking behavior 157–8

R
racing drivers 44–5
Rader, Dennis 158
rape 7, 121, 152–4
rappeling 40
relationships 102
relaxation 58–9
reticular activating system 15
retrospection process 69–71, 72, 139
reversal theory xi, 209, 211n5
Rio Grande, flooding of 137
rioting 147–8
risk-taking
    arousal 107–8
    boredom 145–6
    businesses 208
    cultural evolution 189–91
    eight kinds of 229n29
    excitement 2–3, 8–9
    excitement-seeking state
        207–8
    fire festivals 4–5
    gratuitous 46
    professional obligations 207–8
    professions, risky 40–1
    psychopaths 157–8
    safety-zone frame 130–7
    security/safety 203
    social encouragement of 205–7
    sociology of 229n28
    sports 2–3, 3–4, 57–8, 127–8
    technology 203, 204
    see also bulls, running with
rock-climbing 37
Rumor of War, A (Caputo) 174–5
Ryder, Winona 150

S
safety-zone frame
    definition 54, 77
    excitement-seeking state 55–6
    fallacious 130–7
    game-playing 61–2
    individual differences 62–3
    protective frames, kinds of 54,
        77–9
    as psychological space 56
    seriousness/playfulness 60–3
    sports 56–60
    theaters and stadiums 67
    trauma, exclusion of 54–5
    war 176–8
    work place 55
Saint-Marie-Among-the-Hurons
    fortress 98–9
Samenow, Stanton 160
scarfing (*autoerotic asphyxiation*)
    122–3
Schachter, S. 15
Schwarzkopf, Norman 176
Seductions of Crime (Katz) 159
Sensation Seeking Scale 217n7
sensationalism x
sensory excitement 95
serial killers 158
sexual behavior
    deviant behaviors 120–1
    'excitation transfer' 113
    excitement 8, 119–20
    fantasy 120, 220n6
    Freud on 8, 114
    frustration 119
    major role of 8
    negativism 120–1
    protective frame 60–1
    psychopathic 155–8
    risky 135–6n, 121–4
shark-cave diving 29
Sharp, Jessie 127

shoplifting 150–1
shopping malls 131–2
Singer, J. 15
skiing 43
Skynner, Robin 41
smoking 136–7
soccer hooliganism 65, 132–5
Soviet Union 191
spectators
    detachment frame 64–5,
        137–9
    showing off to 129–30
    theater 66–7
    TV news, as entertainment
        74–5, 162–3, 166–7
    violence 161–2
    war 164–7
speed 103–4
sports
    aggressive 162
    dangerous 3–4, 57–8, 127–8
    excitement-seeking/avoidance
        fluctuations 58
    frustration 102–3
    relaxation 58–9
    safety-zone frame 56–7, 59–60
stage fright 18–19, 24
Stephens, Charles 127
Stockwell Strangler 158
stuntmen 63
surgeons 40–1
Svebak, Sven 86
swimming pools 115–16
sympathetic nervous system 14–15
synergy *see* cognitive synergy

T

Taylor, A.J.P. 192
Telic Dominance Scale 216 n 2
Terence x
terrorism, and publicity 163
test pilots 188–9

theater, and spectators 66–7
Third Man, The (film) 35
Three Mile Island 75, 76
thrill-seekers 91–2
tiger-cage metaphor 31, 37, 185
time, overcoming 104
trauma
    exclusion of 54–5
    post-traumatic stress disorder
        143–4
    safety/danger/trauma zones
        27–9, 31, 42, 65–6
Trial, The (Kafka) 35
Trump, Donald
TV news, as entertainment 74–5,
    162–3, 166–7
Tynan, Kenneth 46
Tyson, Mike 43

U

ultimate fighting 65
Un Chien Andalou (Bunuel) 72
uniforms, and distancing from
    reality 178–80

V

vandalism 7, 146–8, 198
Vendée Globe race 38
Vietnam War 173–5, 177, 180–2
violence
    rape 151
    sexuality 181–4
    as sport 161–2
    wilding 5–6
Voltaire 193
voyeurism 121

W

war
    illusion, the great 176–81
    invisible protection 126
    language of 182, 183–4

military violence, and eroticism
   181–5
psychology of 11
real combat, joy of 171–6
safety zone, illusion of 176–8
soldiers, as actors 178–9,
   180–1
as spectator sport 164–7
and sporting rhetoric 176–8,
   184–5
war games
   board games/computer
      simulations 170–1
   'living the legend' 168–9
   make believe and fantasy 168
   military toys and games 168
   paintball 169–70

retrospection 167
ritualized battles 169–70
Waugh, Evelyn 201
Weldon, Fay 68
Ways of Escape (Greene) 200–1
wilding 5–6
Wilson, E.O. 102
Wordsworth, William 69

X

X games 3–4

Y

Yorkshire Ripper 158

Z

Zillmann, Dolf 112